Women at War,
Women Building Peace

Women at War, Women Building Peace

Challenging Gender Norms

Joyce P. Kaufman
Kristen P. Williams

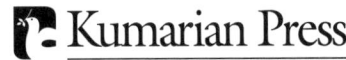

A Division of Lynne Rienner Publishers, Inc. • Boulder & London

Published in the United States of America in 2013 by
Kumarian Press
A division of Lynne Rienner Publishers, Inc.
1800 30th Street, Boulder, Colorado 80301
www.rienner.com
www.kpbooks.com

and in the United Kingdom by
Kumarian Press
A division of Lynne Rienner Publishers, Inc.
3 Henrietta Street, Covent Garden, London WC2E 8LU

© 2013 by Lynne Rienner Publishers, Inc. All rights reserved

Library of Congress Cataloging-in-Publication Data
Kaufman, Joyce P.
  Women at war, women building peace: Challenging gender norms / Joyce P. Kaufman and
  Kristen P. Williams.
    Includes bibliographical references and index.
  ISBN 978-1-56549-560-9 (cloth : alk. paper)
  ISBN 978-1-56549-561-6 (pbk. : alk. paper)
    1. Women—Political activity—History 2. Women political activists—History
  I. Williams, Kristen P., 1964– II. Title.
  HQ1236.K378 2013
  305.4209—dc23   2012043642

British Cataloguing in Publication Data
A Cataloguing in Publication record for this book
is available from the British Library.

Printed and bound in the United States of America

∞   The paper used in this publication meets the requirements
    of the American National Standard for Permanence of
    Paper for Printed Library Materials Z39.48-1992.

    5 4 3 2 1

Contents

Preface vii

1 Challenging Gender Norms 1

2 Women, Conflict, and Political Activism 25

3 Women's Political Activism in Northern Ireland: Protestants and Catholics 57

4 Palestinian Women's Activism and the Israeli-Palestinian Conflict 83

5 Women's Political Activism in Sri Lanka: Tamil Tigers 113

6 Imagined Peace 145

Bibliography 169
About the Authors 183
Index 185

Preface

When sleeping women wake, mountains move.
—Chinese proverb

WAR AND CONFLICT, INTERSTATE AND INTRASTATE, REMAIN EVER PRESENT IN THE twenty-first century. The stories of war—who participates in them, who is affected by them and how—are important to know. Often, these stories of war are gendered in that they are about men as soldiers. When looking at war's impact on women, the stories are about women as victims, as refugees, and their experiences with sexual violence. Yet, women are not just victims, they are also peace activists, they are supporters of war, and they are combatants. In short, like men, women play many and varied roles during war and conflict.

Building on our previous work in which we examined the impact of war on women's citizenship, and particularly ethnically mixed marriages as well as women's peace activism, this book addresses women's political activism in times of conflict. By political activism, we mean the range of actions women take in responding to conflict and war in their societies, which include engaging in peace activism, nonviolent resistance in support of one side of a conflict, and becoming armed combatants and even suicide bombers or martyrs. Along this continuum of political activism, women demonstrate their agency to act. While their agency is constrained by the patriarchal structures (political, economic, cultural, and social) of their societies, they are still able to engage in political activism. We demonstrate women's political activism along the continuum in three case studies: Northern Ireland, Israel-Palestine, and Sri Lanka. What we find is that in all three cases women were indeed political actors at informal and formal political levels, although the challenge of entering the formal political sphere was formidable. We also find that women's political activism during conflict must continue in the postconflict period for a state or society to recover successfully from war and begin the difficult work of reconstruction and peacebuilding.

We are grateful to the two anonymous reviewers whose comments and suggestions strengthened the book significantly, and we are also thankful to the discussants at the annual conferences of the American Political Science Association and International Studies Association for their comments on earlier drafts of this book. We benefited from our experience at a presentation on women combatants, which we gave at USAID in Washington, DC, in June 2011. Our work was also enhanced greatly by Kristen's academic study visit to Israel in January 2012 and invitations to give presentations in Jerusalem and Ramallah, Palestine. Our thanks go to Galia Press-Barnathan, at the Hebrew University in Jerusalem, and to Nader Said, president of the Arab World for Research and Development in Ramallah. In both venues, the audience members asked invaluable questions and provided comments and suggestions that strengthened our understanding of Israeli and Palestinian women's political activism in the context of the Israeli-Palestinian conflict. Joyce's visits to Northern Ireland were again important in enhancing this research. Conversations with Kieran McEvoy and Carmel Roulston were especially helpful for the insight they offered about the role of women. Research at the Linen Hall Library in Belfast enabled us to draw upon newspapers that publicly documented acts of political violence perpetrated by women during the difficult time of the Troubles, and they provided important context, as did some of the primary sources, such as diaries of the women who were imprisoned, which were made available to us. Special thanks once again to Ross Moore for his assistance in locating these documents. We also extend our appreciation to two of our students, Emilie Blechman (Whittier College) and Oana Chimina (Clark University), who assisted us in the research for this book.

We also reserve very special thanks for Jim Lance, our editor at Kumarian Press. This is our second book with him, and we are very appreciative of the support he has given to both of these projects. In noting this, we are grateful to Kumarian Press for permission to reproduce portions of chapters from *Women and War: Gender Identity and Activism in Times of Conflict* (2010). Thanks also go to our production editor, Alexandra Hartnett, and to Jennifer Kern, marketing representative at Kumarian, for their work on getting this book through the production process and out to the wider world. Their excellent work notwithstanding, any errors or omissions are our responsibility.

Finally, we dedicate this book to our families for their support and encouragement as we continue on our joint academic journey of exploring and understanding women and gender in international relations, in times of war and in times of peace. Women's voices matter, and we hope that with this book we have made a contribution, however small, to making those voices heard.

1

Challenging Gender Norms

GENDER NORMS, OR GENDER-BASED EXPECTATIONS, OF WOMEN'S BEHAVIOR include such descriptors as nurturing, caregiving, and peaceful. In cases of interstate and intrastate conflicts, women often engage in peace activism, such as protests, silent vigils, public speeches, and political and economic boycotts.[1] In doing so, women's actions reinforce gender norms, yet peace activism can also be seen as a challenge to gender norms as women move from the perceived private sphere of the home (women's domain) into the public sphere (men's domain). For example, the feminist network Women in Black, which began in Israel as a response to the first intifada, holds silent vigils in public spaces to protest "against any manifestation of violence, militarism or war."[2] This very public display of women's political activism can be seen as challenging existing gender norms.

At the same time, women also serve as combatants, participating in state-sanctioned violence (as members of militaries) as well as non-state-sanctioned violence (members of rebel groups, paramilitary organizations, and militias, and as suicide bombers). This form of political activism—as combatants rather than as peacemakers—challenges gender norms about women's "proper" roles and behavior. A plethora of headlines relatively recently has raised attention to the role of women as active participants in ongoing conflicts. For example, in July 2008 the front page of the *New York Times* ran a story titled "Despair Drives Suicide Attacks by Iraqi Women."[3] What was especially striking about the story was not the fact that the woman identified was the eighteenth female suicide bomber to strike in Diyala province. Rather, the emphasis was on the question of why women in this relatively conservative society are resorting to a type of violence traditionally associated with men. In yet another case, in March 2010 two female suicide bombers were identified as having carried out the deadly attacks on a Moscow subway. Again, the headline is telling: "Russia Says Suicide Bomber Was Militant's Widow."[4] The picture that accompanied the story was of the young woman, seventeen years old, posing with her husband, "a 30-year-old militant leader who lured her from her single mother, drew her into fundamentalist Islam and married her. He was killed by federal forces in December, driving her to seek revenge."[5] The second suicide bomber was "a 28-year-old teacher from a predominantly Muslim region of southern Russia who was married to an extremist leader."[6]

Both of these stories attribute the women's actions in part to their being "lured" by men who drew them into fundamentalism. According to this interpretation, when the men were killed, the women became suicide bombers as a way to get revenge. This depiction suggests that the women's actions were not the result of the choices they made but of decisions made for them by their spouses. While it is true that many suicide bombers, men and women, are motivated by a desire to avenge the death of a loved one, in this case the articles overlook the fact that women *chose* this path and that these women acted for political reasons. Thus, what is surprising is not that some women are turning to suicide bombing as a means of political expression, but rather why so little attention has been given to the role of women who engage in political violence. Using violence as a means of political action or activism is not a new option for women. It is one way in which women who live in circumstances of political violence can express agency. In fact, politically violent action is a way women can engage in politics.

In responding to situations of conflict and war, women have a number of strategies available to them, including becoming politically active to help resolve the conflict through peace activism, becoming actively engaged in support of conflict through nonviolent resistance, engaging in violence in support of the conflict as combatants or even as suicide bombers, or becoming refugees or internally displaced persons. Importantly, these are not mutually exclusive categories. We consider women's responses to conflict and war a form of political activism, which can be considered as taking place along a *continuum of political activism/action*. In this way, there is not a binary of peace and violence, or peace activism and political violence, per se, but a range of actions available to women.

One way women can engage in peace activism is at the local grassroots level in their communities. An example of this is Women in Black in Israel noted earlier. Women's activism in this group is focused on nonviolent action, such as protests, vigils, public speeches, and boycotts. Women can also engage in peace activism through participation in the formal political system, such as the creation of political parties. The Northern Ireland Women's Coalition is one such example. This political party was created to cross communal lines of Protestant/Unionists/Loyalists and Catholics/Nationalists/Republicans to have a voice at the peace negotiations that led to the 1998 Good Friday Agreement to end the conflict in Northern Ireland.

Our previous work looked at women's decisions to work for peace as a conscious choice and form of political activism, sometimes driven by feminist goals (defined as promoting political, social, and economic equality of women and men, and overturning patriarchal political, economic, and social structures) and sometimes by more traditional values (specifically a wife or mother who wants peace in her community). In most cases, the primarily male patriarchal structure of political decision making excluded women from the initial decisions to engage in some form of political violence. Women respond to that situation as political actors—working for peace is one of those strategies.[7]

Yet, as demonstrated by the examples of the suicide bombers in Iraq and Russia noted at the beginning of this chapter, women also choose to engage in political activism in support of conflict and war, again along that continuum: participating in boycotts and protests, conducting surveillance, storing and transporting weapons, and becoming armed combatants and even suicide bombers. In essence, resistance and struggle come in various forms, from nonviolent resistance to overt violence, whether that violence is conducted by the state or by anti-state/nationalist/liberation movements. Moreover, evidence from a range of asymmetric conflicts shows that nonviolent resistance is very rarely only that; rather, as Veronique Dudouet argues, "In most cases, NVR [nonviolent resistance] has been used to various degrees in combination with more classical styles of asymmetric struggle." Examples abound: the African National Congress in South Africa in its struggle to overthrow Apartheid, ethnic Albanians in Kosovo seeking independence from Serbia, and Palestinians seeking to end the occupation in the Israeli-Palestinian conflict.[8]

In this book, we explore cases of women's political activism as an act of political agency during civil or intrastate conflicts (we do not examine interstate wars). Some women choose to work for peace as a way to gain some sense of control over a situation of internal conflict or war, a decision that most were not involved in making, while others clearly opt to support one side or the other in a political and military struggle whether in support of the state or the nationalist/liberation/self-determination movement. (Note that we are not going to address here the circumstances of women who were forced to participate in political violence through coercive means. The very nature of those circumstances means that women did not have choices; we are interested in the decisions women make.) Consequently, our research questions are as follows: (1) *Why* do some women get involved in political activism of any kind (this refers to women's motivations)? (2) *How* do they become involved in political activism (e.g., are they actively recruited by family and friends? Do they join on their own?)? and (3) So what? Why does studying women and women's political activism matter?

We use a gender analysis to understand the why and how of women's political activism in times of conflict and war. This book contributes to the scholarship on women and conflict in a number of ways. Our work is synthetic and draws on existing research to elucidate what we think are some important points about women's decisions to engage in political activism. A great body of research looks at women working for peace, generally and in specific cases, such as in the former Yugoslavia and Israel-Palestine.[9] There are also significant works on women engaging in political violence. For example, the work of Laura Sjoberg and Caron Gentry, Paige Whaley Eager, and Mia Bloom all focus on women and political violence, and they illustrate their arguments with case studies, including Chechnya and Rwanda.[10] A good number of edited volumes address women and political violence from different theoretical and regional or geographical perspectives.[11] Other volumes focus specifically on women suicide bombers, such as the work of Bloom, but also Barbara Victor and Rosemarie Skaine.[12] And other work looks at women as combatants in specific regional or geographic cases, such as that of Miranda Alison (Sri Lanka and Northern Ireland) and Sandra McEvoy (Northern Ireland).[13]

All this is instructive and important research and has been valuable to us as we examine women as political actors responding to conflict. However, in the course of our own work we realized there is a dearth of information that looks at both sides of the issue, that is, why some women choose to work for peace and other women support and engage in conflict, in the same case being studied. Drawing on and synthesizing this research, which looks at one side and the other, will enable us to make an important contribution by allowing us to answer questions about women's choices and decisions regarding situations of civil conflict.

In drawing on the research of others, we are indebted to the qualitative data they have acquired through fieldwork, interviews, testimonials, and so forth, all of which are in line with feminist research methodology. In addition to using secondary sources, we have used primary sources in one of our cases, primarily archival work and interviews in Northern Ireland.[14] Primary and secondary sources enable us to explore and analyze women's motivations and how they became involved in political activism. We recognize the limitations of drawing conclusions from small-N studies, as the qualitative data we cite from the various sources were small numbers of interviews with women. However, this does not negate the findings about women's activism. Women's stories can tell us much about women, gender, and international relations (IR).

The third research question we pose is: So what? Why does studying women and women's political activism matter? This question really gets to the heart of the research in this book. Studying women matters because mainstream IR theories tend to omit women and gender from their analysis of war and peace. Women are everywhere in the world; they are not invisible, and they are affected by wars and conflict. They are also affected by peace. Moreover, studying women matters because women organize *as women* to form women's movements engaged in political activism (one can think of women's organizations dedicated to peace activism but also others, such as all-women militias). This does not mean that all women are the same or they have the same issues and interests. What an exploration and understanding of women's activist organizations can do is recognize, as S. Laurel Weldon demonstrates in her work on women's activist organizations in democracies, that

> claiming that women's organizations represent women as women does not imply that women share an identity or that they share all their interests as women. It merely suggests that women confront some similar issues as women. The system or set of women's organizations can be thought of as a mechanism for articulating women's perspective. . . . There is considerable ideological, racial, class, and other diversity across women's groups, but they focus on a set of overlapping issues that can be thought of as reflecting the social position of women. When women's groups raise these issues for discussion, they provide some representation for women. Again, this account focuses on women's organizations *taken as a group*. It does not claim that any particular organization represents or could represent all women (italics in the original).[15]

In this book we will focus on exploring the motivations for women's political activism and the discourses of political activism. In terms of the motivations for women's political activism, we are interested in the questions of why and how women engage in such activism. What motivates some women to engage in peace activism, nonviolent resistance, and violence? At the same time, we are also interested in the gender discourse surrounding women's political activism. The discourse surrounding women and war is that women are by nature peaceful, while men are aggressive and prone to war. Men are the protectors, and women are the protected. These are essentialist assumptions—that women's peaceful natural disposition is because of their biology, given their childbearing capacity, and they need to be protected by men. When it comes to women engaging in political violence, Sjoberg and Gentry show "that gender discourses dominate today's increasing recognition of and concern for women's violence. In these gendered discourses, deviant women are set up in opposition to idealized gender stereotypes. They are characterized as the exception to clearly understood gender norms."[16] Thus, when women's violence in the international arena is discussed, "traditional gender norms remain intact and thriving."[17] Moreover, when discussing terrorists, warriors, and criminals, the word *women* is used as an adjective that describes the noun. Sjoberg and Gentry assert, "Because women who commit these violences have acted outside of a prescribed gender role, they have to be separated from the main/malestream discourse of their particular behaviour."[18]

Given our overview of the preceding research questions and the importance of gender norms and gender discourses, in the sections that follow we discuss feminist security theory (FST) as a theoretical framework for exploring and analyzing women's political activism in times of conflict and war. We then address the topics of agency and intersectionality, followed by the concluding section, which provides an overview of the subsequent chapters of the book.

FST: Women, Gender, and Security

Traditional, or mainstream, IR theory addresses issues such as war and conflict, peace, international political economy, and state building and national security. For example, realism, particularly its neo- or structural realist variant, looks at the anarchic international system with no world government, the distribution of material power, and a system in which states are concerned about their power relative to others.[19]

In a realist world, gender (and women, for that matter) is not addressed. As J. Ann Tickner notes, "Characteristics associated with femininity are considered a liability when dealing with the realities of international politics." She further asserts, "When realists write about national security, they often do so in abstract and depersonalized terms, yet they are constructing a discourse shaped out of these gendered identities."[20] Pioneering feminist scholars, such as Cynthia Enloe, asked the question when looking at international politics: "Where are the women?"[21] Feminist IR scholars rightly point out that the omission of women and gender in any analysis of issues relevant to IR leaves us with an incomplete understanding of those issues.[22] And when the big issues of mainstream IR such as conflict and peace negotiations are addressed along with any exploration of women as related to those issues, they are most likely done so in very gendered terms: women as victims, women as peacemakers, and women as pacifists. Within this gender order, femininity and women are subordinated to masculinity and men.[23] Mainstream security studies tend to conflate *women* with *gender*. In doing so, as Sa'ar, Sachs, and Aharoni argue, "Men and masculinity [are left] entirely outside the explanatory frame."[24] Using women or gender "as a strictly descriptive attribute" runs the risk of using "essentialist explanations of emotional predispositions and cultural roles." Moreover, "gender as an *analytical* category" is called for by a feminist approach, an approach that "treats the attributes woman/man as historically contingent, rather than as predetermined facts."[25] Consequently, in employing a gender analysis, feminist IR scholarship serves as a challenge to traditional IR to examine the ways "gender differences permeate all facets of public and private life."[26]

We begin with the assertion, as argued by feminist scholars, that assumptions about women's *correct* or *appropriate* behavior are socially constructed where women are assumed to be nurturing, caring, and peaceful. This has contributed to the stereotyping that genders the state and citizenship. As the modern state developed in the West in the eighteenth and nineteenth centuries, participation in the public sphere—the polity—was limited. Only men were allowed to participate. Women were expected to remain in the domestic/private sphere of the home. Moreover, given that the modern state was born from war, according to Charles Tilly, the military was critical to the success and existence of the state.[27] Men are the warriors, women are the protected. And thus, from a very broad IR perspective, the concept of security was, and is, tied to the need to protect the nation-state and the people who live within its borders. Men fight wars to protect innocent civilians—women and children (often used in the same phrase). Yet, as Laura Sjoberg and Jessica Peet show, a "protection racket" is at play: "Women are promised protection from wars by men who then take credit for protecting them, while not actually doing so."[28] Instead, the civilian immunity principle—in which civilians are not to be targeted in times of war and conflict—actually does not protect women. Rather, as Sjoberg and Peet assert, "When feminists argue that 'men' protect 'women' in war, they mean that 'masculinity' protects 'femininity' ideationally, whether or not men (or anyone else) protects women (or anyone else) in real material terms."[29] Additionally, as Catia Confortini states, "The links between military service, citizenship, and the modern state establish a connection between violence, citizenship, and hegemonic masculinity, so that all depend upon each other for permanence and recreation. The capacity or potential for violence is then indissolubly associated with citizenship and the state through an appeal to 'manliness.'"[30] In the end, as Sjoberg and Peet claim, "Women's need for protection justifies wars, but it also justifies the social dominance of masculinity, a requirement for war-fighting."[31]

In thinking about gender and security, feminist IR scholars argue that "gender as a power relation" helps us to understand these concepts more clearly, particularly in understanding gender subordination.[32] In terms of feminist scholarship, no single feminist theory exists. Rather, there are a variety of feminist approaches to security, including liberal feminism, critical feminism, feminist constructivism, feminist post-structuralism, and postcolonial feminism. While the various feminist approaches apply an analysis of women and gender differently, all use gender as a tool of analysis.[33] Moreover, in the IR security subdiscipline of feminist security studies, there are different voices speaking to and about gender and international relations.[34] Some feminist security studies scholars argue for engagement with the mainstream IR literature, while others call for a separation, as they are skeptical that the mainstream IR literature will take gender and women seriously in analyses of IR topics.[35]

While different feminist approaches to security do exist, they do make, as Eric Blanchard asserts, "at least four theoretical moves. First, IR feminists question the supposed nonexistence and irrelevance of women in international security politics, engendering or exposing the workings of gender and power in international relations."[36] Second, feminist security theory (FST) interrogates the claim that the state actually ensures women's "'protection' in times of war and peace."[37] Third, FST questions the discourses that equate women with peace, men with violence. Finally, FST has "started to develop a variegated concept of masculinity to help explain security."[38] In the end, as Jennifer K. Lobasz and Laura Sjoberg remark, "Feminist work addressing security has pointed out gender's key role, *conceptually,* in understanding security; *empirically,* in seeing causes and predicting outcomes; *normatively,* in understanding what is good and bad about security practices; and *prescriptively,* in terms of looking to solve the world's most serious security problems" (italics added).[39]

FST, therefore, argues that "hegemonic understandings of security systematically overlook the practical experiences of insecurity among members of marginalized groups, and among women across the entire social spectrum. . . . Instead of a narrow focus on injuries caused by armed forces and militias, FST argues for much broader definitions that would include injuries perpetrated in the domestic sphere and legitimated by militaristic and patriarchal norms, as well as by the proliferation of arms."[40] In fact, according to Sa'ar et al., FST broadens the definition of security to include "economic development, social justice and emancipation."[41] Thus, in thinking of security as a concept, one must recognize that how security is understood has changed in the sense that it not only relates to traditional military concerns of states but to issues now considered "human security": environmental issues, economic issues in light of globalization, spread of infectious diseases, and human rights, to name a few.[42]

As feminist security theorists repeatedly demonstrate, conflict and war affect the personal security of civilians. The rules of engagement as well as the battlefield's parameters have changed in such a way that the personal security of civilians, namely, women and children, is undermined. These conflicts have also threatened women's physical security: rape is a tool of war and domestic violence in the home, as domestic violence is connected to social or state-sponsored violence. Tickner asserts, "Feminist perspectives on security would assume that violence, whether it be in the international, national, or family realm, is interconnected. Family violence must be seen in the context of wider power relations."[43] The types of conflicts in the contemporary period—intrastate civil wars—have negatively affected women's physical security. Moreover, in times of war, women as civilians are targeted, regardless of the civilian immunity principle, because "insomuch as women are indicators, signifiers, and reproducers of state/nation, belligerents attack *women* to attack the essence of state/nation" (italics in the original).[44]

Women, Structural Violence, and Peace

In thinking of women's security, one can also consider structural violence, a concept first introduced by Johann Galtung. Structural violence refers to a situation in which "violence is built into the structure and shows up as unequal power and consequently as unequal life chances."[45] Building on Galtung's structural violence concept, Cynthia Cockburn notes the relationship between economic distress and political violence. She describes a continuum of violence perpetrated by institutions such as the government and the church. Violence can also be perpetrated by rebel groups. When economic conditions decline, women are negatively affected, particularly when they are single heads of households. At the same time, inequalities in society as well as the state increase not just between sexes and genders but across class lines as well.[46]

In thinking about the complexity of what security and violence mean for women, we also consider peace, peace activism, and political violence. In doing so, we need to define our terms—what do we mean by peace? Peace can mean the absence of war (negative peace).[47] But looking at the issues of peace and war and conflict from the perspective of their impact on women necessitates a broader definition of peace. As V. Spike Peterson and Anne Sisson Runyan note in discussing the rise of peace studies as an academic discipline, "Surely [peace] must be more than simply the time between wars."[48] As many feminist scholars argue, the peace that emerges after a conflict ends is very much a gendered peace. As Donna Pankhurst asserts, a gendered peace is one in which women "suffer a *backlash* against any new-found freedoms, and they are forced 'back' into kitchens and fields" (italics in the original).[49] The evidence of postconflict periods repeatedly demonstrates that the peace process itself and the newly created political institutions do not consider women's needs. What happens instead is that women's rights are limited, and in some cases restricted. The peace that is established does not lead to equality for men and women; instead, discriminatory laws and policies are put in place that reinforce women's unequal status in society. The challenge to existing gender relations that subordinate women to men is difficult to meet when the conflict ends. Instead, the changes to gender norms that women experienced during the conflict are lost because patriarchal societies are not able or not willing to accept and promote the changed gender roles. Pankhurst further states, "The ideological rhetoric is often about 'restoring' or 'returning to' something associated with the status quo before the war, even if the change actually undermines women's rights and places women in a situation that is even more disadvantageous than it ever was in the past."[50] Moreover, violence against women continues even when the official conflict ends.

Feminist scholars, such as Catia Confortini, note that "violence is deeply implicated in the construction and reproduction of gender relations, and in particular in the construction and reproduction of hegemonic masculinity."[51]

The *cycle of violence* refers to domestic violence situations in which there are periods of time when the batterer does not abuse the battered person, but these periods of time "are instrumental to tension buildup in a relationship and always lead to more violence."[52] The cycle of violence in domestic violence can be applied to understandings of periods of violence (war and conflict) and peace within states. In recognizing that gender and power are intertwined, feminist theories claim "that power is an essential feature of society and one that maintains relations of domination and subordination between groups of people."[53] Further, violence and peace are not dichotomous/binaries or "monolithic mutually exclusive categories."[54] As Confortini convincingly argues, "when [mainstream] IR scholars talk about peace, they ignore the wars going inside the home, in the form of domestic violence . . . [because] nonfeminist IR reproduces the gendered opposition between public and private sphere; it establishes its boundaries at the edge of the public sphere, therefore ignoring the feminized domestic life."[55] She demonstrates that feminist scholars have repeatedly shown that "far from being strictly domestic or private matters, instances of violence against women are often related to international relations in unsuspected ways."[56] One need only think of gender-based violence such as rape that occurs during times of war and conflict and military prostitution.[57]

Further, if one considers violence as a process, and "not a static entity,"[58] one can also conceive of violence not as an event in which states enter into war with a beginning and an end, but rather, as Chris J. Cuomo argues, war, violence, and militarism are omnipresent in society even if there is no declared armed conflict.[59] As such, "Neglecting the omnipresence of militarism allows the false belief that the absence of declared armed conflicts *is* peace, the polar opposite of war" (italics in the original).[60] The "pervasive presence and symbolism of soldiers/warriors/patriots shape meanings of gender."[61] Thus, even in supposed periods of peace, violence and militarism are present, and they directly affect women.

Drawing on a range of feminist scholars, Tami Jacoby asserts that peace is defined "as the elimination of insecurity and danger," and as "'the enjoyment of economic and social justice, equality, and the entire range of human rights and fundamental freedoms' or relations between peoples based on 'trust, cooperation and recognition of interdependence and importance of the common good and mutual interests of all peoples.'"[62] In essence, peace is more than just the absence of violence but must also address a much broader range of issues: equality, social justice, and ensuring basic freedoms and fundamental rights for all people in a society (positive peace).

Finally, in looking at the connection between gender, women, and peace, feminist scholars take different positions that enable us to explore and interrogate those connections. According to Miranda Alison, for cultural (or difference) feminists, women have *feminine traits* (women are nurturing and caring, women engage in cooperation), traits that "have been devalued." These feminine traits, however, "are actually superior to 'masculine traits'" such as violence and domination; by "revaluing these feminine traits," peace can be achieved.[63] Ecofeminists argue that oppression of any kind is interrelated (including "war, domestic violence, racism, environmental exploitation").[64] Peace and social justice can only come about when all oppression is ended.[65] Feminists who take a maternalist/motherist view argue that by virtue of being mothers, women are more peaceful than men because "war is antithetical to women's natural childbearing and childrearing role and, by extension, women should organize as mothers to oppose militarism and war."[66]

Alison notes that the problem with the cultural feminist position is that it overlooks the fact that men have also supported peace and engaged in peace activism. Moreover, claiming there are male traits and female traits (and thus essentialism of what it means to be male and female) only serves to maintain "an unhealthy dichotomy and implicitly accepts hierarchal thinking about gender; the hierarchy is simply inverted, with femininity valued over masculinity."[67] Women's willingness to participate in political violence demonstrates the problem with the essentialist and biological determinism position that women/mothers equals peace, thereby overlooking the role that culture and socialization play in terms of what it means to be male/female, masculine/feminine, and perpetuating those dichotomies.[68]

As noted earlier in the chapter, we seek to uncover the gender discourses surrounding women and women's activism in IR: women in the home/private sphere, women are the protected, and women equals peace. In opposition, men are located in the political realm/public sphere, men are the protectors, and men equals war. This overview of FST, examining what is meant by security and peace, and how they affect women, tells us that the line between the public and private spheres is blurred. As Confortini rightly observes, there is a "deeply gendered nature of the violence/peace dichotomy, which reproduces relations of power and subjugation in society."[69] By maintaining and perpetuating separate spheres, those on the margins in IR, such as women, are not deemed worthy of study. Sjoberg states, "The division between political and private is not value neutral; it prioritizes those things understood as political while marginalizing those things understood as personal."⁷⁰ Feminist security theorists and theories have demonstrated that the private and public spheres are not separate spheres.

Agency and Intersectionality

Most political systems tend to be patriarchal, and as such, women generally are removed from the decision-making process for structural, political, or cultural reasons. In cases of war and conflict, oftentimes women have little choice in whether they even are or become part of such a conflict. As Pankhurst writes, "Where there is no front line, as conflict is fought out in people's homes, with light weapons, and where the reason for fighting is the very existence, or at least presence, of people with a differently defined identity (usually ethnic), women have been placed on one side or another whether they actively choose this or not."⁷¹ Yet, while leaders, who tend to be men, make the decisions about whether to go to war, women can and do respond to that conflict situation. Women do have agency even within a patriarchal system. Maud Eduards states that "all human beings, by nature, have agency, the capacity to initiate change, to commit oneself to a certain transformative course of action, independently of historical circumstances."⁷² Given this, people will want "to use this capacity in some way or another, to be an agent rather than a passive being, a victim. Put simply, given the chance, people will try to influence the course of events as much as possible rather than sit back and suffer changes."⁷³ Eduards then applies this notion of agency to women in particular: "Because women are said to be closer to nature than men, and nature is defined as unconscious and passive, one position holds that *women do not have agency*. The other position is that women have inborn procreative and caring qualities, that *they have a specific female agency*. Both views deny women the possibility to challenge and change their condition as women. Agency is regarded as a property of subjects, and consequently a male prerogative" (italics in the original).⁷⁴

This idea of women's agency is also reflected in the work of Jennifer Leigh Disney, who in turn draws on the work of Jacqui Alexander and Chandra Mohanty to talk about "the importance of 're-presenting' women not as victims or dependents but as agents of their own lives."⁷⁵ She then quotes Alexander and Mohanty, who define agency as "the conscious and ongoing reproduction of the terms of one's existence while *taking responsibility for* this process" (italics added).⁷⁶

We are interested in understanding women's perspectives and whether they see their actions and political activism as feminist or not, as that will help us to understand their motivations (the why question). In her analysis of Palestinian women's activism, for example, Richter-Devroe notes that "contextualized culturally specific gender roles in the political culture of resistance can be empowering for women. Although it is true that they are not derived from and informed by a clearly defined feminist agenda, they are nevertheless a first step in mobilizing women's political agency."[77] We concur with Disney's statement that "while not all women's activism may be explicitly *feminist*, much of women's activism around class, gender, economics, sexuality, violence, culture, ideology, and materiality in the productive and reproductive spheres of life does involve the exercise of *feminist agency*" (italics in the original).[78] At the same time, we can define feminist agency as an attempt by women and women's organizations to overturn patriarchy and political, economic, and social structures of male dominance and women's subordination. Disney defines feminist agency as women's "transformation from mobilization to participation to organization."[79] In looking at national liberation movements, she shows that women mobilize as women in organizations, and they express feminist agency when they "integrate a feminist analysis of women's oppression into the vision and practice of social change of revolutionary movements."[80] For the Republican women in Northern Ireland and women combatants in the Liberation Tigers of Tamil Eelam (LTTE) in Sri Lanka who perceived themselves as feminists, according to Alison, "their feminism is inextricably intertwined with their respective nationalist communities" and the challenge for these self-identified feminists is how to make inroads within their nationalist movements "to push a feminist agenda."[81]

At the same time that we recognize and acknowledge that women have agency, we also acknowledge that such agency is constrained, as Alison argues, "by the structures and prevailing discourses of our societies and the events of our lives."[82] Sjoberg and Gentry argue that in understanding women's agency and choices, "gendered lenses of feminist research suggest a relational autonomy approach" in that "every choice is not completely free in a world of intersubjective construction and power disparity."[83] One can see this relational autonomy and constrained agency in women's movements. For example, Vanessa Farr notes that Palestinian women have organized in women's movements for decades, although they have not been part of the formal political structure. And as evidence of their constrained agency, citing Kuttab, she notes that "Palestinian women's movements face a central dilemma: the reality and necessity of their political engagement in resistance to the occupation contrasts strongly with the continued, and growing, impacts of conservative gender ideologies that aim to constrain their movements and choices."[84]

In addition to women expressing agency (whether feminist agency or not), recognizing that women have different experiences related to their class, ethnicity, gender, nationality, race, sexuality, and so forth leads us to recognize that not all women have the same interests, and therefore the term *women* or *woman* is problematic. The *intersectionality* of class, race, gender, and sexuality matters in using a gender analysis to account for women's behaviors and actions.[85] As Cockburn avers, intersectionality and positionality relate to "the way individuals and groups are placed in relation to each other in terms of significant dimensions of social difference." The social dimensions of power are class, gender, and race.[86] This intersectionality is all the more important in studying conflicts and security, which is not often addressed in mainstream IR theories. As Sachs, Sa'ar, and Aharoni demonstrate, "civilians' coping with organized political violence is mediated by their locations within webs of power relations, predominantly gender, class, and ethno-nationality. The process of responding to the political situation is intertwined with overall complexes of resources and responsibilities, and these differ significantly in women and men, rich and poor, or members of the majority and members of marginalized minorities."[87] They argue that "the intersectional approach to gender implies that 'women' should be perceived as a heterogeneous category" in which women's experiences in conflict can only be understood by taking into account class, ethnicity, and nationality.[88]

Conclusion

In this chapter we propose our primary research questions: Why and how do some women engage in political activism, whether in the form of peace activism, nonviolent resistance, or outright violence? And why should we study women and women's activism? To begin to answer these questions, we look to FST and feminist scholarship. FST offers a corrective to the limitations of mainstream IR scholarship regarding conflict, security, and women in several ways: (1) it uses a gender analysis to understand conflict, war, and security, and women's responses to those conditions (thereby antiessentialism of the theory: gender is a social construct, and women's peace activism is not because women are inherently or by nature peaceful);

(2) it offers a broader understanding and definition of security beyond security that is just focused on the nation-state in light of what *security* means for women in a society (i.e., Cockburn's continuum of violence: domestic violence, state violence, international violence); (3) it includes intersectionality of dimensions of power and difference, including gender, race, ethnicity, nationality, sexuality, and socioeconomic status; and (4) it recognizes that women are not just victims of violence and war but also have agency (albeit constrained agency) to act and do so sometimes in the form of political activism that includes peace activism, nonviolent resistance, and political violence.

Chapter 2 examines in detail women's activism along a continuum of political activism. In this chapter we explore the motivations of women to become political actors, assessing whether women's motivations to pursue the path of peace activism differ from those engaging in violence (the why question). In addition to considering women's motivations, we also look at factors, or variables, to account for the women themselves, such as marital status, age, ethnicity, and socioeconomic status. Moreover, the intersectionality of class, race, ethnicity, and so forth, can tell us much about different women and their experiences with conflict. Without a full appreciation of the complexity, the intersectionality, of these factors, we cannot fully understand what motivates some women to engage in political activism. In answering the how question, we also consider the factors that mattered in understanding women's recruitment into activism. Related to this, we also take into account the willingness of organizations (particularly rebel or terrorist organizations) to allow women to take an active role as combatants and even suicide bombers, as well as the role of the society or community in supporting and condoning such actions by women.

Chapters 3 through 5 provide case studies of women responding to conflict. The cases were selected for several reasons. First, all three case studies are intrastate conflicts focused on political, cultural, social, and economic struggles (with goals of national self-determination). Second, an asymmetry of power exists between the state and the nationalist/ethnic group. Third, geographic variance—Europe, the Middle East, and South Asia—can help with generalizability. Fourth, the outcomes are different: two of the conflicts are now concluded, although tensions remain, while one of the conflicts is ongoing. In the case of Northern Ireland, the conflict ended with the negotiation and signing of the 1998 Good Friday Agreement. In the case of Sri Lanka, in 2009 government forces defeated the Tamil minority that had long been seeking independence from the Sinhalese majority. The Israeli-Palestinian conflict is ongoing, with Palestinians seeking an end to the Israeli occupation of the West Bank and the formation of an independent Palestinian state in the West Bank and Gaza.

Northern Ireland is explored in chapter 3. In this instance, the shorthand version of "the Troubles," which the conflict came to be called, as a religious conflict of Catholic versus Protestant overlooks the critical aspects of this fight as a political and economic struggle, as well as a struggle for political power and national identity (and an end to what Catholics/Nationalists/Republicans perceive as British occupation of Northern Ireland). The chapter contains examples of women who worked on each of the two sides to try to end the conflict and bring about peace—or, at the very least, cross-communal understanding—as well as women acting in support of the conflict. In that case, the support could range from giving tacit approval to the fighting or picking up arms and becoming part of the violence. Similarly, women worked for peace informally but also within the political system; the creation of the Northern Ireland Women's Coalition gave women the opportunity to have a seat at the table when the 1998 Good Friday Agreement was negotiated.

Chapter 4 examines Palestinian women's political activism. There are many examples of Palestinian women who worked for peace alongside Israeli women or in Palestinian-only organizations; there are also examples of Palestinian women actively engaged in the struggle for Palestinian statehood. For Palestinians, activism to end the occupation ranges from nonviolent resistance (i.e., academic and cultural boycott of Israeli universities and academics, economic boycott of Israeli goods) to armed combatants and suicide bombings. Our focus here is on Palestinian women who do not live in, nor are citizens of, Israel but rather reside in the Palestinian territories (Gaza Strip and the West Bank). The contested status of these territories, which the Palestinian people see as the basis for a state (the Israeli government calls them *disputed territories*, while the international community calls them *occupied territories*), are the focus of the issue that has generated the violence, perpetrated both by the Israeli state and Palestinians. Hence, the issues surrounding Palestine and the Palestinians are tied to self-determination and the essence of what, in IR terms, defines a nation-state.

In chapter 5, we explore Tamil women who belong to the LTTE in Sri Lanka as combatants and as peacemakers, but also as peace builders as the society is reconstructed after years of civil war. This was a nationalist struggle for Tamil independence from the Sinhalese-dominated majority that went on for 26 years, ending only in 2009. Although women in this case also worked for peace, most of the attention has been given to women combatants, especially suicide bombers. Thus, unlike the case of Northern Ireland, for example, where women who worked together across communal lines have been featured most prominently to the general exclusion of women combatants, Sri Lanka is the mirror image of Northern Ireland and represents a case where the focus has been on women combatants and suicide bombers rather than those who worked for peace.

The concluding chapter 6 returns to the original questions asked in this chapter and, based on our research in the case studies, seeks to answer them. In chapter 6 we also address women and the postconflict period, including the role of (and barriers to) women's participation at the negotiating table, as well as the challenges faced by female combatants for their reintegration into society, particularly disarmament, demobilization, and reintegration programs. For lasting peace, postconflict reconciliation is a necessary element.[89] We also offer suggestions for areas of future research.

Notes

1. On nonviolent resistance strategies, see Veronique Dudouet, *Nonviolent Resistance and Conflict Transformation in Power Asymmetries* (Berlin: Berghof Research Center for Constructive Conflict Management, 2008), 5–6, accessed January 23, 2010, http://www.berghof-handbook.net/documents/publications/dudouet_handbook.pdf.

2. "About Women In Black," Women in Black, accessed December 27, 2011, http://www.womeninblack.org/en/about.

3. Alissa J. Rubin, "Despair Drives Suicide Attacks by Iraqi Women," *New York Times*, July 5, 2008, A1.

4. Clifford J. Levy and Ellen Barry, "Russia Says Suicide Bomber Was Militant's Widow," *New York Times*, April 2, 2010, A1.

5. Ibid.

6. Clifford J. Levy, "Second Bomber in Moscow Attacks Is Identified," *New York Times*, April 6, 2010, A1.

7. See Joyce P. Kaufman and Kristen P. Williams, *Women, the State and War: A Comparative Perspective on Citizenship and Nationalism* (Lanham, MD: Lexington Books, 2007); and Joyce P. Kaufman and Kristen P. Williams, *Women and War: Gender Identity and Activism in Times of Conflict* (Sterling, VA: Kumarian Press, 2010).

8. Dudouet, *Nonviolent Resistance*, 9. For a quantitative analysis of the effectiveness of strategic nonviolent resistance between nonstate and state actors from

1900 to 2006, see Maria J. Stephan and Erica Chenoweth, "Why Civil Resistance Works: The Strategic Logic of Nonviolent Conflict," *International Security* 33, no. 1 (Summer 2008): 7–44.

9. See Sanam Naraghi Anderlini, *Women Building Peace: What They Do, Why It Matters* (Boulder, CO: Lynne Rienner, 2007); Cynthia Cockburn, *From Where We Stand: War, Women's Activism and Feminist Analysis* (London: Zed Books, 2007), 141; Swanee Hunt, "Moving Beyond Silence: Women Waging Peace," in *Listening to the Silences: Women and War*, ed., Helen Durham and Tracy Gurd (The Netherlands: Koninklijke Brill BV, 2005), 251; Donna Pankhurst, "The 'Sex War' and Other Wars: Towards a Feminist Approach to Peace Building," *Development in Practice* 12, no. 2–3 (May 2003), 161; and Donna Pankhurst, ed., *Gendered Peace: Women's Struggles for Post-War Justice and Reconciliation* (New York: Routledge, 2008).

10. Laura Sjoberg and Caron E. Gentry, eds., *Women, Gender and Terrorism* (Athens: University of Georgia Press, 2011); Laura Sjoberg and Caron E. Gentry, *Mothers, Monsters, Whores: Women's Violence in Global Politics* (London: Zed Books, 2007); Paige Whaley Eager, *From Freedom Fighters to Terrorists: Women and Political Violence* (Burlington, VT: Ashgate, 2008); and Mia Bloom, *Dying to Kill: The Allure of Suicide Terror* (New York: Columbia University Press, 2007).

11. See, for example, Linda Ahall and Laura J. Shepherd, eds., *Gender, Agency and Political Violence* (Basingstoke, UK: Palgrave Macmillan, 2012); Wenona Giles and Jennifer Hyndman, eds., *Sites of Violence: Gender and Conflict Zones* (Berkeley: University of California Press, 2004); Caroline O. N. Moser and Fiona C. Clark, eds., *Victims, Perpetrators or Actors: Gender, Armed Conflict and Political Violence* (London: Zed Books, 2001); Wenona Giles, Malathu de Alwais, Edith Klein, and Neluka Silva, eds., *Feminists Under Fire: Exchanges Across War Zones* (Toronto, Canada: Between the Lines, 2003); and Susie Jacobs, Ruth Jacobson and Jennifer Marchbank, eds., *States of Conflict: Gender, Violence and Resistance* (London: Zed Books, 2000).

12. Bloom, *Dying to Kill*; Barbara Victor, *Army of Roses: Inside the World of Palestinian Suicide Bombers* (New York: Rodale Press, 2003); Rosemarie Skaine, *Female Suicide Bombers* (Jefferson, NC: MacFarland, 2006).

13. See, for example, Miranda Alison, *Women and Political Violence: Female Combatants in Ethno-National Conflict* (New York: Routledge, 2009); Miranda Alison, "Women as Agents of Political Violence: Gendering Security," *Security Dialogue* 35, no. 4 (December 2004): 447–63; Miranda Alison, "Cogs in the Wheel? Women in the Liberation Tigers of Tamil Eelam," *Civil Wars* 6, no. 4 (Winter 2003): 37–54; Sandra McEvoy, "Loyalist Women Paramilitaries in Northern Ireland: Beginning a Feminist Conversation about Conflict Resolution," *Security Studies* 18, no. 2 (April 2009): 262–86.

14. During an academic study visit to Israel and the West Bank in January 2012, Kristen spoke informally with Israelis (Jews and Arabs) and Palestinians

about the Israeli-Palestinian conflict. While not formal interviews, the conversations were extremely helpful as we conducted the research for this book.

15. S. Laurel Weldon, *When Protest Makes Policy: How Social Movements Represent Disadvantaged Groups* (Ann Arbor: University of Michigan Press, 2011), 15–16.

16. Sjoberg and Gentry, *Mothers, Monsters, Whores*, 7.

17. Ibid.

18. Ibid., 9.

19. Kenneth N. Waltz, *Theory of International Politics* (New York: Random House, 1979). Other mainstream IR theories include liberalism (and its neo variant) and social constructivism. In the case of liberalism, international institutions serve as mechanisms for state cooperation; in social constructivism, self-help and anarchy are social constructions that influence how states behave. In none of these are gender and women the focal points of analysis.

20. J. Ann Tickner, *Gender in International Relations: Feminist Perspectives on Achieving Global Security* (New York: Columbia University Press, 1992), 41.

21. Cynthia Enloe, *Bananas, Beaches and Bases: Making Feminist Sense of International Relations* (Berkeley: University of California Press, 1989).

22. For excellent discussions of feminist IR theory, see Enloe, *Bananas, Beaches and Bases*; Christine Sylvester, *Feminist Theory and International Relations in a Postmodern Era* (Cambridge: Cambridge University Press, 1994); J. Ann Tickner, *Gendering World Politics: Issues and Approaches in the Post–Cold War Era* (New York: Columbia University Press, 2001); Brooke A. Ackerly, Maria Stern, and Jaqui True, eds., *Feminist Methodologies for International Relations* (Cambridge: Cambridge University Press, 2006); V. Spike Peterson and Anne Sisson Runyan, *Global Gender Issues in the New Millennium*, 3rd ed. (Boulder, CO: Westview Press, 2010).

23. On gender order and power, see Catia Confortini, "Galtung, Violence, and Gender: The Case for a Peace Studies/Feminism Alliance," *Peace and Change* 31, no. 3 (July 2006): 355.

24. Amalia Sa'ar, Dalia Sachs, and Sarai Aharoni, "Between a Gender and a Feminist Analysis: The Case of Security Studies in Israel," *International Sociology* 26, no. 1 (January 2011): 55, 56.

25. Ibid., 64.

26. J. Ann Tickner, "You Just Don't Understand: Troubled Engagements between Feminists and IR Theorists," *International Studies Quarterly* 41 (1997), 614.

27. Charles Tilly, *Coercion, Capital and European States* (Cambridge, MA: Blackwell, 1992). See also Kaufman and Williams, *Women, the State and War*, 12.

28. Laura Sjoberg and Jessica Peet, "A(nother) Dark Side of the Protection Racket," *International Feminist Journal of Politics* 13, no. 2 (June 2011): 167.

29. Ibid.

30 Confortini, "Galtung, Violence, and Gender," 355.

31. Sjoberg and Peet, "A(nother) Dark Side," 168.

32. Laura Sjoberg, "Seeing Gender in International Security," June 5, 2012, accessed August 16, 2012, http://www.e-ir.info/2012/06/05/seeing-gender-in-international-security/.

33. For a comprehensive description of each of these feminist approaches, see J. Ann Tickner and Laura Sjoberg, "Feminism," in *Theories of International Relations: Discipline and Diversity*, ed. Tim Dunner, Milya Kurki, and Steve Smith (Oxford: Oxford University Press, 2006), 185–202.

34. A special issue of *Politics & Gender* included articles by different scholars and their take on the state of feminist security studies. See the special section "State of Feminist Security Studies: A Conversation" in *Politics & Gender* 7, no. 4 (2011). On the need for engagement with other mainstream security studies scholars, including critical scholars, see the articles by J. Ann Tickner ("Feminist Security Studies: Celebrating an Emerging Field"), Lauren Wilcox ("Beyond Sex/Gender: The Feminist Body of Security"), and Valerie M. Hudson ("But Now Can See: One Academic's Journey to Feminist Security Studies"). For the need to keep feminist security studies and security studies separate, see articles by Annick T. Wibben ("Feminist Politics in Feminist Security Studies") and Carol Cohn ("'Feminist Security Studies': Toward a Reflexive Practice"). For more on a discussion of how security is framed by feminist IR/security scholars, see Christine Sylvester, "Tensions in Feminist Security Studies," *Security Dialogue* 41, no. 6 (2010): 607–14.

35. Laura Sjoberg, "Looking Forward, Conceptualizing Feminist Security Studies," *Politics & Gender* 7, no. 4 (2011): 600.

36. Eric M. Blanchard, "Gender, International Relations, and the Development of Feminist Security Theory," *Signs* 28, no. 4 (Summer 2003): 1290.

37. Ibid.

38. Ibid.

39. Jennifer K. Lobasz and Laura Sjoberg, "Introduction," *Politics & Gender* 7, no. 4 (2011): 573.

40. Sa'ar et al., "Between a Gender," 51.

41. Ibid., 53.

42. For more on human security as it relates to state security, see the United Nations Office for the Coordination of Humanitarian Affairs, "Human Security for All," http://www.unocha.org/humansecurity/about-human-security/human-security-all.

43. J. Ann Tickner, *Gender in International Relations* (New York: Columbia University Press, 1993), 58. This relationship is stressed by Cynthia Cockburn in her book *The Space between Us: Negotiating Gender and National Identities in Conflict* (London: Zed Books, 1998), and is a relationship noted by others as well. See, for example, Laurence McKeown and Simona Sharoni, "Formations and

Transformations of Masculinity in the North of Ireland and in Israel-Palestine," unpublished paper, 2002, http://www.simonasharoni.com/Docs/MasculinityUnpublished.pdf; also, Kaufman and Williams, *Women, the State and War*, 173–74, which summarizes our findings on this issue.

44. Sjoberg and Peet, "A(nother) Dark Side," 172.

45. Johann Galtung, "Violence, Peace and Peace Research," *Journal of Peace Research* 6, no. 3 (1969): 171.

46. Cockburn, *From Where We Stand*, 190–91. For more on the continuum of violence and violence as a choice, see Cockburn, *Antimilitarism: Political and Gender Dynamics of Peace Movements* (Basingstoke, UK: Palgrave Macmillan, 2012).

47. According to Galtung, "Violence, Peace," negative peace refers to the absence of violence, while positive peace refers to social justice. See Confortini, "Galtung, Violence, and Gender," 335.

48. Peterson and Runyan, *Global Gender Issues*, 179.

49. Pankhurst, "'Sex War,'" 161. See also, Pankhurst, "Introduction: Gendered War and Peace," in *Gendered Peace: Women's Struggles for Post-War Justice and Reconciliation*, ed. Donna Pankhurst (New York: Routledge, 2008), 1–30.

50. Pankhurst, "'Sex War,'" 161. Megan MacKenzie finds that in the postconflict period in Sierra Leone, female combatants were worse off. See MacKenzie, "Empowerment Boom or Bust? Assessing Women's Post-Conflict Empowerment Initiatives," *Cambridge Review of International Affairs* 22, no. 2 (June 2009): 199–215.

51. Confortini, "Galtung, Violence, and Gender," 336. For a critique of hegemonic masculinity as a way to understand (men's) violence toward women, see Donna Pankhurst, "Post-War Backlash Violence against Women: What Can 'Masculinity' Explain," in *Gendered Peace: Women's Struggles for Post-War Justice and Reconciliation*, ed. Donna Pankhurst (New York: Routledge, 2008), 308–10. She argues that "the concepts of masculinity, hyper-masculinity, hegemonic masculinity, and crisis of masculinity, do not help us with understanding the variety of behaviour patterns" (p. 310).

52. Confortini, "Galtung, Violence, and Gender," 337.

53. Ibid., 342.

54. Ibid., 346.

55. Ibid.

56. Ibid.

57. For more on the cycle of violence and what happens to women during and after conflict, see Fionnuala Ní Aoláin, Dina Francesca Haynes, and Naomi Cahn, *On the Frontlines: Gender, War, and the Post-Conflict Process* (New York: Oxford University Press, 2011).

58. Confortini, "Galtung, Violence, and Gender," 357.

59. Chris J. Cuomo, "War Is Not Just an Event: Reflections on the Significance of Everyday Violence," *Hypatia* 11, no. 4 (Fall 1996): 30–31.

60. Ibid.

61. Ibid., 32.

62. Tami Amanda Jacoby, *Women in Zones of Conflict: Power and Resistance in Israel* (Quebec: McGill-Queen's University Press, 2005), 13.

63. Alison, *Women and Political Violence*, 85.

64. Ibid.

65. Ibid.

66. Ibid., 86.

67. Ibid., 89.

68. Ibid., 94.

69. Confortini, "Galtung, Violence, and Gender," 349. For more on the blurring of the private and public spheres as related to women and armed conflict, see Maria Stern and Malin Nystrand, *Gender and Armed Conflict* (Stockholm: Swedish International Development Cooperation Agency, April 2006), 44–46.

70. Laura Sjoberg, "Conclusion: The Study of Women, Gender, and Terrorism," in Sjoberg and Gentry, *Women, Gender and Terrorism*, 233.

71. Pankhurst, "Women, Gender and Peacebuilding," 7.

72. Maud L. Eduards, "Women's Agency and Collective Action," *Women's Studies International Forum* 17, no. 2–3 (1994): 181.

73. Ibid.

74. Ibid., 182.

75. Jennifer Leigh Disney, *Women's Activism and Feminist Agency in Mozambique and Nicaragua* (Philadelphia, PA: Temple University Press, 2008), 41.

76. Ibid.

77. Sophie Richter-Devroe, "Gender, Culture, and Conflict Resolution in Palestine." *Journal of Middle East Women's Studies* 4, no. 2 (Spring 2008): 52.

78. Disney, *Women's Activism*, 34.

79. Ibid., x.

80. Ibid., 2.

81. Alison, *Women and Political Violence*, 231.

82. Ibid., 120.

83. Sjoberg and Gentry, *Mothers, Monsters, Whores*, 16–17. See also Sjoberg and Gentry, "The Gendering of Women's Terrorism," in Sjoberg and Gentry, *Women, Gender, and Terrorism*, 57–80.

84. Vanessa Farr, "UNSCR 1325 and Women's Peace Activism in the Occupied Palestinian Territory," *International Feminist Journal of Politics* 13, no. 4 (December 2011): 545.

85. On intersectionality, see Floya Anthias and Nira Yuval-Davis, *Racialized Boundaries: Race, Nation, Gender, Colour and Class and the Anti-Racist Struggle* (London: Routledge, 1992); Flavia Agnes, "Transgressing Boundaries of Gender and Identity," *Economic and Political Weekly* 37, no. 36 (2002): 3695–98; Giles and Hyndman, *Sites of Violence;* Leslie McCall, "The Complexity of Intersectionality," *Signs* 30, no. 3 (Spring 2005): 1771–1800; Cockburn, *From Where We Stand*; Peterson and Runyan, *Global Gender Issues*.

86. Cockburn, *From Where We Stand*, 7.

87. Dalia Sachs, Amalia Sa'ar, and Sarai Aharoni, "'How Can I Feel for Others When I Myself Am Beaten?' The Impact of Armed Conflict on Women in Israel," *Sex Roles* 57 (2007): 595.

88. Ibid. Their work examines the impact of armed conflict on Israeli women—Jewish and Palestinian women living in Israel proper—and within these two groups they examine class and nationality and how they intersect with gender.

89. Dudouet, *Nonviolent Resistance*, 18.

2
Women, Conflict, and Political Activism

In December 2011 the United States announced it had extradited a Bosnian Muslim woman, Rasema Handovic, to Bosnia to stand trial for killing six Bosnian-Croat civilians as part of the mass killings of Croat civilians in Bosnia and Herzegovina in April 1993 during the Bosnian-Croat War of 1993–1994. She and her companion, Edin Dzeko, who was also extradited, were alleged to have belonged to a Bosnian army unit that attacked the Bosnian-Croat village of Trusina, killing eighteen people. Witnesses say that Handovic personally shot some of the victims in the head.

This case is at odds with many of the assumptions surrounding that war, not the least of which are the gendered assumptions of women, especially Bosnian Muslim women, as victims. Eyewitnesses claimed she was clearly a combatant rather than a victim. In this case, a Bosnian Muslim woman "is one of only a few women accused of war crimes committed during the Bosnian conflict."

After she and Dzeko fled to the United States, both became naturalized American citizens. Nonetheless, the United States authorized their extradition to stand trial on war crimes.

AS WE DISCUSS IN CHAPTER 1, FEMINIST SCHOLARS MAKE AN IMPORTANT contribution to international relations theory by examining women's political activism that opposes war, militarism, and patriarchy. Such a gender analysis also explains women's political activism that supports and reproduces patriarchy, war, and militarism.[2] In using a feminist and gender analysis in examining women's activism, we show that such activism confronts gender norms about women's behavior. Whether women engage in working for peace or in acts of resistance and political violence, they challenge existing gender norms in times of conflict (and postconflict) by participating in the public sphere in two ways: (1) women's participation in peace activism and peace negotiations, which are overtly political acts, and (2) women as combatants and supporters of conflict, thereby challenging the gender norm of women as peaceful. (We recognize that the private and public spheres are not, in fact, a dichotomy or binary; the line between them is blurred.)

An underlying gendered (and essentialist) assumption is that women's political activism will be in support of peace and that women will use nonviolent means (such as protests, vigils, boycotts, and public speeches) to make their point. However, we argue that women's activism can also support a conflict through nonviolent resistance and as armed combatants. There is no presumption that women's political activism will always be working for peace, which is the more traditional—and gendered— assumption about women's behavior during conflict. Also important to recognize is that often it has been difficult for women to challenge the existing political system, especially in times of war and conflict, even to work for peace, something that is seen within the purview of "women's nature" (a gender norm). This challenge is magnified when women choose to support one side of a conflict and pick up arms.

The exploration of the gendered assumptions as related to women's political activism is the focus of this chapter. We begin with a discussion of women and peace activism, examining the motivations of women activists and how peace activism itself challenges gender norms, even though such activism also reinforces the essentializing role of women as peaceful and nurturing. We then move to a discussion of women engaging in nonviolent resistance and political violence in support of a conflict, including taking up arms and becoming suicide bombers. As with peace activism, we examine women's motivations for engaging in political activism in support of conflict, including activism as expressed through violence, again a challenge to gender norms. In this type of activism, in addition to entering the public sphere, women's activism upends gendered and essentialist notions of women as peaceful. If women are willing to engage in political violence, what does this say about essentialist claims that *women equals peace* because of women's biology as reproducers, caregivers, and nurturers?

Returning to the words of Sjoberg and Gentry, "Women, like men, are capable of violence. As women's freedoms increase, so will their violence.

Women, like men, commit violence for a variety of reasons, some rational and some irrational."[3] In short, women's actions and reasons for committing acts of political violence are not necessarily different from those of men. What makes it appear to be different is the fact that we, society and culture, do not generally attribute these violent characteristics to women, nor do we assume that women will resort to acts of violence to settle a difference, either personally or in the larger political realm. Clearly, these gendered assumptions are belied by the realities.

In addition, scholars developing theories of individual violence focused on men. When women were considered in the context of these theories, Sjoberg and Gentry assert "*not only* that these theories omitted women, but that their genderings made them inadequate to explain *both* men's and women's violence" (italics in the original).[4] Thus, we cannot necessarily assume *either* that any theory that explains political violence in general can be attributed to the motivations of *both* men and women, nor can we similarly assume that women have different motivations than men. Importantly, any examination of women's involvement in political conflict must be contextual, with an eye toward understanding women's reasons for engaging in these acts. To accomplish this, we also need to be aware of the fact that just as it is impossible to generalize across all men's motivations for violence, it is impossible to discern all women's.

For example, in the case of Northern Ireland, the focus of chapter 3, Valerie Morgan states that "in examining women's attitudes to conflict and responses to physical violence it seems clear that these have spanned the whole range from active support of paramilitaries to direct campaigning for peace. Certainly a blanket assertion that women oppose physical violence in pursuit of political ends [is] a serious oversimplification."[5] Or, as Cindy Ness reminds us, we must keep in mind "that violence is also always driven by conditions, context and language that are unique to the setting in which it emerges."[6] These comments suggest that the conclusions we draw here are specific to the cases we use, yet we hope to be able to identify characteristics that will provide some guidance in moving beyond those cases, so we can better understand women's decisions to become politically active.

In our research we also note that women's ability to take up arms is contingent on whether the male leaders of political organizations will allow them to do so and whether the society supports women in these roles. We also provide examples to illustrate women's political activism, although specific cases are examined in more detail in subsequent chapters. What is important about these examples is that in all of them some women chose to work for peace and resolve the conflict, while others opted to engage in acts of nonviolent resistance and political violence. We come full circle with our research questions: *Why* do some women get involved in political activism (what are their motivations)? *How* do they become involved in political activism?

As asserted in chapter 1, we see women's political activism along a continuum: women engage in peace activism at the informal/grassroots level, they engage in peace activism in formal big P politics (e.g., forming political parties, participating in peace negotiations), they engage in activism in support of a conflict through nonviolent resistance (e.g., protest, preparing documents and leaflets for distribution, gathering intelligence), and they engage in support of a conflict through political violence (e.g., becoming armed combatants, suicide bombers). In essence, we recognize that women's political activism is not a binary or dichotomy of peace versus violence. Rather women's activism does fall along a continuum. For the purposes of illustration of women's political activism in this chapter and the case chapters that follow, however, we do separate peace activism and political violence in discussing and assessing women's motivations (the why question) and the mechanisms by which women became politically active (the how question). The next section focuses on women as agents of peace and looks at women's motivations, feminist and traditional, for their decisions to engage in political activism. The section that follows examines women as agents of violence, looking at women's motivations for nonviolent resistance and political violence in support of one side of a conflict.

Women as Agents of Peace

States depend on the creation of a national identity that places women at its center, as does the term *mother country*, for example. Yet, women are also excluded from participating in political decisions, including the decision for war. The social construction of ethnic and national identities has contributed to the civil conflicts that have emerged since the end of the Cold War in places as varied as Bosnia, Rwanda, Sudan, Somalia, and Sri Lanka, to name a few. Thus, identity and nationalism become important coalescing forces that can perpetuate violence. Feminist scholars have noted that nationalism is gendered in so far as women's gendered roles in the private sphere are linked to the public sphere of the nation, the body politic. Women are expected to serve in the role "as biological reproducers of group members" through state policies that restrict contraception and prohibit abortion.[7] State policies can also provide rewards to women for having more children. Religious and social norms and laws encourage women to serve "as reproducers of group members and their cultural forms."[8] Moreover, women are also considered "participants in political identity struggles" in that not only do they serve as symbols of group identity but they also support and participate in nationalist causes.[9] Often these images and identity of ethnicity and nationalism are built around the representations of women who need to be "protected" by their men and become a rationale for violence.

Krishna Kumar argues that intrastate conflicts "share five broad characteristics relevant to women and gender studies."[10] First, warring parties intentionally commit violence against civilians. Second, civil conflicts lead to the displacement of large numbers of people. Along with that, sometimes traditional gender roles of both women and men are redefined in such a way that "the family institution comes under severe stress, resulting in divorce and desertion."[11] The third characteristic she identifies is "women's own participation in civil wars [that] contributes to the redefinition of their identities and traditional roles."[12] And women, as well as men, are victims of violence (and are perpetrators of violence).[13] Fourth, the belligerent parties intentionally "destroy the supporting civilian infrastructure."[14] And last, civil wars "leave a legacy of anger, bitterness, and hatred among the belligerent groups that is difficult to heal."[15] If the state has not been partitioned when the conflict ends, then the parties to the conflict are not separated and instead will "continue to face each other daily."[16] Further, intrastate conflicts alter the battlefield in the sense that violence permeates the home in a number of different ways: the emergence of paramilitaries that affect a community, an increase in domestic violence, and of course rape and sexual violence as tools of war, which all mean that intrastate war intrudes on the private lives of citizens in ways that interstate wars may not.

In cases of civil or intrastate conflict, one group is set in opposition to another group within a state. Ethnic, religious, tribal, and national conflicts upend previously harmonious relationships. Neighbors and former friends can become enemies. Family members from different ethnic or religious groups can also become enemies.[17] The expectation is that women must take a side as the conflict erupts. At the same time, conflicts can provide women with the opportunity for political activism, thereby expressing power and agency as they work toward resolving the conflict and establishing peace.

Women have been active in working for peace at the national and international levels, and examples are abundant in the literature. A long history of women's politicization and activism is linked to women's peace movements, including the creation of the Women's International League for Peace and Freedom in 1915 during World War I. Intrastate conflicts may speed up this process. The evidence also shows that historically women have played important roles in encouraging peace. Women's activism in support of peace has taken a variety of approaches, including grassroots efforts to raise attention to the causes of peace through the creation of groups such as Women in Black in Israel, as well as formal political efforts and involvement at peace negotiations such as the Northern Ireland Women's Coalition.

Clearly, women have an important role to play during a conflict in negotiating the peace that will end the conflict, in helping to create a social and political structure that will dominate after the conflict ends, and in playing a role in the postconflict social and political process, especially the formal political process, which can help avoid or avert conflicts in the future. According to Peterson and Runyan, women "have long been involved in analyzing how to stop war and how to create peace, though they have received no attention for these activities in past and most contemporary international relations literature. Instead, their peace efforts have been ignored or trivialized—largely by men who stereotype women as soft-headed, irrational pacifists. This characterization is political because it excludes women's perspectives from the study of war and peace."[18]

Women's perspectives are important because women may see issues of war and peace differently from men. Their own experiences with war and conflict are often not the same as men's experiences with war and conflict. Women are affected by gender-based violence in ways that men are not (sexual violence/rape; disruption of family life when needing to find food and shelter for their families, etc.). Given these different experiences, women may have issues of importance to bring to the negotiations regarding peace and what the postconflict society might look like.

In most cases, however, when the conflict ends, the patriarchal structure of society is not transformed in such a way that leads to women's equality nor to women's access to the formal political system. Moreover, often the barriers to women's participation in the formal political system prior to, as well as during and following, conflict are imposed on them by gendered social and political realities. Costs and time commitments necessary to run for office, access to networks or mentors who can help provide critical introductions, and meetings scheduled at times when women cannot attend (e.g., those with child care and school-aged children) are but a few of the barriers that inhibit women's involvement with the formal political system. Consequently, for many women, their activism is at the grassroots level where they can find areas of commonality despite political differences and therefore where they can really have an impact. This is consistent with what Elisabeth Porter noted in the case of women in Northern Ireland in which she talks about women's narratives that help build a "dialogue across difference."[19] Specifically, she writes, "Women constantly share each other's life stories and the myriad of details that make up mundane ordinary lives, shared over the telephone, when walking the children to school, over coffee when borrowing a household item or clothes. Talking through our narratives with those who come from different traditions, communities and regions is crucial to break the barriers of distrust that too often are based on fear cultivated through ignorance."[20] Hence, building trust and participation in the community becomes an important step toward political involvement, inclusion, and reconciliation.

Building a dialogue across difference provides a means for women to engage in peace activism. Some women oppose war by virtue of their motherist position (which builds on a more traditional and, hence, essentialist social role). Women become peace activists because as wives and mothers they feel the effects of the conflict directly, and their traditional role as mothers and wives becomes the basis of commonality and opens the door to women's political activism. Examples include Israel's Parents Against Silence and the Vietnam-era U.S. group Another Mother for Peace.[21] This broad generalization risks essentializing women's roles as peacemakers. At the same time, however, it is also the case that women identified themselves not as feminists or activists. Instead, as wives and mothers they believed it was their responsibility to pursue peace (an end to conflict). Other women oppose war based on motivations that are explicitly feminist: opposition to the militaristic decisions made by predominantly male leaders and with the stated goal of ending the patriarchal structure of their society. Examples of this approach include Women's Peaceful Road in Colombia and Women in Black in Belgrade.[22]

Women opposed to war have an *immediate goal*—to end the conflict. Women became involved in political activism not only because they were affected personally by war and conflict, but because they often felt they had a particular perspective to bring and a role to play. Whether taking a feminist or a more traditional approach, women's perspectives and understandings of security tend to be much broader than seeing peace as the end of conflict. For many women, they seek to address the root causes of the conflict. The important point is that regardless of the particular ideological approach taken (feminist versus motherist/traditional), the result was the same: women *choosing* to work actively for peace during the conflict.

It is also important to recognize, however, there are often differences in the long-term goals of those motivated by traditional gender roles and those motivated by feminist goals. Although these are broad categorizations, in general, feminist activists seek to change the patriarchal structure of society that places masculinity and men hierarchically above femininity and women in all aspects of society (political, social, cultural, and economic) and hinders women's equality. For feminists, a more just and equal society is required when the conflict ends, not a return to the prewar status quo, which often leaves women in unequal economic, social, and political positions. On the other hand, in general, women motivated by traditional gender roles and behavior, namely, protecting their families and communities, do not seek to change the patriarchal structure explicitly, though they still seek an end to the conflict.

These differences in motivations (traditional versus feminist) are manifested in the types of women's movements, as noted previously. Some women's movements are explicitly feminist, while others are not. According to Beckwith, women's movements provide important entry points for "democracy at the level of citizen participation."[23] This makes democracy more inclusive. Women's movements "generally extend mass participation and thus contribute to democratic development."[24] Given that "all women share the common experience of political exclusion as a class," they also "share a common focus as they organize: to challenge and to transcend their political exclusion as they struggle for specific goals."[25] This activism challenges the state and civil society to respond to the demands of women's movements, groups not normally included in the formal power structures of the state.[26]

Beckwith cautions, however, that "definitions of women's movements sometimes serve to conflate feminist movements and women's movements."[27] Antifeminist and right-wing women's movements also address women's issues and their gendered experiences. Yet the goals of these movements are not to challenge and alter the patriarchal structure of society. As noted previously, feminist movements seek to alter existing patriarchal power arrangements and can be considered a subset of women's movements broadly defined.[28] In defining women's movements as *"social movements where women, organized explicitly as such, are the major actors and leaders and make gendered identity claims the basis for their actions"* (italics in the original),[29] Beckwith argues that what women's movements have in common is that women's issues, decision making, leadership, and gendered experiences are the fundamental issues.[30]

As mentioned at the outset of this section, many intrastate conflicts revolve around countries' issues of ethnic and nationalist identities. Examples of women's peace activism abound that show that women sometimes put their nationalist identity above their gender identity, but there are also examples of women pushing their gender identity (a form of a dialogue across difference—in this case differences in national or ethnic identity but similarity in gender and positioning as women) or identity as women above nationalist or ethnic identity.[31] Women and women's groups have integrated positions that pertain to issues of gender as part of their campaign for peace. One excellent example is Women in Black, initially founded in Israel in 1988 following the first intifada by Palestinians in 1987. These women participated in silent vigils each week to protest the Israeli occupation of Gaza and the West Bank, and they continue to hold silent vigils each Friday afternoon in Jerusalem protesting war, militarism, and human rights abuses. Women in Black is explicitly feminist in its outlook, as its website makes clear: "It is evident . . . that we have a feminist understanding: that male violence against women in domestic life and in the community, in times of peace and in times of war, are interrelated. Violence is used as a means of controlling women."[32] It is also dedicated to crossing ethnic and national lines to foster cooperation in support of justice and peace: "We work for a world where difference does not mean inequality, oppression or exclusion. Women's voices are often drowned out in mixed actions of men and women. When we act alone what women say is really heard."[33] The group's website also claims that women have a different perspective about war, given the impact that war and conflict have on women, which is often quite different from the impact on men.

In recognizing this difference, however, Women in Black's peace activism does not support the essentialist view that women are "natural born peace-makers"; rather, the group's website notes that "women often inhabit different cultures from men, and are disproportionately involved in caring work. We know what justice and oppression mean, because we experience them as women. Most women have a different experience of war from that of most men. All women in war fear rape. Women are the majority of refugees. A feminist view sees masculine cultures as specially prone to violence, and so feminist women tend to have a particular perspective on security and something unique to say about war."[34]

Yet another example is the Coalition of Women for Peace (CWP), also located in Israel. According to its website,

> The Coalition of Women for Peace is a *feminist* organization against the occupation of Palestine and for a just peace. Founded in November 2000, after the outbreak of the Second Intifada, CWP today is a leading voice in the Israeli peace movement, bringing together women from a wide variety of identities and groups. *CWP is committed to ending*

the occupation and creating a more just society, while enhancing women's inclusion and participation in the public discourse. CWP initiates public campaigns and education and outreach programs, working to develop and integrate a feminist discourse on all levels of society.[35] (italics added)

Women also come together through their traditional gender identity in which they engage in peace activism as mothers or wives or both. These identities are perceived as less threatening to the patriarchal structure in society. In times of conflict, women are motivated to move from the private sphere of the home into the public sphere, and many find it liberating and empowering. What this means, as feminist scholars continue to assert, is that the private-public sphere divide is less rigid than is assumed, and can be seen more as a continuum with women crossing the two spheres.[36] Examples of peace activism in support of explicitly traditional gender roles include Parents Against Silence, uniting Israeli parents against Israel's invasion of Lebanon in 1982. Women of the Mothers of the Plaza de Mayo used their identity as mothers to challenge Argentina's military regime, which responded to political dissent through the policy of the "disappeared"—literally people were taken from their homes and never seen again.[37] According to Swanee Hunt and Cristina Posa, a maternal identity enables women to transcend international borders and find common ground on the means to promote peace, particularly a peace that will benefit their communities: "And since women know their communities, they can predict acceptance of peace initiatives as well as broker agreements in their own neighborhoods."[38] This maternal identity is related to what Sara Ruddick calls "maternal thinking" and "maternal practice" rooted in social practice and not biology.[39] It is in the act and practice of caring for children that "mothers typically find it not only natural but compelling to protect and foster the growth of their children."[40] In turn, women engage in maternal thinking, which leads many women, because of their perceived commonalities, to unify in support of pacifism and antimilitarism, and thus oppose war.[41]

In both cases, as explicitly feminist or traditional motivations for peace activism, women act—they are agents in their political activism. While it may be the case that women are more comfortable taking traditional, or essentialist, roles, or that such activism is considered less threatening to the existing patriarchal structure, the problem for women's peace activism that uses gender essentialisms, in effect, "reinforces patriarchal values and hierarchies."[42] As Elissa Helms reminds us, and other feminists have noted, when women's movements use their members' identities in terms of their traditional domestic roles as wives and mothers, these movements "are too easily co-opted by patriarchal, male-dominated nationalist movements."[43] In addition to the possibility of being co-opted by male-dominated nationalist movements, many scholars have also shown that when the conflict ends, women are expected to go back to their domestic duties in the home and not participate in the peace negotiations or the postconflict reconstruction of the society. This happened in places such as Algeria, Nicaragua, and Zimbabwe.[44]

In writing about women's political activism in Northern Ireland, Monica McWilliams identified five stages of women's involvement (she was one of two women representing the Northern Ireland Women's Coalition at the peace talks). Women became more political as well as more politicized over time, and this coincided with the increase of political violence. Women's political activism in Northern Ireland was connected to the civil rights movements of the 1960s and 1970s, the feminist struggles of the 1970s and 1980s in the United States and elsewhere, and then to "the recent campaigns by women's groups as they struggle for increased recognition in the new peace processes which may determine the political future of Northern Ireland."[45] She describes a process of increased involvement by women starting within a broader (i.e., civil rights) movement. The process then continued with the underlying goal of improving conditions in society. Importantly, McWilliams's stages of women's involvement have applicability in addition to the case of Northern Ireland.

Porter identifies a number of reasons the community is considered a safe place for women's political activism. She argues that the community is essential to the lived experiences of national identity in terms of the cultural, economic, political, and social dynamics of people's narratives. It is the community that "open[s] the political space to where women's activism lies."[46] While this type of women's activism in the community can be seen as narrowly encompassing and often connected to perceived women's issues (e.g., child care, education, rape counseling, and welfare rights), at the same time community activism enables women to gain experience organizing around a particular issue, often with women in groups that would otherwise be in conflict.

Hence, according to Bouta et al., women's organizations "form an essential part of civil society and have the potential to promote women's leadership, to build awareness of women's rights, and to contribute to gender equality."[47] Community-based women's organizations can play an important role in women's politicization. In this role, women are also motivated to act and to transcend the structural barriers that make it difficult for them to enter the formal political system. Moreover, many of these community-based organizations provide an opening for women to engage in cross-community activism as an inroad to peace activism.[48] In this way, women's activism challenges gender norms of remaining in the domestic/private sphere, and instead propels them into the public sphere of political action. This tells us something as well about answering the how question: how did women get politically active? For many, it became a gradual process, and for most, it started with engaging in activism in their communities.

Women as Agents of Resistance and Political Violence

Women play many roles that support the conflict short of actually taking part in acts of political violence (part of the continuum of political activism), including gathering intelligence, hiding weapons, and fighting. But there are also myriad examples of women who go beyond supporting the conflict in some way to actively engaging in acts of violence as combatants: women suicide bombers in Iraq and Israel; female members of the Liberation Tigers of Tamil Eelam (LTTE) in Sri Lanka; American military women engaged in various acts of abuse and torture at the Abu Ghraib prison in Iraq. Female combatants have been active in Algeria, El Salvador, Eritrea, Ethiopia, Mozambique, Namibia, Nepal, Nicaragua, South Africa, and Zimbabwe. In the contemporary period, scholars have reported that about 30–40 percent of fighting forces in many of the ethnic-separatist groups around the world are women. As part of that participation, women have played leadership roles (although they do not actually attain the top leadership positions).[49] These actions challenge the gender norms of women as peaceful and nurturing. Yet, as feminist scholars repeatedly argue, the assumption that women are peaceful while men are aggressive is problematic. In fact, Tickner takes on the myth of "the association of women with peace" and warns that "many contemporary feminists see dangers in the continuation of these essentializing myths that can only result in the perpetuation of women's subordination and reinforce dualisms that serve to make men more powerful."[50] Women do support "men's" wars.[51] In our earlier work, we found considerable evidence that some women did support the causes of war in Bosnia, Israel, and Northern Ireland.[52] This point is made by a number of other authors and in other cases as well. As Sjoberg and Gentry claim in their introduction, "Women, like men, sometimes see violence as the best means to political ends."[53] Hence, stereotypes aside, not all women's political activism is in support of the causes of peace and conflict resolution. The reality is that for some women, the most effective way to express political agency is to take action in support of a particular side or cause, resorting to violence if or when necessary.

In some cases, in fact, the assumptions of gender norms or stereotyping have allowed women to act in support of the conflict. These gendered constructions put women into a unique position to act for the cause and to engage in actions that support ongoing political violence generally beyond suspicion. As Miranda Alison asserts, even when women take on nontraditional gender roles, such as involvement in nationalist struggles, often these women also make use of "conservative gender constructions and stereotypes to pursue their objectives against the state or their perceived enemy." In cases such as Afghanistan and Algeria, "women have used local cultural expectations about what clothing is appropriate for them to secretly transport small arms and explosives."[54]

Cindy N. Ness attributes some of the social and cultural changes that are contributing to political violence by women to "a fading demarcation of the public and private spheres (particularly in the West), a growing recognition of (and dependence on) the political utility of women, and a significant lessening of the divide between combatant and noncombatant status in war zones." In her view, these have contributed to "the democratization of violence," where political violence is no longer the purview of the state—or of men.[55]

Moreover, the prominence of women engaging in resistance and political violence grew as did the number of intrastate wars, conflicts that often had their origins in ethnic, religious, tribal, or other forms of national divisions, or as wars of independence against a colonial power. As leaders emerged to promote these identities, so also emerged a particular notion of the state and the citizen. Thus, women's gender identities became vulnerable to redefinition and along with that, a change in their roles in the society. In effect, as groups fought for their independence, recognition, self-determination, or sovereignty, they needed every available person to help with the cause. In many of these traditional societies where a woman's role was fairly well defined, the exigencies of the time and the cause superseded that role. Women's imagery (e.g., fight for the mother country as a rallying cry for men) was no longer sufficient. Rather, women were actually needed to fight. In other words, when it comes to the role of women as combatants, achieving the ends becomes the most important goal, superseding social or cultural norms.

As this chapter and the ones that follow demonstrate, three actors matter when examining women's engagement in resistance and political violence: the women themselves, the leaders of the organizations, and the society or community. We are interested in exploring the motivations (the why question) and characteristics of the women themselves who choose to support conflict, including those who choose to be combatants. Our research shows that while women may be highly motivated to participate in resistance struggles and political violence, their ability to do so is in many ways contingent on the willingness of the leaders of those organizations to accept women's combatant roles as well as the norms or values of the society or community that supports the organization.

Considering our research questions: why do some women choose to engage in acts of resistance and political violence, even going to the extreme of becoming suicide bombers? and how do they become politically active? As the literature shows, women's motivations for political violence are personal and political.[56] They may act for personal reasons, perhaps a family member has died or suffered from the enemy's actions and therefore women seek to avenge that family member's death. Women may also act for political reasons—in support of the cause (i.e., nationalist liberation movement; jihad). As with the blurring of the private and public spheres, these motives are also sometimes blurred—if avenging the death of a family member who also was engaged in political violence, then the revenge motive is inherently political. Regardless of whether the motivations are personal or political or both, women express agency in their actions.[57]

One of the most basic reasons women choose to become belligerents is survival; that is, they feel that only by joining with the military (or paramilitary) force can they be assured of protection, at least from an enemy. The importance of survival and the belief that fighting is the best way to protect their family and their community as well as themselves cannot be underestimated. For example, when the literature discusses older married women who opt to become combatants, worry for their children was the motivating factor for their participation as fighters, whereas for women who were younger and single, their femininity was the focus.[58] Alison's interviews with members of the LTTE, Irish republicans and Irish loyalists revealed that "a clear motivating factor . . . has been concern for their respective families and wider communities. In both Sri Lanka and Northern Ireland there exists a very strong sense of family, of community and of communal loyalty, which has deepened in both places through the experience of war."[59] Women engage in resistance and take up arms because of family and the community.[60] She further finds that many women's personal experiences of "the death or arrest of loved ones, usually men" became a motivating factor for women to act.[61]

The image of motherhood and protecting the children is also a very powerful motivator. Part of the attraction for women in Nicaragua was "the image of mothers protecting their children as part of a divine order. One Sandinista official said in 1980, 'give every woman a gun with which to defend her children.'"[62] Goldstein adds that "good mothers were expected to be 'Patriotic Wombs' that would provide soldiers for the revolution and happily send them off to die for the cause."[63] He further notes that "the image of the woman holding a rifle and a baby is found in liberation movements across the third world. It combines the roles of motherhood and war, harnessing women for war *without* altering fundamental gender relations" (italics in the original).[64] In this depiction, the image of woman as combatant was conflated with the image of woman as mother. Women were expected to be both. Or another interpretation might be that a woman could conform to the traditional gender role of mother and still fight for the cause.[65] Thus, fighting for a cause was another responsibility women were *expected* to take on in addition to all their other work. Goldstein also states that "women's combat participation, although glorified during the [Vietnam] war as a model of self-sacrifice for the nation, was downplayed and largely forgotten after the war, as in other countries."[66]

It is also important to note that being a member of the women's cadre, whether as part of the LTTE, the Sandinistas, the IRA, and so on, meant that women were part of a select group and that they would be provided for. Hence, participating as part of elite combat units represented one way to ensure that women's basic needs—food, clothing, shelter—would be met. It was a way to further their education, which often had been disrupted by the conflict, and to ensure that subsequent generations would not suffer as they did. For example, Alison cites women who give disruption to their education as one of the reasons they joined the LTTE, and, specifically, they wanted to make sure that "this disruption [will not] happen to future generations and wanted to do something to end this."[67] Often, fighting for the cause also meant fighting for social issues, such as child care and health care. In other words, women fighting for one set of political issues often benefited from the implementation of other sets of policies as well.

Consequently, political motivations are also at work in understanding and explaining women's decisions to become politically active. Women, as do men, support national liberation, self-determination movements. And, as Alison argues, there is "an interplay between ideological and practical, experience-based motivations for women to enlist as combatants."[68] Women are political actors; engaging in political activism is a form of politics.

In considering the political motives that are feminist, one can look at women in the left-leaning secular revolutionary/terrorist groups that emerged in the 1960s and 1970s. Ness makes the point that although the "typical terrorist" was male, "several of the most active left-wing terrorist groups during this period had a strong female presence."[69] Here she gives a number of examples of women, such as Ulrike Meinhof of the Baader-Meinhof group, Leila Khalid of the Popular Front for the Liberation of Palestine, and Fusako Shigenobu, founder and leader of the Japanese Red Army. In giving these examples, Ness also noted, "From modern terrorism's beginnings, women have tended to be more active as leaders and members of groups that have worked to overturn traditional values, rather than those seeking to restore old ones—stated another way, they have been less likely to play an active role in right-wing groups that idealize the past and incorporate sexism into the political ideologies."[70] This, in turn, suggests that "left-wing groups are ideologically more suited to justify and advocate women assuming combatant and other non-traditional roles because they premise that fundamental problems in the political and social institutions of society require a radical break with the past."[71] In these cases, women were ideologically driven to make changes, as were men, and the very leanings of the organizations made it possible for them to take a leadership role in doing so.

It should also be noted that the emergence of these women as leaders of these left-leaning organizations coincided with the advance of the women's movement (second-wave feminism), a basic premise of which was to advocate the philosophy that women should not be bound to traditional women's roles and that women and men would benefit from situations of equality.[72]

Confronting traditional values in the name of a political cause can be seen in the case of Northern Ireland, where women, it seemed, played a greater activist role on the side of the Republican/Nationalist (Catholic) side than they did on the Unionist/Loyalist/Protestant side. Or, as Alison notes, "Republicans viewed the conflict as a revolutionary war of resistance against the state, so there was a role for many people to play, including women."[73] She quotes a loyalist ex-prisoner and community worker who said that in effect two different wars were going on in Northern Ireland: "In contrast [to the Republicans], 'loyalist paramilitaries were never about buildin' a revolutionary movement. They were involved in a low-intensity counter-terrorist war against republicans. Now, what role is there for women to play in that?'"[74] Writing about the Protestant/Unionist women and Catholic/Republican women, Rachel Ward and Rosemary Sales reflect on the importance of symbolism as well as the "tradition of struggle" that energized Catholic women to political activism while similarly constraining Protestant women.[75] Sales contends that "Protestant women have remained much less visible. The public face of the Protestant community is overwhelmingly male, represented by male political and church leaders, many of them with strongly anti-feminist views."[76] And yet, as Sandra McEvoy demonstrates in her work, Protestant-Loyalist women, while perhaps seemingly invisible, did engage in political activism, including "conducting surveillance" and "storing arms and munitions in their homes."[77]

Consequently, fighting a "people's war" requires broad mobilization for the cause and opens a window of opportunity for women to act.[78] Working for peace was not an option; liberation of the country from the political oppressors was seen as the primary motivating goal. Gender became less important than willing bodies. The Sandinistas of Nicaragua are an example of women being actively recruited into and becoming part of the military front. According to Goldstein, "Women were particularly attracted to the Sandinista front because, as a movement that grew up in the feminist era, the front had a strong women's organization which advocated policies that helped women."[79] Importantly, perceiving one's role as participating in the fight for a cause becomes a powerful motivator for women as well as men to act. For women, that also might mean women's liberation as well, a gender-specific motivation.

In addition to women's liberation and feminist motivations, research also shows that there are other gender-specific motivations for women's political activism in support of conflict. For example, sexual violence experienced by Tamil women in Sri Lanka at the hands of the Sri Lankan military affected their decision to join the LTTE. Alison found in her interviews with LTTE members that "fear and reality of rape" were reasons for joining the organization.[80]

Acceptance of Women as Combatants: Further Challenging Gender Norms

In addition to the question of women's motivations, we also want to explore and understand how women become politically active. In many cases, women were actively recruited (often by other women). The use of particular women's organizations to enlist women to a cause appears to be fairly widespread. Where they differ, however, is how many of these auxiliary organizations were then expanded to allow or even encourage women to become combatants. In the case of Northern Ireland, for example, "In the late 1960s, younger women joining Cumann na mBan (the IRA women's auxiliary organization) began expressing disillusionment with their subsidiary role and argued for their integration into the IRA itself; sympathetic male IRA officers eventually gave them military training."[81] This led gradually to women being "seconded" into the IRA, "militarily active, but without status as full members. With the later IRA restructuring, women were accepted into the organization on an equal basis with men."[82]

Before a woman can be accepted as a combatant, the group's rules of engagement often have to change for her to be accepted. As Goldstein notes in the case of Vietnam, "Although they might take part in fighting, . . . women's main function in the war was to provide cheap labor."[83] And it was in the glorification of woman as mother that women were mobilized to fight for the cause.[84] Consequently, in many cases, tying women's traditional role as mothers to their roles in political violence makes it less difficult for the society to accept women in a violent role.

The works of Paige Whaley Eager and Carole Lilly and Jill Irvine about the role femininity plays as a factor for women combatants in different societies further support this assertion about the connection to women's traditional roles and the gender norms about women. Drawing on the given societal norms of femininity as well as mythology and symbolism allows these women to be accepted as members of the larger group rather than be seen as threatening, which is important especially in more traditional societies as well as necessary if they are really to be integrated into the larger force.[85] For example, Eager notes that in Sri Lanka and Palestine, both extremely patriarchal, "The leadership of these groups has to rationalize these otherwise forbidden acts by women so as not to upset the dominant cultural and gender norms."[86] She then lists the ways women's participation is rationalized, including the ways the dire situation requires desperate measures and the assumption that "once normal times reemerge or the glorious past is recaptured, then women will return to their 'normal' roles."[87] Lilly and Irvine assert that "more often, however, stories about women warriors sought to reassert their femininity in an attempt to reconcile the contradiction between these women's activities and the nationalist view of gender roles."[88] Women's femininity became part of the focus and descriptors of women combatants, and also explained the willingness of the organization and society at large to accept their roles as political actors.

Sometimes women are targeted for combat roles "because of their desire to prove themselves, which encourages male soldiers to do their best."[89] But often, women's roles simply evolved from dependent to supporter to combatant, thereby making it easier to accept the idea of woman as combatant. Or, put another way, "The boundaries between the three roles are often blurred because women combine the roles. They are fighters, spies, cooks, mothers, and wives at the same time. They fulfill multiple roles that cannot be separated."[90]

As discussed in more detail in chapter 4, the acceptance of women's combatant roles in Islamic fundamentalist groups also posed a challenge to these groups in terms of their ability and willingness to revise or redefine their norms. Women's participation in holy wars, according to Ness, results from two main factors. First, policies and prohibitions on women's ability to act in these conflicts had to be changed, given that these organizations needed to recruit women for such activism. Second, to include women's participation, women themselves had to be willing to participate in these conflicts.[91] Once jihadist leaders, whether Palestinian, Chechen, or other, determined the need to reinterpret jihad as a total war, women could then participate more explicitly, and thus women would be able to fulfill their duties to Islam. Such a reinterpretation began only in the early 1990s. The decision to expand definitions of jihad that included women enabled Islamist organizations to recruit and use women in combatant roles from then on, including the Palestinian Islamic Jihad organization in its conflict with Israel.[92] In 2003 indications were that even Al Qaeda, which had resisted the use of women as combatants, was starting to move in that same direction. In reality, "were Al Qaeda to deploy female operatives, these women would have an easier time evading security measures. Most important to note is that the prohibitions that kept Islamic females from participating in *jihad* have been significantly loosened and fewer hurdles, religious or cultural, stand in the way of their involvement now."[93]

There are caveats, to be sure, about whether women's participation in resistance and political violence lead to women's changed gender roles and empowerment. For example, Kim Jordan and Myriam Denov's analysis of the LTTE found that even though the organization had an ideological commitment to women's liberation, and

> while public approval and rhetoric regarding LTTE women suggests an acceptance of women "as equals," the glorification of the women fighters can be seen to reinforce the perception of females as the symbolic nurturers of society . . . [and] while females may benefit from more egalitarian relations within the LTTE than within traditional Tamil society, women's empowerment is made possible through the adoption of masculine behaviours as opposed to consciously attempting to "feminize" the

military subculture. This reinforces the assertion that female actors are permitted in armed conflict as long as their inclusion does not disrupt the masculine image of warfare.[94]

We can apply these caveats about the LTTE to other cases. In some cases, such as in El Salvador and Sudan, women actually were able to gain positions of leadership and responsibility in the military or paramilitary structures as well as in the government. But as Bouta et al. also noted, "Such gender changes at the micro level are often not accompanied by corresponding changes in political or organizational influence, and they do not fundamentally alter patriarchal ideologies."[95] Hence, in some cases, while women can gain positions of leadership and responsibility *during* conflict, they were excluded from the decisions to engage in violence and were blocked from continuing in positions of political power and influence after the conflict ended. In comparing women combatants with women suicide bombers, Dorit Naaman astutely notes, "Women fighters challenge the patriarchal army order in more profound ways than suicide bombers, ways that are harder to dismiss or subvert."[96] She quotes Leila Khaled, the Palestinian member of the Popular Front for the Liberation of Palestine, in her comments about religious leaders accepting Palestinian female suicide bombers: "When the religious leaders say that women who make those actions are finally equal to men, I have a problem. Everyone is equal in death—rich, poor, Arab, Jew, Christian, we are all equal. I would rather see women equal to men in life."[97] Women's engagement in political violence threatens to upend the gender order when the conflict is over because the women are likely to want to remain politically active and maintain the equality they may have gained during the conflict, whereas women suicide bombers are less threatening to the gender order because they are not alive to make such demands. At the same time, as we see in the next section on female suicide bombers, while women have engaged in this particular kind of violence, it does not necessarily translate into women's equality.

Suicide Bombers/Martyrs

While very few people, men and women, become suicide bombers, this particular form of political violence by nonstate actors has interested scholars, policymakers, and the public at large. Given the interest and fascination with this extreme form of violence, this section focuses on this particular type of political activism along our continuum. A suicide bomber sacrifices his or her life to bring death to the enemy as well as raise the visibility of "the cause," often through martyrdom. The increasing prevalence and visibility of suicide bombers have contributed to more women undertaking this extreme form of combat and have also led to the need for more women willing to do this. The increase in the number of women suicide bombers, in turn, increases the profile of the women who engage in this action as well as the visibility of their cause.

What is also striking about stories of women who become suicide bombers is the gendered discourse that permeates much of the analysis of this type of activism. The advent of female suicide bombers resulted in, and in part was a result of, a change in the social and political order, so that, as Ness notes, "What would otherwise be interpreted as aberrant behavior becomes contextualized in a history of accepted ideas. The female martyr is constructed as embracing culturally accepted gender norms at the same time that she steps outside of them—she is modest, chaste, and a purveyor of family honor in her personal life, whereas she is fierce, courageous, and the equal of men in the name of the cause."[98] While it is often her very femaleness that allows a woman to be so effective in this role, it is also important to remember that women take on this role in what are generally patriarchal and male-dominated societies and structures. Thus, one might ask whether women are taking part in this behavior not only for a cause but also as a statement as women and as a challenge to gender norms.

Since the first suicide attacks carried out by women in Lebanon in 1985,[99] the number of women suicide bombers participating in various campaigns has increased, including in Chechnya, Israel, Sri Lanka, and Turkey. Women suicide bombers acting for the LTTE in Sri Lanka and the Kurdistan Workers Party (PKK) in Turkey are some of the cases most often cited of secular/nationalist groups; the cases of Chechnya, Hamas, the al-Aqsa Martyrs' Brigade, and Islamic Jihad are among the religious causes most often studied to explore this phenomenon. According to Mia Bloom, "Worldwide, approximately 17 groups have started using the tactical innovation of suicide bombing, with women operatives accounting for 15 percent of those attacks."[100] Bloom also cites the work of Rohan Gunaratna, a terror expert who claims that "almost 30 percent of suicide attackers are women."[101] And, if news reports are any indicator, we now find women suicide bombers in the ongoing conflicts in Afghanistan and Iraq, as well as in Russia.

So why are women willing to die for a cause? Are women motivated to engage in this most extreme act of political violence because of feminist goals? What other factors might account for this? We noted earlier that women are motivated for personal and political reasons to engage in nonviolent resistance and political violence, and this is true of suicide bombers as well.

According to Robert Pape, "The profile of a suicide bomber resembles that of a politically conscious individual who might join a grassroots movement more than it does the stereotypical murderer, religious cult member, or everyday suicide."[102] He continues to explain that suicide terrorism "is commonly a form of altruistic suicide, in which high levels of social integration and respect for community values can lead successful individuals to commit suicide *out of a sense of duty*" (italics added).[103] For many men and women, that sense of duty is expressed through nationalism and self-determination for one's group—political motivations. For example, the PKK in Turkey used suicide attacks as an expression of a nationalist movement and a nationalism that "can be demonstrated in terms of gender." As Bloom notes, "Turkey provides a distinctive manifestation of suicide terror in the Middle East because of the role played by young, female bombers. Eleven of the fifteen PKK suicide attacks were carried out by women."[104]

Here the case of Chechnya is especially illustrative. Speckhard and Akhmedova identify one of the main motivations for suicide bombers: "a serious *personal trauma* that in nearly every case involved the death, torture, and/or disappearance of a close family member, and often witnessing violence to family members at the hands of Russian forces."[105] Speckhard and Akhmedova are very explicit, stating that "our main finding in the Chechen sample is that deep personal trauma and the desire for revenge within the context of a nationalistic battle were the strongest motivating forces behind suicide terrorism."[106] This pattern can be seen in other cases as well.

These personal motives are intensified when the woman herself had been brutalized, tortured, or raped, which, especially in the more religious groups, not only brought dishonor but also would exacerbate the desire for revenge. Bloom writes that "sexual violence against women—and the ensuing social stigma associated with rape in patriarchal societies—appears to be a common motivating factor for suicide attackers. Kurdish women allegedly raped in Turkey by the military have joined the PKK, while Tamil women allegedly raped by the Sinhalese security services and military join the LTTE. . . . According to the Hindu faith, once a woman is sexually violated she cannot get married or have children. Fighting for Tamil freedom might have been seen as the only way for such a woman to redeem herself."[107] In the case of Dhanu, a Sri Lankan woman who was the suicide bomber who killed Rajiv Gandhi in 1991, "Motivation probably came directly from revenge; reportedly, her home in Jaffna [Sri Lanka] was looted by Indian soldiers, she was gang-raped, and her four brothers were killed."[108] These examples certainly support the claim that personal loss and revenge for that loss are important motivating factors for women as well as men in resorting to acts of political violence.

In some cases, women do become suicide bombers as a feminist statement, as a way of gaining access in an otherwise patriarchal society. Bloom quotes Leila Khaled of the PLFP explaining that "violence was a way of leveling the patriarchal society through revolutionary zeal—the women would demonstrate that their commitment was no less than those of their brothers, sons or husbands. Strategically, women were able to gain access to areas where men had greater difficulty."[109]

Sjoberg and Gentry raise a number of critical questions about the conclusions Bloom and Victor draw in their respective studies of the motivations of women suicide bombers, and their critiques and warnings might be equally as applicable to any study of women suicide bombers.[110] In Bloom's case, Sjoberg and Gentry warn that "the reduction of women's reasons for political violence to the personal (and even sexual) sphere is problematic. . . . These accounts emphasize women's motivations for engaging in suicide terrorism as different to men's, as associated with their femaleness rather than humanity, and as personal rather than political."[111] The danger inherent in this approach is that it minimizes the impact of women's choices and denies the political agency that should be ascribed to those choices.

In her study of Palestinian women suicide bombers, Victor focuses on the specific—and personal—reasons for women's actions. Sjoberg and Gentry again pose some important questions about her approach, noting that "Victor persists in treating women differently [from men]. To Victor, Palestinian female suicide bombers are marginalized, divorced, ridiculed and isolated, and influenced by the death and/or humiliation of a male relative."[112] Ultimately this leads Sjoberg and Gentry to assert that the logical conclusion would be that "men can be sane and suicide bombers, while clearly women must be insane to be suicide bombers."[113] Yet, as the contributors to an edited volume by Sjoberg and Gentry also show, in a myriad of cases (including Al Qaeda, Chechnya, the Kashmir militant movement, LTTE, Peru's Shining Path), "all include accounts that suggest that both personal and political influences are at work in the decision to join insurgent and terrorist movements and to act as members of those organizations."[114] Moreover, testimonials left by suicide bombers from various countries have expressed political motivations. In reading and viewing such testimonials, Tanya Narozhna concludes,

"These testimonials shatter the commonplace myth that excessive personal grief pushes some women on the path of political violence in the form of martyrdom/suicide bombings. Rather, these final messages emphasize how deeply and strongly private lives and individual identities of female martyrs/suicide bombers are bound up with the destiny of their national groups in political, social and cultural terms. They point to the false separation between the personal and the political, individual and collective."[115] Consequently, it is important to remember that women have chosen to engage in these actions for a variety of reasons. They are choices made by women as political actors and agents.

Characteristics of Suicide Bombers:
Marriage, Motherhood, Age, and Class
Research shows no common characteristics across or within cases. For example, Pape found that the ages of the "average" suicide bomber varied, ranging from fifteen (a male attacker in Lebanon) to fifty-two (a woman in Chechnya). The majority of the bombers (55 percent) were between the ages of nineteen and twenty-three, and 32 percent were twenty-four or older.[116] One of Pape's findings when gender is considered was that on the whole, women suicide attackers "were significantly less likely to be in their late teens and early twenties and more likely to be in their mid-twenties and older."[117] Here, Pape speculates the reason has to do with marriage and prospects for marriage. His assumption, and it clearly is a gendered one, is that women will engage in suicide acts as they get older because it reflects "the declining prospects for mature women in traditional societies."[118]

We contend that when specific cases are examined, the age at which a woman makes this choice has less to do with marriage per se and more to do with the perceived needs of the organization or women's relationship to motherhood. For example, in the LTTE, marriage for women was prohibited before age twenty-five,[119] and women who joined the women's suicide wing were personally chosen by Velupillai Prabhakaran, the leader of the Tamil Tigers. Prabhakaran tended to select "young people aged between 14 and 16, and about three females for every two males. Women and young boys are often preferred to men for the simple reason that they're not subject to the same kinds of movement restrictions and body searches."[120]

Moreover, women LTTE suicide bombers, the female Black Tigers, were neither married nor mothers. For the organization, there was a connection between motherhood, sacrifice, and women. An unmarried woman without children makes the ultimate sacrifice when she becomes "a human bomb."[121] And in the case of the PKK in Turkey, women suicide bombers tended to be unmarried and between the ages of seventeen and twenty-seven. Bloom also notes that these women were not educated, were from poor families, and "had no professional skills, and no great prospects."[122]

These two cases, female suicide bombers in the LTTE and the PKK, stand in contrast to the Chechen case in which the women suicide bombers who were (or had been) married left children behind. According to Speckhard and Akhmedova, "Chechen militant Wahhabis are known to believe that it is better to martyr oneself after having fulfilled life obligations, including having children. This is in direct opposition to the practice of Lebanese and Palestinian groups that generally favor(ed) sending unmarried and childless men, and in many cases, refused to send women at all until—at least in the Palestinian case—it became tactically advantageous and perhaps even necessary to do so."[123] Thus, from this brief analysis, it appears that motherhood may be a factor in some cases, but it is not a factor that is universal. In some cases, motherhood was an advantage in that the woman had already produced offspring and therefore was fulfilled in some way, while in other cases, becoming a suicide bomber prior to having children was evidence of a greater sacrifice for the cause.

Support from the Community for Female Suicide Bombers/Martyrs

Regardless of the mission, suicide bombing as a tactic must be supported by the group or it will actually work against the cause. In understanding the importance of public support, the work of Khalil Shikaki is instructive. In looking at the ways in which society views suicide attacks, he writes, "To support or oppose violence and suicide attacks is of course a matter of policy preference. As a society, societies make policy preferences all the time. They support the peace process or they support violence."[124] In his estimation support is derived from the perception of the threat from the other (Israel, in the case of the Palestinians) and the cost-benefit analysis associated with the suicide attacks. Both of these are emotional reactions to the situation that contribute to the calculation of whether there will be support for this type of action.[125] Without ongoing support from the group the attacks are supposed to be helping, the tactic will not be effective, whereas while there is public support, the tactic will continue to be used.

Ness (drawing on Schalk) develops the idea that "secular and religious militant groups utilize surprisingly similar rhetorical strategies to condone females carrying out suicide missions," where actions "are not viewed as a rupture from the 'decent' behavior but, rather, a transition whereby an old gender value is seen as being given new expression."[126] Furthermore, using women in this role significantly increased not only the number of people who could commit such attacks but the greater chances for success, since women are far less suspect than men. It took time, attitudinal or doctrinal changes, and practical considerations before organizations would permit women to undertake this extreme form of action. And the literature provides any number of reasons why it was in their best interest to employ women in this capacity.

Conclusion

Along the continuum of political activism, women challenge existing gender norms in times of conflict in two ways. First, women's participation in the public sphere in peace activism and peace negotiations challenges gender norms because women move from the private sphere into the public sphere (although as we continue to assert, these spheres are not really separate: what happens in the home is often political, and what happens in the public sphere affects the private sphere). Second, women engaging in nonviolent resistance and political violence as combatants challenges the gender norm of women as peaceful and also challenges the gender norm of women remaining in the private sphere as such women do move from the private to the public sphere (again, these spheres are not really separate: a woman hiding weapons in her home, the private sphere, is acting politically, thus she is in the public sphere). Yet, as this chapter has demonstrated, challenging the existing political system—and thus the existing gender norms—especially in times of war and conflict, is difficult for women regardless of the type of political activism in which they engage.

We also showed in this chapter that women's actions and reasons for committing acts of political resistance and violence are not different from those of men. What makes it appear to be different is the fact that these violent characteristics are not usually attributed to women, nor is it assumed that women will resort to acts of violence to settle a difference, either personally or in the larger political realm. These gendered assumptions and gendered discourses are contradicted by the realities.

We also need to acknowledge that we cannot and should not generalize across all men's motivations for violence, nor generalize all women's motivations as well. Yet, as demonstrated in the case studies that follow, one of the more interesting findings is that women's responses when asked why they work for peace and when asked why they chose to engage in political violence are similar. Moreover, as the literature shows, women's motivations for political resistance and violence are personal and political.

Examples abound: the ETA Basques in Spain,[127] Palestinians in the Occupied Territories, Kosovars in Kosovo, and the LTTE in Sri Lanka. In all these cases, *women and men* are motivated by nationalism and self-determination (and they often do not see their actions as violent but as forms of resistance).

The findings also show there is no uniformity in the factors that describe the women who participate in political violence. Some are married, some are not. Some have children, some do not. For example, members of the LTTE tended not to be married or mothers, whereas in the Chechen case, women suicide bombers were or had been married and left children behind. Some are young, as in the PKK, and others middle aged. Some are educated and some are not. Some are working class, while others are middle class.

What the literature also shows is that along the continuum of political activism when the nationalist cause has been won and the conflict has ended, women are expected to resume their traditional gender roles and return to the private sphere. Very rarely are women brought into the formal political structure: what happens is that gender roles and norms remain entrenched even if they were suspended for the duration of the fight. Gender norms, while they may be challenged, particularly in times of conflict and war, are rarely overturned. We see this in the case chapters that follow.

Notes

1. "Bosnia: U.S. Extradites Woman Accused of War Crimes in the 1990s," *New York Times,* December 28, 2011, A7.

2. Cockburn, *From Where We Stand,* 240–41.

3. Sjoberg and Gentry, *Mothers, Monsters, Whores,* 4.

4. Ibid., 176.

5. Valerie Morgan, *Peacemaker? Peacekeepers? Women in Northern Ireland 1969–1995* (Londonderry, UK: INCORE, 1996), 4, http://cain.ulst.ac.uk/issues/women/paper3.htm.

6. Cindy D. Ness, "The Rise in Female Violence," *Daedalus* 136, no. 1 (Winter 2007): 85.

7. Ibid., 43.

8. Ibid.

9. V. Spike Peterson, "Gendered Nationalism: Reproducing 'Us' versus 'Them,'" in *The Women and War Reader,* ed. Lois Ann Lorentzen and Jennifer Turpin (New York: New York University Press, 1998), 45. See also Peterson, "Sexing Political Identities/Nationalism as Heterosexism," *International Feminist Journal of Politics* 1, no. 1 (1999): 34–65; Floya Anthias and Nira Yuval-Davis, "Introduction," in *Woman-*

Nation-State, ed. Nira Yuval-Davis and Floya Anthias (London: Macmillan, 1989), 1–15; Nira Yuval-Davis, *Gender and Nation* (London: Sage, 1997).

10. Krishna Kumar, "Civil Wars, Women, and Gender Relations: An Overview," in *Women & Civil War: Impact, Organizations, and Action*, ed. Krishna Kumar (Boulder, CO: Lynne Rienner, 2001), 6–7.

11. Ibid., 6.

12. Ibid.

13. Ibid., 7.

14. Ibid.

15. Ibid.

16. Ibid.

17. Women in ethnically or religiously mixed marriages was one of the variables we examined in Kaufman and Williams, *Women, the State, and War*, 96–103. Marriage is one way states gender citizenship, and as we saw in the cases we examined, generally the woman suffers when she marries outside her group. She is often ostracized by her own family for marrying outside the group and is never really accepted by her husband's family because she is one of "the other." In some cases, as we saw in the former Yugoslavia, that situation led directly to violence against women.

18. V. Spike Peterson and Anne Sisson Runyan, *Global Gender Issues in the New Millennium*, 2nd ed. (Boulder, CO: Westview Press, 1999), 179.

19. Elisabeth Porter, "Participatory Democracy and the Challenge of Dialogue across Difference," in *Gender, Democracy and Inclusion in Northern Ireland*, ed. Carmel Roulston and Celia Davis (Basingstoke, UK: Palgrave, 2000), 158.

20. Ibid.

21. Joshua S. Goldstein, *War and Gender* (Cambridge: Cambridge University Press, 2001), 327. See also Catia Confortini, "Feminist Critical Methodology, Decolonization and the Women's International League for Peace and Freedom (WILFP), 1945–75," *International Feminist Journal of Politics* 13, no. 3 (September 2011): 349–70.

22. Cynthia Cockburn, "Gender Relations as Causal in Militarization and War," *International Feminist Journal of Politics* 12, no. 2 (June 2010): 142–43.

23. Karen Beckwith, "The Comparative Politics of Women's Movements," *Perspectives on Politics* 3, no. 3 (September 2005): 588.

24. Ibid., 589.

25. Ibid.

26. Ibid.

27. Karen Beckwith, "Beyond Compare? Women's Movements in Comparative Perspective," *European Journal of Political Research* 37, no. 4 (2000): 436.

28. Ibid., 437–38.

29. Beckwith, "Comparative Politics," 585.

30. Beckwith, "Beyond Compare?" 437. For more on women's movements in democracies, see Weldon, *When Protest Makes Policy*.

31. Kaufman and Williams, *Women, the State, and War.*
32. "About Women in Black."
33. Ibid.
34. Ibid.
35. "About CWP," Coalition of Women for Peace, accessed January 30, 2010, http://www.coalitionofwomen.org/?page_id=340&lang=en.
36. Tickner notes that feminist scholars, such as Carole Pateman, have continuously argued that the public-private divide is problematic in that the division into two spheres, and women's roles in them, only reinforces the notion that women remain in the private sphere, while the public sphere is reserved for men. In so doing, this assumes that the public sphere—where the men are located—is more important than the private sphere. Tickner, "You Just Don't Understand," 622.
37. Begona Aretxaga, *Shattering Silence: Women, Nationalism, and Political Subjectivity in Northern Ireland* (Princeton, NJ: Princeton University Press, 1997), 115; Anderlini, *Women Building Peace*, 38–39.
38. Swanee Hunt and Cristina Posa, "Women Waging Peace," *Foreign Policy* 124 (May–June 2001): 41.
39. Sara Ruddick, "Maternal Thinking," *Feminist Studies* 6, no. 2 (Summer 1980): 342–67. For other works by Ruddick on maternal thinking and feminism, see Sara Ruddick, "Thinking about Mothering—and Putting Maternal Thinking to Use," *Women's Studies Quarterly* 11, no. 4 (Winter 1983): 4–7; Sara Ruddick, "Feminist Questions on Peace and War: An Agenda for Research, Discussion, Analysis, Action," *Women's Studies Quarterly* 12, no. 2 (Summer 1984): 8–11.
40. Ruddick, "Maternal Thinking," 344.
41. For a critique of Ruddick's maternal thinking, see Alison Bailey, "Mothering, Diversity, and Peace Politics," *Hypatia* 9, no. 2 (Spring 1994): 188–98.
42. Elissa Helms, "Gender Essentialisms and Women's Activism in Post-War Bosnia-Herzegovina," in *Feminists under Fire: Exchanges across War Zones*, ed. Wenona Giles, Malathi de Alwis, Edith Klein, and Neluka Silva, with the assistance of Maja Korac, Djurdja Knezevic, and Zarana Papic (Toronto: Between the Lines, 2003), 181.
43. Helms, "Gender Essentialisms," 192.
44. Azza Karam, "Women in War and Peace-Building," *International Feminist Journal of Politics* 3, no. 1 (April 2001): 10.
45. Monica McWilliams, "Struggling for Peace and Justice: Reflections on Women's Activism in Northern Ireland," *Journal of Women's History* 6–7, no. 4–1 (Winter–Spring 1995): 18.
46. Elisabeth Porter, "Identity, Location, Plurality: Women, Nationalism, and Northern Ireland," in *Women, Ethnicity, and Nationalism: The Politics of Transition*, ed. Rick Wilford and Robert L. Miller (New York: Routledge, 1998), 48.
47. Tsjeard Bouta, Georg Frerks, and Ian Bannon, *Gender, Conflict, and Development* (Washington, DC: World Bank, 2005), 73.
48. Kaufman and Williams, *Women and War*, 102.

49. Cindy D. Ness, "In the Name of the Cause," in *Female Terrorism and Militancy: Agency, Utility and Organization*, ed. Cindy D. Ness (New York: Routledge, 2008), 16.

50. Tickner, *Gender in International Relations*, 59.

51. Ibid., 59.

52. Kaufman and Williams, *Women, the State, and War*.

53. Sjoberg and Gentry, *Mothers, Monsters, and Whores*, 4.

54. Alison, "Women as Agents," 456. See also Alison, *Women and Political Violence*.

55. Ness, "Rise in Female Violence," 85.

56. For an exploration of women's motivations for terrorism, see Sjoberg and Gentry, *Women, Gender, and Terrorism*.

57. Laura Sjoberg discusses the "beautiful soul" narrative surrounding women fighters and the political and personal reasons women participate in political violence. Sjoberg, "Women Fighters and the 'Beautiful Soul' Narrative," *International Review of the Red Cross* 92, no. 877 (March 2010): 53–68, accessed January 30, 2011, http://www.icrc.org/eng/assets/files/other/irrc-877-sjoberg.pdf.

58. Carole S. Lilly and Jill A. Irvine, "Negotiating Interests: Women and Nationalism in Serbia and Croatia, 1990–1997," *East European Politics and Societies* 16, no. 1 (2002): 122.

59. Alison, *Women and Political Violence*, 224.

60. Ibid.

61. Ibid., 225.

62. Goldstein, *War and Gender*, 81.

63. Ibid.

64. Ibid.

65. Ibid., 82.

66. Ibid., 80–81.

67. Alison, "Cogs in the Wheel?" 42.

68. Alison, *Women and Political Violence*, 224.

69. Ness, "In the Name of the Cause," 13.

70. Ibid.

71. Ibid.

72. Ibid., 14.

73. Alison, "Women as Agents," 454.

74. Ibid.

75. Rachel Ward, *Women, Unionism and Loyalism in Northern Ireland: From "Tea-Makers" to Political Actors* (Dublin: Irish Academic Press, 2006), 15. See also Rosemary Sales, *Women Divided: Gender, Religion and Politics in Northern Ireland* (New York: Routledge, 1997), 5.

76. Sales, *Women Divided*, 5.

77. McEvoy, "Loyalist Women Paramilitaries," 270.

78. See Goldstein, *War and Gender*, 80.

79. Ibid., 81. The Sandinista National Liberation Front took power in Nicaragua in 1979 following the overthrow of president Anastasio Somoza Debayle. The Sandinistas remained in power until elections in 1990.

80. Miranda Alison, "'In the War Front We Never Think That We Are Women': Women, Gender, and the Liberation Tamil Tigers of Eelam," in Sjoberg and Gentry, *Women, Gender, and Terrorism*, 137.

81. Alison, "Women as Agents," 451.

82. Ibid.

83. Goldstein, *War and Gender*, 80.

84. Ibid., 80–81.

85. Eager, *From Freedom Fighters to Terrorists*, 138. Also, see Lilly and Irvine, "Negotiating Interests," 109–44.

86. Eager, *From Freedom Fighters to Terrorists*, 138–39.

87. Ibid., 139.

88. Lilly and Irvine, "Negotiating Interests," 122.

89. Bouta et al., *Gender, Conflict, and Development*, 13.

90. Ibid., 15.

91. Ness, "In the Name of the Cause," 18.

92. Karla J. Cunningham, "The Evolving Participation of Muslim Women in Palestine, Chechnya, and the Global Jihadi Movement," in *Female Terrorism and Militancy: Agency, Utility, and Organization*, ed. Cindy D. Ness (New York: Routledge, 2008), 85; Jessica Davis, "Women and Radical Islamic Terrorism: Planners, Perpetrators, Patrons?" Canadian Institute of Strategic Studies, STrategic Datalink 136, May 2006, http://www.opencanada.org/wp-content/uploads/2011/05/SD-136-Davis.pdf.

93. Ness, "In the Name of the Cause," 21.

94. Kim Jordan and Myriam Denov, "Birds of Freedom? Perspectives on Female Emancipation and Sri Lanka's Liberation Tigers of Tamil Eelam," *Journal of International Women's Studies* 9, no. 1 (November 2007): 57–58.

95. Bouta et al., *Gender, Conflict, and Development*, 55.

96. Dorit Naaman, "Brides of Palestine/Angels of Death: Media, Gender, and Performance in the Case of the Palestinian Female Suicide Bombers," *Signs* 32, no. 4 (Summer 2007): 950.

97. Ibid.

98. Ness, "In the Name of the Cause," 22.

99. Clara Beyler, "Messengers of Death—Female Suicide Bombers" (Herzliya, Israel: International Institute for Counter-Terrorism, 2003), 2. Beyler, however, gives no reason for women's participation in these attacks, nor have we been able to find very much information about this group. In this case, though, it is known that the attack was politically motivated and was followed immediately by five other women who were sent to Lebanon believed to be acting on behalf of the Syrian Socialist National Party.

100. Mia Bloom, "Mother. Daughter. Sister. Bomber." *Bulletin of the Atomic Scientists* 61, no. 6 (November/December 2005): 56.

101. Bloom, "Mother. Daughter." 56.

102. Robert A. Pape, *Dying to Win: The Strategic Logic of Suicide Terrorism* (New York: Random House, 2005), 200.

103. Ibid., 200–201.

104. Bloom, *Dying to Kill*, 102.

105. Anne Speckhard and Khapta Akhmedova, "Black Widows and Beyond: Understanding the Motivations and Life Trajectories of Chechen Female Terrorists," in *Female Terrorism and Militancy: Agency, Utility, and Organization*, ed. Cindy D. Ness (New York: Routledge, 2008), 110.

106. Ibid.

107. Bloom, "Mother. Daughter." 59.

108. Pape, *Dying to Win*, 226.

109. Bloom, "Mother. Daughter." 58.

110. Sjoberg and Gentry, *Mothers, Monsters, Whores*, 136–37.

111. Ibid., 136.

112. Ibid., 137.

113. Ibid.

114. Sjoberg and Gentry, *Women, Gender, and Terrorism*, 234.

115. Tanya Narozhna, "Power and Gendered Rationality in Western Epistemic Constructions of Female Suicide Bombings," in *Gender, Agency and Political Violence*, ed. Linda Ahall and Laura J. Shepherd (Basingstoke, UK: Palgrave Macmillan, 2012), 90.

116. Pape, *Dying to Win*, 209.

117. Ibid.

118. Ibid.

119. Ness, "In the Name of the Cause," 21.

120. Charu Lata Joshi, "Sri Lanka: Suicide Bombers," *Far Eastern Economic Review*, June 1, 2000, http://www.essex.ac.uk/armedcon/Countries/Asia/Texts/SriLanka011.htm.

121. Arjuna Gunawardena, "Female Black Tigers: A Different Breed of Cat?" in *Female Suicide Bombers: Dying for Equality?* ed. Yoram Schweitzer (Tel Aviv: Jaffee Center for Strategic Studies, Tel Aviv University, 2006), 84, http://www.e-prism.org/images/memo84_Female_suicide_bombers_-_Jaffee_Center_-_Aug06.pdf.

122. Bloom, *Dying to Kill*, 102.

123. Speckhard and Akhmedova, "Black Widows," 107.

124. Khalil Shikaki, "The Views of Palestinian Society on Suicide Terrorism," in *Countering Suicide Terrorism* (Herzliya, Israel: Institute for Counter-Terrorism, 2000), 100, http://www.ict.org.il/Portals/0/51563-Countering%20suicide%20Terrorism.pdf.

125. Ibid., 100–101.

126. Ness, "In the Name of the Cause," 21.

127. For work on women armed activists in ETA (Euskadi ta Askatasuna), the Basque separatist movement, see Carrie Hamilton, "The Gender Politics of Political Violence: Women Armed Activists in ETA," *Feminist Review*, no. 86 (2007): 132–48.

3

Women's Political Activism in Northern Ireland: Protestants and Catholics

The writings of Dolours and Marion Price, two Catholic/Republican sisters imprisoned for their violent role in the Troubles, offer some insight into their thoughts on what they had done. In 1973 the sisters were arrested, tried, and convicted of a car bombing of the Old Bailey and other sites in London. They were sentenced to twenty years in prison and were released in 1980, having served seven years of their term. Both remained politically active, and they spoke out against the Good Friday agreement. In one of their letters from prison they wrote, "Then, of course, the death of a British soldier is also sad. Because he's just some kid who doesn't even know why he is in Ulster let alone why he has to die. At least our Volunteers know what they are giving their lives for, that's the difference between the idealist and the cannon fodder of the British government."[1]

IN HER STUDY OF PROTESTANT LOYALIST WOMEN IN NORTHERN IRELAND, Rachel Ward notes that although "nationalism can explain the motivation to political action it does not so easily illuminate the roles in which the women are engaged. However, society is shaped by nationalism, and this in turn contributes in some way to the hurdles that the women face to taking on a more public political role."[2] In taking on that public role, as noted earlier in this book, women have a number of choices. In Northern Ireland we see examples of women who chose to work for peace at different levels (e.g., community, national, and even international) versus those who engaged directly on one side or the other in support of the violence of the Troubles. Women in Northern Ireland have become known for the former example, and two were awarded a Nobel Peace Prize.[3] However, the reality is that women opted to work for peace and engage in political violence on both the Protestant/Unionist/Loyalist and Catholic/Republican/Nationalist sides of the Troubles.

As we discussed in chapter 2, women choose to support conflict, to pick up arms and become combatants for reasons of nationalism and nationalist liberation just as men do. What is different, however, is that for men such action is seen as natural, whereas for women it is seen as extraordinary, because such behavior is seen as deviating from the gender norms of women as peaceful and nurturing. Furthermore, before women can engage in such actions, they often must depend on men to approve those actions. We see this same pattern with Northern Ireland. In fact, in this case, women who chose to engage in acts of political violence were dependent on men, whereas women who opted to work for peace often did it *in spite of the men*, which often resulted in hostility toward those women, as seen in the reaction to the Northern Ireland Women's Coalition (NIWC) during the negotiations surrounding the 1998 Good Friday Agreement.[4]

In the case of Northern Ireland, the shorthand approach is to look at the political violence that characterized the Troubles as a religious divide: Catholic versus Protestant. However, the reality is that the divisions were economic and political as well as religious regarding access to power and political decision making. Working-class women especially felt the effects of economic downturns as well as the violence, and they had the least access to the formal political system and the fewest options to escape. And these were often the women who stepped in and became active along the continuum of political activism on the Protestant and Catholic sides (given space considerations and simplicity, we use the terms Protestant, Unionist, and Loyalist interchangeably; the same for Catholic, Nationalist, and Republican). The very nature of the violence, which reached deep into communities and even into homes and families, meant that few women were not touched by it in some way. Women were not secure in their homes and communities, and as we noted in the last chapter, this tells us much about how we define and understand what it means to be secure and insecure.

Women Working for Peace and In Support of Political Violence: Challenging Gender Norms

In Northern Ireland women worked across communities at the grassroots level during the Troubles to improve understanding and build trust at that level.[5] It is also an example of women who came together to work within the formal political system to create a political party at the national level, the Northern Ireland Women's Coalition (NIWC), to get a seat at the table when the Good Friday Agreement was negotiated.[6] Thus, this case of women's political activism is an example of women making a difference at a number of levels politically, along the continuum of activism, despite the fact that the structure of the political system is basically patriarchal and traditional. However, Northern Ireland also represents a case in which women not only worked for peace, but some were actively engaged in support of the conflict on both sides of the divide, resorting to acts of political violence.

To understand the role women played during the period known as the Troubles, it is important to understand the history (see map, Figure 3.1). Armed conflict has been part of the history of Northern Ireland since the early part of the twentieth century, affecting women personally and adversely, especially in the 1960s and 1970s, because of economic decline and the concomitant rise in sectarian violence. Unemployment and poverty increased for women in Northern Ireland; the degradation of the quality of life coupled with the generally harsher conditions exacerbated by the violence contributed to the growth of women's political activism, especially at the community level. In some cases, particularly in the late 1960s and the early 1970s, women's political activism focused on social justice as part of a broader civil rights movement to end discrimination in housing, and against the arbitrary internment of some of the Irish nationalists without legal charges or trial. However, in other cases, women's activism took the path of supporting the conflict, going so far as their being directly engaged in acts of political violence at times. One critical aspect of the increasing activism was the clear confluence of public and private issues, as feminist scholars repeatedly claim that the public-private divide is not so clearly demarcated.

To put women's roles into perspective, it is important to remember that Northern Ireland is a relatively traditional/patriarchal society in which women generally did not play a major political role. Further, as Morgan wrote in 1995, at that time Northern Ireland was "amongst the most rural and traditional areas in western Europe. . . . A relatively high proportion of the population live in small towns, hamlets and on scattered farms, the traditional family unit remains the norm in many areas and religious belief and observance rates are much higher than in most other EU countries. These characteristics cut across the Protestant/Unionist/Loyalist–Catholic/Nationalist/Republican divide and meant that throughout the community women's roles are still frequently defined in terms of responsibilities to home, family and church."[7] The traditional nature of the society and the

Figure 3.1 Map of Ireland and Northern Ireland

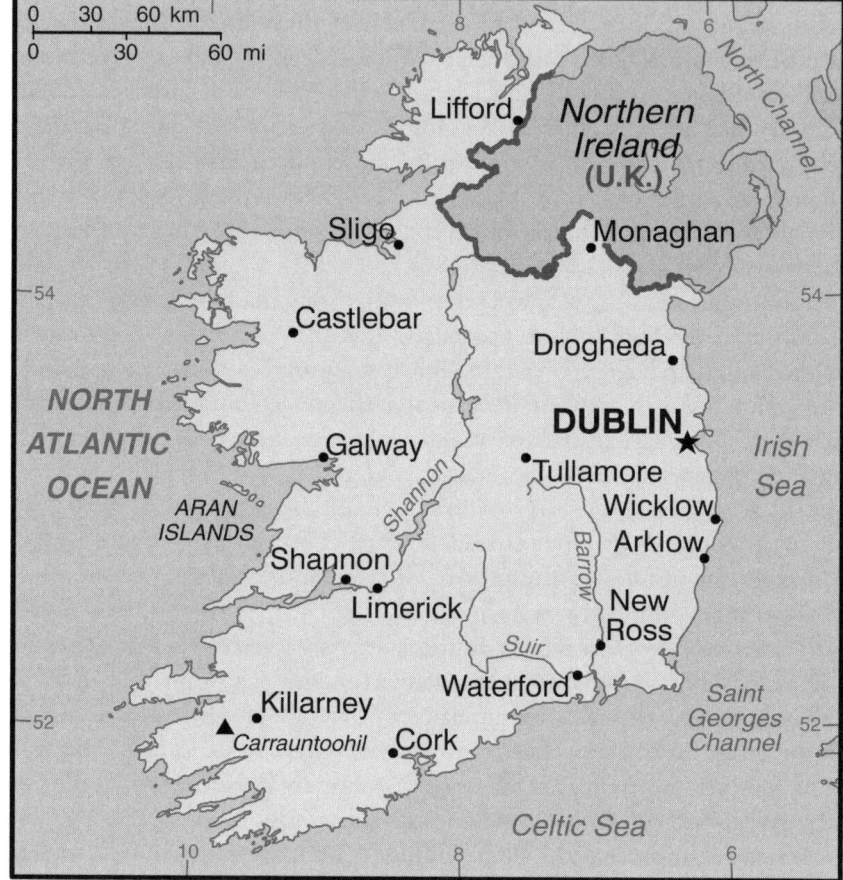

Courtesy University of Texas Libraries.

important role of the church seemed to suggest that the "good woman" image would be paramount, that is, someone who devotes herself to home and family. The often-idealized projection of women "includes a role as natural peacemakers, but precludes active involvement in making that peace at a constitutional level."[8]

Thus, although the political divisions between Catholic and Protestant took their toll on women, in general women were not seen, nor did they see themselves, as major players by either side in the conflict. Or, as Carmel Roulston notes, "Women, it seems, do not fit comfortably into mainstream politics as presently organized, and there are no guarantees that the women who manage to make their way into parliaments and governments will be able—or willing—to act in ways significantly different from their male colleagues."[9] In other words, if women were to play a role in politics in Northern Ireland, they would have to do so on different terms from men's.

If they chose to become politically engaged, women responded to the situation of violent conflict that was wracking their society along the continuum of political activism as peace activists, nonviolent resisters, and for some, as combatants. There are ample examples of women who chose to pursue all these courses of action, although in our research thus far, we did not find any explicit examples of women who first worked in support of the conflict and then opted to work for peace (unlike male political leaders such as Gerry Adams, Martin McGuinness, and Ian Paisley).[10]

Women Working for Peace

In the case of Northern Ireland, there are two general models of women who worked across the community divide to try to bring an end to the violence of the Troubles. One model, which appears to be the more common by far, is the example of women who opted to work at the community level to reach across the Catholic/Protestant division, which is where they believed they could have the greatest impact. It was the area that touched them most directly, and it also allowed them to build on issues they had in common, many of which were tied to traditional needs for women in areas such as education, health care, and domestic violence. The other case, which was more unusual, was of women who chose to work in the formal political process to try to bring about peace at the national level.

We wrote in previous research that "the concern of many women, and what spurred many on to political activism, was the belief that no one was addressing the root causes of the violence. Women did not want to 'work for peace' per se. Rather, they saw the violence as a symptom of larger structural issues within the society that needed to be addressed before the violence would end. And they believed that those changes needed to start with a commitment to fair treatment and equality for all citizens."[11]

Cynthia Cockburn, among others, describes the ways the social and economic divisions that existed in Northern Ireland ultimately brought together women on both sides of the political and religious divide, allowing them to transcend their differences: "There are, however, three things the two working-class communities share: *poverty, violence* and *political neglect*. And women of those communities experience all three in a distinctive, gendered, way" (italics in the original).[12]

The common experience of those critical factors—poverty, violence, and political neglect—allowed women in Northern Ireland to start working together at the community level. Ultimately, their shared concerns and common experiences led to the creation of community-based women's projects that were about basic necessities, which are about politics, although many of the women involved did not see their work as political. It is also important to note that many of the women who participated in this community-based activism were working-class women, often with minimal levels of education and with few options; for economic or personal reasons they could not leave their community, and, therefore, the most viable option available to them was to find ways to make the situation better or at least tolerable. Despite the differences that might exist in the society, women in Northern Ireland were united and mobilized into action by their common desires and dreams for a better society after the conflict ended.

Women's community-based activism focused on areas of common concern to women, namely, child care, domestic violence, economic issues, and health. At the same time, this activism was connected to the larger women's movement. As in other countries, such as the United States, the feminist movement in Northern Ireland dates from the 1960s: "As in other parts of the world, the feminist movement in Northern Ireland had initially hoped to foster a unitary women's identity that could transcend the polarized ethnic divide between Catholic and Protestants, nationalists and loyalists."[13] Women in Northern Ireland were caught in a double bind. Religious affiliation was a mark of their identity and their presumed political affiliation.[14] At the same time, "the feminist/women's movement recognized that there were problems and issues common to all women that could better be addressed if women worked together."[15]

Initially, many of the existing community-based organizations were made up of Catholic or Protestant women but not both, thereby mirroring the divisions that existed in the broader society. Over time, the organizations began to cross communal lines. There are numerous examples of women who became politicized and engaged in nonviolent political action beyond the behind-the-scenes role as a result of the direct impact of the political violence on them, their families, and communities. While they did not work for peace per se, they did work hard to cross the communal divisions to build the trust necessary to ultimately bring lasting peace to (or at the very least, lessen the violence in) their society. For example, as Swanee Hunt and Cristina Posa write, women "have helped calm the often deadly 'marching season' by facilitating mediations between Protestant unionists and Catholic nationalists. The women bring together key members of each community, many of whom are released prisoners, as mediators to calm tensions. This circle of mediators works with local police throughout the marching season, meeting quietly and maintaining contacts on a 24-hour basis."[16]

In addition to women's political activism focused on the community, women also sought to participate in the formal political system to end the conflict. In response to the dearth of women in the formal political process, the NIWC was created in 1996 as a "cross-community party, founded on human rights, inclusion and equality."[17] From the outset, the NIWC was designed to "bring a voice of common sense and a new approach to traditional problems in Northern Ireland."[18] As Kate Fearon and Monica McWilliams assert, the NIWC was born out of the "frustrations and aspirations of women from a diverse range of backgrounds and affiliations. For many years, the majority of those women had been concerned about the exclusion of women from mainstream politics in Northern Ireland. All of them hoped that the opportunity to create a lasting peace would not be wasted and believed that women had particular experiences and insights that could help move the process forward."[19]

The NIWC was successful in its bid to make sure that women were seated at the table when the Good Friday Agreement was negotiated. Two women were elected to serve as representatives of the party, and according to their own stories, they endured a great deal.[20] In 2006 the NIWC was disbanded. Yet it did provide an important lesson for women's participation in the future. Women became more effective actors as well as political agents, as "they and the local electorate began to realize that they no longer had to depend on their elected, mostly male representatives, but could start to negotiate their own rights of citizenship."[21] In fact, the NIWC "had managed to do something that had eluded the women's movement in Northern Ireland for many years: unite and organize around an identity as women."[22]

Thus, in the case of Northern Ireland, we see numerous examples of women who chose to respond to the political violence by working across the community divide primarily as grassroots activists. We also saw examples of women who chose to work within the political system to try to influence the peace negotiations in the hope that the resulting change would alter the structures that initially led to the outbreak of violence. Whether at a community level or through the formal political structure, though, women made it clear they were acting as *women*, often stressing how their roles as wives and mothers were affected by the violence in such a way to provoke a response.

One of the other important lessons, however, was how few of the women who were involved with the NIWC or worked for peace at the national level continued in formal politics after the signing of the agreement and the subsequent disbanding of the party in 2006. Part of this was because of perceptions, such as the assumption that the NIWC existed outside the mainstream, and once the agreement was signed there was no reason for the group to continue. No doubt this was one of the reasons the NIWC could not get representatives elected to government at any level, and its members finally decided to disband. However, other factors have to be considered as well. For example, in an interview with Patricia Lawsley, Northern Ireland commissioner for Children and Young People and an active member of the Social Democratic and Labor Party,[23] she talked about the fact that it is "not cheap to be a politician" and that anyone needs to have funding to continue to run for office.[24] And men generally have more access to that funding. But also women often do not take the opportunity to get involved and were—and still are—not good at promoting themselves. Her goal was to see women involved more in politics, "not as a token gesture but for the contributions that they can make."[25] That said, any woman who gets involved must also realize that it will be a lonely path.

Margaret Ward, director of the Women's Resource and Development Agency in Belfast, provided another key insight into the reason women have not been as involved in the formal political process. Given the patriarchal structure of the political system and the male-dominated political parties, many women felt that they could play a greater and more important role by working informally, rather than through the formal political system.[26] This point was echoed by Jane Morrice, former member of the Northern Ireland Assembly (1998 through 2003) and a member of the NIWC. She said the informal path allows women to "do what we do best." Her point is not that women should stop trying for a place at the top, nor should they stop trying to change society from the bottom up. But given the political realities, what women can do effectively is continue to hold the government accountable and continue to push for those things that are important to them. And that is often more effectively done from outside the formal political system than from within.[27]

A universal issue is the patriarchal and male-dominated structure of the political parties, which worked against the promotion of women. In the case of the Republican (Catholic) women associated with the Irish Republican Army (IRA) and Sinn Féin, some were permitted leadership roles. However, in no case could we find women directly involved with the initial decisions that contributed to the outbreak of the violence nor of women who really were able to succeed as true party leaders; decisions were generally made by men. The issue facing women, then, was how to respond to the political situation they were placed in, which they did either by working for peace, generally in their own communities but also at the national level, or by actively supporting the cause to the point of engaging in acts of political violence.

Women, Nonviolent Resistance, and Political Violence

As in other countries, Northern Ireland has examples of women being actively involved in the violence on both sides of the conflict. One of the points Ruth Jacobson makes about women's roles in supporting violence is that the women might not have done so overtly, but rather they engaged in activities that *provoked* violence, often justified by the need to ensure their children's future. She asserts that "while only a few women have exercised their agency to inflict violence, considerably larger numbers have seen 'our children's future' as their reason for *supporting* activities which have a virtual certainty of *provoking* violence, such as Orange marches through highly contested areas" (italics added).[28] The need to protect and ensure the children's future and taking a position because of their role as mothers are among the reasons women give for their political activism.

Actions in support of the cause, condoning or even becoming actively engaged in perpetrating violence, can be seen on both sides, although the roles women played in each were bounded to some extent by gendered social and cultural constraints. Here the structure of the formal religious traditions played a role, a point explored by Cockburn and Rachel Ward among others. About Belfast, Cockburn says (but with a claim that can be extrapolated more broadly to all of Northern Ireland), "Conventional gender relations in working-class Belfast are heavily subordinating of women. The Catholic Church exploits the political situation to retain a firm grip, instilling fear of sexuality, inhibiting women from questioning tradition.

The Protestant churches and the Orange Order and similar loyalist organizations are oppressively patriarchal."[29]

In her study of Protestant/Unionist women, Ward writes, "Women are constrained by the conservative influence of the Churches on society and, while Catholic women have been able to take advantage of the 'tradition of struggle,' to be active in community politics, Protestant women have 'remained much less visible.'"[30] She adds that the sectarian divisions have in turn been experienced differently by the women in each of the two communities, and "this is seen in the *gendered symbolism*, in which republicanism has drawn upon the 'tradition of strong Gaelic women' to depict a more active role for women, while there 'is no equivalent symbolic role for women in Protestantism'" (italics added).[31] Thus, women on both sides had to negotiate a role for themselves that was consistent with the dominant culture and tradition and, in many cases, with the approval of the male leaders.

Women, Political Violence, and the Catholic/Republican/Nationalist Cause
As long ago as the 1970s and the early years of the Troubles, women were enlisted in the Provo organization (Provisional IRA Council) specifically in support of the violence as a means to challenge the state, in this case the United Kingdom.[32] Women carried weapons to Provo snipers by hiding weapons in their clothes. When the sniper was ready to fire his gun, the woman would hand it to him. After he fired his shot, the sniper would give the gun back to her. Because there were no regular policewomen in the Royal Ulster Constabulary (RUC), the armed police force in Northern Ireland (perceived to be Protestant and pro-Unionist, and thus identified with the state, Britain), and the RUC did not have significant numbers of female searchers, Catholic women were able to provide support for male IRA members.[33] An article from the *Daily Telegraph* in April 1974 supports this assertion: "The recent rash of incendiary devices in shops is being blamed on women who are taking advantage of the difficulty in searching girls thoroughly. Some are thought to be concealing the bomb materials on intimate parts of their bodies."[34] And although we could not find any record of Irish women suicide bombers, records document that women carried bombs under their dresses, pretending to be pregnant to avoid detection.[35] This presages what we see in chapters 4 and 5 with women suicide bombers in Palestine and Sri Lanka. Those assumptions of gender norms that placed more of the burden for violence on men (and because they did not have policewomen, another gendered factor) worked to the advantage of women in support of the conflict on the Catholic side.

In her study of women's activism in Northern Ireland, Sharon Pickering writes that on the Catholic side of the divide, the experiences of the civil rights campaign of the late 1960s to early 1970s gave way to more public and often violent expressions of political activism by women. One woman activist she interviewed said she was politically active in 1969 as a member of community groups "trying to bring a lot of changes to the community. . . . [1969] was a great period of advancement of women who came onto the streets in equal numbers to their male counterparts and who did all sorts of things that women really don't do, or were never permitted to do. They made petrol bombs; I remember getting arrested for Molotov cocktails, and seeing women in Westland Street sitting down filling milk bottles which we had stolen out of the local dairy and making Molotov cocktails."[36]

She explains how these bombs were thrown at the members of the RUC and describes how "there was a great upsurge in women taking their part alongside the men and *defending* their area" (italics added).[37] Pickering then elaborates on the comment about women working to "defend" their area: "Women's violent and illegal actions were directed at *protecting* the safety and wellbeing of their communities from the RUC and British Army" (italics added).[38] In short, one of the reasons Catholic nationalist women claimed they were becoming politicized and engaging in acts of political violence was the perceived need that they had to protect and defend their community against the oppression of the British state, in this case exemplified by the RUC and the military.

O'Ballance gives us other examples of women who became critical parts of the IRA campaign of violence in the 1970s, especially with the bombings that accelerated in 1973 and 1974. And in so doing women clearly moved beyond the "protecting" arena to becoming more aggressive, hence moving along the continuum of political activism. Here too women were uniquely situated to play a role, especially as the size of the bombs became smaller and therefore easier to place. "They [the bombs] could be carried by women and positioned unobtrusively in the target premises. This partly solved the Provo problem of bomb carriers."[39] In this way, women used existing gender norms and challenged those norms as well by taking advantage of assumptions about women's roles as being nonviolent yet at the same time challenging those gender norms as the women participated in resistance and political violence.

Pickering makes another important point about this aspect of women's political activism when she says that as the Troubles progressed into the mid- to late 1970s, "the activism of nationalist and republican [Catholic] women outside the home continued to be informed by the transformation of life within the home as men were arrested and women were largely left to rear children, maintain the home, and support their imprisoned husbands, fathers, brothers and sons."[40] This serves as another example of the ways the public domain, in this case tied to the political violence of the Troubles, invaded the private realm of the home and contributed to the politicization of women. Pickering also notes that although they were "slower to mobilize and were less politically active than their nationalist counterparts," Protestant Unionist women became politically active as well, although this generally did not take place until the 1980s.[41]

An interview with political scientist Carmel Roulston reinforced this idea when she described the ways the politicization of the family led to the politicization of the women, perhaps more so than men. Her argument is that during the Troubles, men could be broadly recruited through the schools, their football (soccer) clubs, and so on. Further, since much of the IRA insurgency grew from the neighborhoods, it was possible for men to draw upon friendship networks successfully, as well as the family. But recruitment of women into the cause was far more circumspect, especially in this traditional society. Therefore, a lot of the recruitment of women came through the family, often using women's traditional roles to the women's advantage; the family could be trusted (which helps answer the how question).[42] An example of this can be seen with the Price sisters, mentioned at the beginning of this chapter. They came from a Catholic community and a family of staunch Republicans and IRA members. According to one news account, "When their mother, Crissie, died, her coffin was flanked by an IRA colour party. An aunt, Bridie Dolan, was blinded and had her hands blown off while moving hand-grenades in 1938."[43] These familial connections worked more to the advantage of the Republican side where women were omnipresent. In contrast, Loyalist women who actively participated in the violence often were demonized, as were the Republican women once their roles in the violence became public.

The headlines from two columns, one from the *Sunday World*, published in the Republic of Ireland, the other from the British tabloid *Daily Mail*, illustrate the gendered discourse of the demonization of the women who perpetrated violence on the Republican side. The *Sunday World* headline, "Where Women's Lib Means Guns," includes a photo with the caption, "A teenage girl squints down the sights of this weapon, which fires a tiny .223 bullet," and another photo with a caption that reads, "The miniskirt brigade in action."[44] The *Daily Mail* ran a column titled "The Frightening Cult of the Violent Woman," which attributes the rise of women's violence in part to the fact that "mothers and wives, becoming increasingly delinquent, fail to imbue moral sense in families, or act as a restraining influence."[45] And William Whitelaw, secretary of state for Northern Ireland, "had no hesitation in pointing a condemning finger at the role of female subversives and law breakers or in assuring the House of Commons that the Security Forces were making every effort to bring these women to justice."[46] But as also noted in a column in the *Newsletter*, a Unionist-leaning paper published in Belfast, "The broader issue of the part they [women] will play and the disruptive influence they will bring to bear in the society of the future as *wives and mothers* remains untouched. Therein lies the greatest danger" (italics added).[47]

The message clearly was that not only were more women becoming involved as terrorists, but that part of the reason for this was their failures as wives and mothers, the traditional roles women are supposed to play. Following that logic, there is the danger this pattern will be repeated because of these women's failures. Thus, not only were women demonized for their violent acts but also because of their inability to be "good" wives and mothers; in short, they failed society in any number of ways. But there is another aspect to this image of women as well: the demonization of women who perpetrated acts of violence during the conflict meant that it was far more difficult for them to be integrated back into society after the conflict ended, leading to another set of issues for women as well as for the reconstruction of society after the Troubles officially ended.

It should also be noted that in 1974, the British newspaper *Daily Mail* reported, "A new top security prison for women only is to be built in Northern Ireland to house hardened female terrorists." It was built to hold fifty women, including "a young offenders' center for girls aged between 16 and 21."[48] This is yet another indicator of the increase in the number of women engaged in acts of political violence and the expectation that this would continue.

Reading newspaper accounts of women's involvement during the conflict is instructive and clearly supports the increasing roles women played as the violence escalated. They also underscore the reasons women's active involvement in political violence on the Republican side increased over time as more of the IRA men were killed or imprisoned, leaving a void that women could fill. Furthermore, reading the same account in various newspapers, depending on their political leaning, offers a very different picture of or slant on the events.

The number of articles that featured women as combatants or committing acts of political violence increased considerably from the late

1960s to the early 1970s; by the mid-1970s, such stories can be found very regularly in various newspapers. In 1973 a story in the Belfast *Telegraph*, the only evening paper, described the events surrounding the detention in Belfast of a nineteen-year-old woman, "the first woman to be served with an interim custody order which enables the State to detain her." According to the story, the move came "at the start of a campaign by the Army and police to neutralize the women's IRA, who have helped bolster up the Provisionals since internment. Security chiefs have known for a long time that the women's section of the IRA has been playing a major role in helping to transport arms and explosives."[49]

A few days later, the major papers all covered the appointment of Máire Drumm as president of the Provisional Sinn Féin.[50] She was described in the British newspaper the *Guardian* as "a Belfast housewife" and "mother of five," and in the Belfast *Daily Telegraph* as "a militant Republican leader."[51] The *Guardian,* however, also noted that as one of a number of officers, "Sinn Fein is run by its executive council and Mr. [Rory] O'Brady with the other vice president, Mr. David O'Connell, remain the two most influential figures."[52] Thus, despite the prominent position of this woman, the newspaper accounts make it clear that the men make the decisions. Drumm had gained prominence as a leader in the IRA at a Sinn Féin rally in July 1971 when she said that '" it is not enough to throw stones and bottles and it is a waste of time shouting up the IRA. The important thing is to join. Sure we want to see the British soldiers go home, but we want them to go home in their coffins.'"[53] For that and a similar speech in Belfast, she received two six-month sentences and was sentenced again following a speech in Dublin. Her husband and son were both imprisoned for their work with the IRA, again reinforcing the relationship between the home and family and the political realm, and the confluence of personal and political motivations for women's activism.

The year 1975 seemed to be a turning point in the media descriptions and coverage of the role of women as perpetrators of political violence, a trend that continued and even increased subsequently. The *Daily Mirror*, a British tabloid, published a column in December 1975 sensationalizing the role of women as combatants for the IRA but also naming other women who were identified that year as participating in acts of political violence outside Northern Ireland. Among those were Sara Jane Moore, who was awaiting trial for attempting to assassinate U.S. president Gerald Ford, and Ulrike Meinhof, of the Baader-Meinhof Gang in West Germany, who was accused of mounting a number of terror attacks that killed U.S. servicemen and a German policeman. The article states, "The year of violent women—that was 1975. The year when the so-called weaker sex learned that *guns and bombs could make them more than equal. For the first time, the female Irish terrorists began to steal the headlines of horror from the gunmen*" (italics added).[54] The article continues its list with: "Girls like 19-year-old Marion Coyle, now awaiting trial for her part in the Herrema kidnap, and her cousin Marlene, 21, who is on the Scotland Yard wanted files. And when such girls are jailed, they can riot like men."[55]

By 1976 the headlines about the role of women became more sensational and more frequent: "IRA Girl Bombers Go to War" and "IRA Send in the Girl Bombers."[56] Each offers its own description of an incident in which two teenage girls were described as planting explosives in a Chinese restaurant in Lurgen, County Armagh, Northern Ireland. But what is especially revealing in the second article, drawn from the British paper the *Daily Mail*, was the comment that "Army sources believe the Provos may be starting to run short of men volunteers in the North Armagh area."[57] Clearly, the implication is that the shortage of men meant that the IRA had to turn to women to do the work, but also that the women would step in and take on the roles as needed.

What is also revealing in looking at the newspaper accounts is that there is a significant change in the patterns of what the women did over time, going from serving as couriers to transporting weapons and bombs to serving as guards during the commission of an act of political violence, then "luring" soldiers to their deaths (women "picked up" soldiers specifically to take them to apartments or locations where they would then be murdered), to actually picking up arms and engaging in acts of violence themselves as they moved along the continuum of political activism. From 1975 on, such accounts were almost commonplace. For example, Marjorie Proops, who worked as a columnist for the *Daily Mirror*, started tackling serious subjects, including abortion and drug addiction. In some of her columns she addressed the role of women as participants in the violence, reflecting the events of her time. But this is also an indicator of popular interest in the topic, albeit often from a biased—and gendered—perspective. In a column about Marion Coyle, a volunteer in the Provisional IRA who was arrested and imprisoned for kidnapping an industrialist, Proops wrote, "There was nothing frail, feminine or helpless about this savage young woman. And she isn't as untypical of women, generally, as most would like to believe." According to one psychiatrist Proop mentions, "Women are much more ruthless than men, when driven to it. . . . if women are now showing the claws they have kept sheathed for so long, it's because they now feel they've as much right as men to demonstrate their feelings."[58]

And while women have always been part of the struggle, "it's only when they are on the side of the baddies that they're denounced as unfeminine and unnatural. Thankfully, the majority of women fight aggressively only on behalf of their men and their children."[59] This last phrase too is revealing, suggesting it is permissible for a woman to fight for her family but not for a political cause. Women's agency is denied through the gendered discourse of women's activism.

In addition to the increase in the number of stories and the fact that women were actively engaged in these acts of violence, the actors also seemed to get younger, another indicator of the need for more people who could be recruited and who had a lower chance of being detected. In an early case of an "underwear bomber," schoolgirls, aged about fourteen, "evaded civilian searchers by carrying the explosives in their bras and pants," and then placed the bombs in a bag under a table in a Wimpy restaurant in Belfast City Centre causing extensive damage. About a month earlier, young girls followed a similar pattern and placed a bomb in the Londonderry town center.[60]

While using women, especially young women, was condemned by many, they without doubt played a key and visible role in perpetrating acts of political violence throughout the most active years of the Troubles, especially on the Catholic/Nationalist/Republican side. As the number of men available decreased, the role of women became more important and prominent. This pattern is repeated in a number of cases.

Women, Political Violence, and the Protestant/Unionist/Loyalist Cause
It becomes evident that although many of the acts of political violence were attributed largely to the Republican side, women on both sides engaged in acts of political violence in support of their causes. Although women on the Loyalist side "have a clearly demarcated place in loyalist culture, which is informed by a traditional view of the role of women in society and is difficult to defy,"[61] they, too, took part in acts to support the conflict, moving beyond supporting the Orange [Protestant] marches to volunteering as members of the paramilitaries.

However, in many ways, their participation was far more constrained by cultural and social norms than was the case on the other side. As Rachel Ward stresses in her work, "There are patriarchal pressures to conform to a traditional gender role due to influential politicians, clergy and even husbands' expectations of women."[62] This point is also stressed by Joanne Nagel, who studied masculinity and nationalism in general and who writes that "the scripts in which these roles are embedded are written primarily by men, for men, and about men, and that women are, by design, supporting actors whose roles reflect masculinist notions of femininity and of women's proper 'place.'"[63] She also provides a distinction between cases of nationalist struggles and military occupation (antistate, liberation movements) that further helps elucidate the differences in perspective between the approach taken toward the role of women on the Republican and on the Loyalist sides.

One can argue that the general distinction given by Nagel is analogous to the case of Northern Ireland, where the Republican side clearly saw its country as being occupied by British forces. Pickering elaborates on this point when she says, "Women from the nationalist tradition mobilized out of necessity, out of both personal and communal experiences of injustice, often perpetrated by government agencies, especially by the RUC and British Army. . . . The overtly political nature of women's mobilization and the intensity of efforts to support those groups/campaigns deemed *anti-state* by the RUC and British Army were the major factors behind the contingent politicization of the women" (italics added).[64] Thus, whereas the Republican women were used to provide cover for the men's acts of political violence, including drawing upon their roles as wives and mothers and then actively engaging in acts of violence, Loyalist women generally aided their side in the struggle by supporting their men through far more traditional means that were sanctioned by a patriarchal system.

On both sides, however, it is also clear that women were brought into the struggle more actively when their numbers were needed, albeit to serve different roles. For example, women in the Loyalist Orange Order (Protestant) "have been invited to parade because there is a need for numbers to enhance their visibility. They are therefore being brought in from their cozy social sphere to fulfill a political need, which could be utilized in the future."[65] But another distinction that can be seen here is in the types of organizations Loyalist women were involved in, many of which were "sisters of . . ." or the "women's branch/auxiliary of . . ." Clearly, the main focus was on the men's organizations, with the women's branches serving an auxiliary role. And while "membership does have an underlying political connotation," according to Ward, the main focus of the women's branches tended to be more overtly social rather than political.[66] Ward goes on to say, "While the Orange Order is perceived as a political organization because of its connection to the UUP [Ulster Unionist Party], the women's association avoids the 'political' aspect of Orangeism. For one respondent, her lodge was 'more like a social club.'"[67] In general, these women were bound by the constraints of *gendered symbolism*, which has been translated beyond attitudes and into the types of actions that women engaged in: "Many unionist women remain in the background of politics, taking up a supportive, auxiliary position, 'doing their bit' but remaining relatively invisible to the public sphere."[68]

However, despite the prevalent attitudinal and social gender norms, some Loyalist women were willing to move beyond their traditional place and engage in acts of resistance and political violence in support of their side of the conflict, thereby challenging the existing gender norms of women's behavior. Sandra McEvoy, who interviewed Loyalist women in paramilitaries, suggests that those women also saw themselves as "responsible for defending their communities from armed Republicanism."[69] In other words, some of their perceptions of the need to defend themselves and their communities mirrored the comments made by the Catholic/Republican women. And like the Republican women, they could justify their involvement by citing the need to protect and defend their home, community, and family.

McEvoy also found that women often formed their own units in the Ulster Defense Association (UDA), one of two major Protestant paramilitary organizations (the other is the Ulster Volunteer Force, or UVF), with a membership as high as three thousand women at one point.[70] Clearly, these organizations went beyond the social and cultural orientations noted by Ward and others that show the continuum of women's political activism in times of conflict. These women's tasks ranged from "transporting arms, munitions, and intelligence in baby carriages, purses, cars, and on their bodies" (which we saw with Republican women) to "cleaning crime scenes . . . transporting LPO contraband in and out of detention facilities; . . . carrying out punishment beatings on behalf of the organization; and armed robbery."[71] In fact, in *Ulster Home Cooking*, a cookbook "prepared by Ulster-women *for* Ulster-women," one of the "household hints" includes how to remove blood stains.[72] While this could have been innocent, when published by the DUP during the height of the Troubles, it could also have been more sinister in meaning.

It appears that on this side of the Troubles, as with the other side, women were actively engaged in a range of activities in support of the political violence. But it is far more difficult to find information, let alone publicly released articles about women who actively perpetrated acts of violence on the Loyalist side. This finding itself supports the literature that indicates women's roles were far less obvious and violent acts committed by Loyalist women were not as celebrated as they were on the other side;

that is, women were *invisible*, a word often used in this context. But this does not mean that women were not involved.[73]

The fact that there is little public information about women combatants on the Loyalist side committing acts against members of the Republican/Nationalist side does not mean that the topic does not draw interest. For example, the role of women in the paramilitaries was a theme of playwright Gary Mitchell, who himself lived (and lives) in a Protestant housing estate in Belfast. According to one review of his play *Loyal Women*, which was produced in London in 2003, "Other playwrights, notably Martin McDonough, have suggested that the attraction of the IRA could be the feeling of masculinity it confers on men who can make up, with violence and rhetoric, their sexual and emotional failings. In this play, the Women's Ulster Defense Association likewise compensates for vanishing family and social ties."[74] Thus, in this depiction of the women's UDA designed for a popular audience, the focus is on the women where "the reality of violence, like space, is seen as gendered, and is directed inward, against other women. In this closed world, light years away from any lingering images we may have of 'peace women,' women display a limitless potential for violence against other women."[75] What makes this especially compelling is that the play is set in the post–Good Friday Agreement period, at a time when Northern Ireland was supposed to be moving toward reconciliation. Yet, clearly it is designed to show the divides that remain and the impact those divisions had and continue to have on the women who had engaged in violence.

In her work on Loyalist women paramilitaries in Northern Ireland, McEvoy concluded that "Women members of the LPOs [Loyalist paramilitary organizations] were blending their traditional roles as wives and mother with that of armed political participants."[76] Somehow, that blending made the combatant role for women more palatable. Thus, as in the case of women working for peace, an important coalescing symbol was motherhood, but in this case, it was mothers with guns to protect their children as well as to produce more children for the cause.

Interestingly, one of McEvoy's findings was that some women justified joining the paramilitaries because of concern about the impact the early peace agreements would have on their communities.[77] In fact, the various agreements actually spurred the level of violence on the Loyalist side out of fear of what the agreement would mean to the Loyalists, but also, from the belief that the other side had won, that is, that the perceived IRA violence had paid off. This assertion also supports the need for women to be included at all stages in negotiating an end to conflict and a peace agreement. Thus, ideally there should be a confluence of women working for peace and those who perpetuate and support the violence.

Resurgence of Violence after the Good Friday Agreement

While the 1998 Good Friday Agreement ushered in a new period of peace, violence perpetrated largely by extremist factions on both sides continues. For example, between June and July 2011, sectarian violence exploded in Belfast, initiated in part by members of the UVF. The loyalist side continued with their parades, or marches, which further enflamed the already tenuous mood; riots broke out in Belfast when Protestants prepared to begin their annual marches, which always incite the Catholic side. According to a BBC news reporter, "There is a presence in the area of a faction of the pro-British loyalist Ulster Volunteer Force, a paramilitary organization which signed up to the peace process but is becoming disillusioned. They are flexing their muscle."[78]

Neil Jarman, of the Institute for Conflict Resolution, who has studied Northern Ireland, noted that "attempting to establish how the trouble starts after a previous lull is extremely difficult."[79] In an interview with the BBC during the violence that broke out in June 2011, he said, "If you talk to one side you will get one story and if you talk to the other, they will tell you something entirely different. . . . What we do know is that often there are sporadic bits of trouble which are so relatively small that they often go unreported by the media. But they are the source of significant tension in the area and can lead to something much worse like we've seen in the last 24 hours. . . . It was too simplistic to see the trouble purely in terms of two communities unable to live alongside each other."[80] Rather, he attributed some of the problem to the resurgence of the paramilitaries asserting themselves.[81]

It is important to note that the resurgence of violence is not confined to one side or the other. In April 2010 the Real IRA, a hard-line splinter group that broke from the IRA in 1997 in opposition to the agreement, claimed responsibility for a car bomb planted outside the Northern Ireland headquarters of Britain's security service, MI5: "The attack seems to have been timed to coincide with the transfer of policing and justice powers from London to Belfast."[82] In response to the attack, Northern Ireland secretary Shaun Woodward said the "democratic transition stands in stark contrast to the activity of a criminal few who will not accept the will of the majority of people to Northern Ireland."[83] Although the Northern

Ireland Assembly voted in March 2010 for the transfer, not all members were in favor of the move.[84] In his news analysis, reporter Mark Simpson wrote, "The timing and location of the bombing were designed to try to create the biggest possible international headlines and the deepest political impact. . . . And making it explode shortly after midnight, less than an hour after policing and justice powers were transferred from London to Belfast, was a key part of the potentially lethal plan. . . . On a day when a new political era is starting at Stormont, dissident republicans wanted to highlight one of the weaknesses of the peace process—the threat of further violence."[85]

Conclusion

Northern Ireland is a case where women were able to find a way to become engaged in cross-communal activities by working together in pursuit of common goals, just as they were able to make inroads in working for peace through the formal political structure. Either approach was difficult as women negotiated an established patriarchal system and, in some ways, challenged the existing gender norms of women remaining in the private sphere of the home and family. Of the different approaches, though, it clearly was easier for women to work together at the community level than to try to breach the formal political structure, in large part because of the existing gender norms of women's roles and position in society and the structural barriers to their participation at the formal political level. At the same time, however, women's participation in the formal political system, namely, through the work of the NIWC, leads to "a more comprehensive understanding of the realities of conflict and the meaning of security" as the Good Friday Peace Agreement was being negotiated.[86] Similarly, women who chose to engage in nonviolent resistance and political violence, regardless of sides, had to fight to have more than a subsidiary or support role. Acceptance of those roles was conferred by men in the power structure, often grudgingly, and with the recognition that women could play roles and do things the men themselves could not because of prevailing gender norms (women could hide weapons in their baby carriages, for example, and not be suspect). Thus, women who wanted to be actively engaged in the fight for the cause—and thereby challenge gender norms—had to depend on men to allow them to do so. Even with the social and political constraints, however, women still were able to express their agency in their political activism. And women's agency and activism were motivated by personal and political reasons, whether in the name of working for peace or in support of their side of the conflict.

As the record shows, according to Morgan, in the case of Northern Ireland,

> Some women have made a notable contribution to reducing physical and structural violence—as have some men. But equally their actions have often served to reproduce the divided community rather than challenging it. It would be more accurate to say that women have been both peace makers and peace preventers and that the range of their attitudes and responses has been as wide and as varied as that of men. . . . it does seem more reasonable to try to understand these differences [between men and women] as manifestations of the different historical, social, political and economic roles of women and of men than as evidence of a general feminine orientation to peacemaking.[87]

Women have been instrumental in doing much of the work at the community level needed to transform the culture (cycle) of violence necessary for the country to move beyond the conflict, yet they have also been systematically excluded from working at the national level, either by choice or by omission. And without their involvement, one can easily ask whether true and lasting peace and reconciliation in Northern Ireland will ever really be possible.

Notes

1. Dolours died in January 2013 of a suspected drug overdose. Dolours and Marion Price, "Death of a Soldier," in *Venceremos Sisters: Prison Writings of the Price Sisters* (Belfast: Cathal Brugha Cumann, 1974), Linen Hall Library, Belfast.

2. Ward, *Women, Unionism and Loyalism*, 147–48.

3. In 1976 Betty Williams and Mairead Corrigan were awarded the Nobel Peace Prize for their work in promoting peace and nonviolence in Northern Ireland through the creation of a cross-communal organization known as Peace People.

4. For a description of what the women of the NIWC experienced, see, for example, Baroness May Blood, *Watch My Lips, I'm Speaking* (Dublin: Gill and Macmillan, 2007). For more background about the NIWC, see Kate Fearon, *Women's Work: The Story of the Northern Ireland Women's Coalition* (Belfast: Blackstaff Press, 1999).

5. See Kaufman and Williams, "Northern Ireland: The Impact of 'The Troubles,'" in *Women, the State, and War*, 157–190; and Kaufman and Williams, *Women and War*.

6. Kaufman and Williams, "Northern Ireland."
7. Morgan, "Peacemaker? Peacekeepers?," 3.
8. Ibid.
9. Carmel Roulston, "Democracy and the Challenge of Gender: New Visions, New Processes," in *Gender, Democracy and Inclusion in Northern Ireland*, ed. Carmel Roulston and Celia Davies (New York: Palgrave, 2001), 29.
10. One of the things that is most interesting about this dichotomy is the fact that there are examples of *men* who were involved first in perpetrating the violence and then in working in support of the negotiations to bring about an end to the Troubles. Gerry Adams, leader of Sinn Féin, stands as one major example, as does Martin McGuinness, who went from being a military leader of the Provisional Irish Republican Army to deputy first minister of Northern Ireland. Ian Paisley is an example on the other Protestant, pro-Unionist side. According to Sandra McEvoy, part of the reason is that "In Northern Ireland, combatant women are being systematically excluded from peace processes," which she claims "reifies gender stereotypes, while marginalizing a part of the population that feminists have sought to empower." McEvoy, "Beginning a Feminist Conversation," 282. In addition, we suspect that part of this might also be because of the difficulty women have working in the formal political system in Northern Ireland under any set of circumstances.
11. Kaufman and Williams, *Women, the State, and War*, 170.
12. Cockburn, *The Space Between Us*, 53.
13. Aretxaga, *Shattering Silence*, 7.
14. Kaufman and Williams, *Women, the State, and War*, 175.
15. Ibid.
16. Hunt and Posa, "Women Waging Peace," 42. "Marching season" refers to the period of time, usually in late spring/early summer, when Protestants march or "parade" to commemorate the victory of King William of Orange over Catholic King James at the Battle of the Boyne in 1690, consolidating his reign over England, Scotland, and Ireland. This was also seen as the primacy of Protestant rule over Catholic rule.
17. Northern Ireland Women's Coalition, accessed June 13, 2007, http://www.niwc.org (site discontinued) .
18. Ibid.
19. Kate Fearon and Monica McWilliams, "Swimming against the Mainstream: The Northern Ireland Women's Coalition," in Roulston and Davies, *Gender, Democracy and Inclusion*, 117.
20. See for example, Fearon, *Women's Work*; and Blood, *Watch My Lips* for first-person accounts of their experiences. Also see Kaufman and Williams, "Women, Political Activism, and Conflict," in Kaufman and Williams, *Women and War*.
21. Fearon and McWilliams, "Swimming against the Mainstream," 131–32.
22. Ibid., 132.

23. The SDLP is a nationalist party that proclaims the importance of a united Ireland but also stands in solid opposition to violence as a political tool, http://www.sdlp.ie/index.php (accessed January 17, 2012).

24. Patricia Lawsley, interview by Joyce P. Kaufman, Belfast, Northern Ireland, November 11, 2007.

25. Ibid.

26. Margaret Ward, interview by Joyce P. Kaufman, Belfast, Northern Ireland, November 20, 2007.

27. Jane Morrice, interview by Joyce P. Kaufman, Belfast, Northern Ireland, November 21, 2007.

28. Ruth Jacobson, "Women and Peace in Northern Ireland: A Complicated Relationship," in *States of Conflict: Gender, Violence and Resistance*, ed. Susie Jacobs, Ruth Jacobson, and Jennifer Marchbank (London: Zed Books, 2000), 181.

29. Cockburn, *The Space Between Us*, 74.

30. Ward, *Women, Unionism and Loyalism*, 15.

31. Ibid.

32. O'Ballance, *Terror in Ireland*, 130.

33. Ibid., 159.

34. "Ten Women Held in Dawn Raids," *Daily Telegraph*, April 13, 1974.

35. "The Deadly Secret of Mum-to-Be," *Daily Mirror*, July 7, 1973; also, Stuart Greig, "Women Join the Snipers and Bombers," *Daily Mail*, September 24, 1973.

36. Sharon Pickering, *Women, Policing and Resistance in Northern Ireland* (Belfast: BTP Publications, 2002), 69–70.

37. Ibid., 70.

38. Ibid., 71.

39. O'Ballance, *Terror in Ireland*, 189.

40. Pickering, *Women, Policing and Resistance*, 101.

41. Ibid., 112.

42. Carmel Roulston, interview by Joyce P. Kaufman, Belfast, Northern Ireland, December 16, 2010.

43. "Marion Price: Voice of Extremism," *Telegraph*, December 12, 2000, 2012, http://www.telegraph.co.uk/news/uknews/1378002/Marion-Price-voice-of-extremism.html.

44. "Where Women's Lib Means Guns," *Sunday World*, March 3, 1974, Linen Hall Library, Belfast.

45. Jane Gaskell, "The Frightening Cult of the Violent Woman," *Daily Mail*, March 26, 1973, Linen Hall Library, Belfast.

46. "Women Apart," *Newsletter*, March 29, 1973, Linen Hall Library, Belfast.

47. Ibid.

48. James Grylls, "New Jail for Women," *Daily Mail*, December 7, 1974, Linen Hall Library, Belfast.

49. "Swoop Thought to Have Sent IRA Girls on the Run," *Belfast Telegraph*, January 2, 1973, Linen Hall Library, Belfast.

50. The Provisional executive of Sinn Féin was set up in 1970 to function from headquarters in Dublin in the Republic of Ireland and reflected a split within the IRA.

51. Simon Hoggart, "Woman Nationalist Is New Leader of Provisional Sinn Fein," *Guardian*, January 8, 1973; Hugh David, "Threat by New Provo Leader," *Daily Telegraph*, January 8, 1973.

52. Hoggart, "Woman Nationalist."

53. Ibid.

54. Paula James, "Gunning to the Front," *Daily Mirror*, December 17, 1975, Linen Hall Library, Belfast.

55. Ibid.

56. John Ware, "IRA Girl Bombers Go to War," *The Sun*, September 2, 1976, Linen Hall Library, Belfast; "IRA Send in the Girl Bombers," *Daily Mail*, September 2, 1976.

57. "IRA Send in the Girl Bombers."

58. Marjorie Proops, "Women Deadlier than the Male—Sometimes," *Sunday Mirror*, November 9, 1975, Linen Hall Library, Belfast.

59. Ibid.

60. "Pantie Bombers Blow Up Café," *Daily Mirror*, January 8, 1977.

61. Ward, *Women, Unionism and Loyalism*, 119.

62. Ibid., 148.

63. Joanne Nagel, "Masculinity and Nationalism: Gender and Sexuality in the Making of Nations," *Ethnic and Racial Studies* 21, no. 2 (March 1998): 243.

64. Pickering, *Women, Policing and Resistance*, 109.

65. Ward, *Women, Unionism and Loyalism*, 149.

66. Ibid., 147.

67. Ibid., 146.

68. Ibid., 148.

69. McEvoy, "Loyalist Women Paramilitaries," 263.

70. Ibid., 269.

71. Ibid., 270.

72. *Ulster Home Cooking* (Londonderry: DUP Center, n.d.), Linen Hall Library, Belfast.

73. Interestingly, one of the few very public acts of violence committed by Loyalist women was the murder of Anne Ogilby, a Protestant woman who was beaten to death in South Belfast in July 1974 by a group of ten women and one man, all associated with the UDA, one of two ultraright Loyalist organizations (the other was the UVF). She was killed because she was suspected of having had an affair with an imprisoned UDA man, Billy Young, who was the estranged husband of another UDA member. While this is not a case of women in one group committing an act of political violence against members of the other group, this does demonstrate a case of women engaging in violence in the context of an intrastate conflict. See "Battered to Death in UDA Club: Allegation," *Belfast Telegraph*,

August 7, 1974, Linen Hall Library, Belfast; and Ciaran Barnes, "Battered and Dumped in Stockman's Lane, Murder Still Has Power to Shock," July 7, 2008, http://saoirse32.blogsome.com/2008/07/24/p111157/.

74. Rhoda Koenig, "Loyal Women, Royal Court Theater, London," *Independent*, November 13, 2003, http://www.questia.com/library/1P2-1817660/theatre-loyal-women-royal-court-theatre-london-00999.

75. Wesley Hutchinson, "Engendering Change in the UDA: Gary Mitchell's Loyal Women," *Estudios Irlandeses*, no. 0 (2005): 70, http://cain.ulst.ac.uk/estudiosirlandeses/hutchinson05.pdf.

76. Sandra McEvoy, "Women Loyalist Paramilitaries in Northern Ireland: Duty, Agency and Empowerment. A Report from the Field." Paper presented at the Annual Meeting of the International Studies Association, Chicago, February 2007, 7.

77. Ibid., 272.

78. Mark Simpson, "Photographer Shot in Second Night of Belfast Rioting: Analysis," BBC News Northern Ireland, June 22, 2011, http://www.bbc.co.uk/news/uk-northern-ireland-13869210.

79. Conor Spackman, "East Belfast Interface: A Familiar Pattern Continues," BBC News Northern Ireland, June 21, 2011, http://www.bbc.co.uk/news/uk-northern-ireland-13860978.

80. Ibid.

81. Ibid.

82. Mark Simpson, "Real IRA Admits Northern Ireland MI5 Base Bomb," BBC News Northern Ireland, April 12, 2010, http://news.bbc.co.uk/2/hi/8614723.stm

83. Ibid.

84. Ibid.

85. Ibid.

86. Avila Kilmurray and Monica McWilliams, "Struggling for Peace: How Women in Northern Ireland Challenged the Status Quo," *Solutions* 2, no. 2 (February 28, 2011), http://www.thesolutionsjournal.com/print/893.

87. Morgan, "Peacemakers? Peacekeepers?" 9.

4

Palestinian Women's Activism and the Israeli-Palestinian Conflict

> *In late March, a macabre music video appeared on a television show for Palestinian children. "Duha," 4, as pale as a porcelain doll, is sitting on a bed, watching her mom dress before leaving home. "Mommy, what are you carrying in your arms instead of me?" the girl sings. The next day, Duha gets the answer from the evening news. It turns out her mother was carrying explosives and had blown herself up, killing four Israelis. The final scene shows the girl wistfully rummaging through her dead mother's bedside table. She finds a hidden stick of dynamite and picks it up. The implicit message is that someday Duha will follow her mother into blazing martyrdom.*[1]

IN THIS CHAPTER WE EXPLORE PALESTINIAN WOMEN WHO ARE AT VARIOUS POINTS along the continuum of political activism. Our focus is on Palestinian women who reside in the occupied territories of the West Bank and Gaza, which are currently under Israeli control (while Israel did withdraw from Gaza in 2005, it remains in control of the airspace and territorial waters). Hence, the issues surrounding Palestine and the Palestinians are tied to self-determination and the end of the Israeli occupation of those territories.

Here we explore the role of women in what they see as this nationalist struggle for statehood and independence, bearing in mind that this conflict is far from over. As we begin this analysis it is important to remember that there are Palestinian women who worked for peace alongside Israeli women or in Palestinian-only organizations. There are also examples of Palestinian women actively engaged in the struggle for Palestinian statehood from nonviolent resistance in supporting the cause to serving as suicide bombers, which are the images often popularized in the press.

Palestinian women's activism is not new and has a long tradition. According to Simona Sharoni, as early as the fall of the Ottoman Empire and the concomitant emergence of Palestinian nationalism, Palestinian women began to organize. At this time, "Women's activism did not take place within the frameworks of exclusive women's groups; women who mobilized in support of the national struggle were mostly related to men who were politically involved."[2] This is instructive for a number of reasons.

First, Palestinian women were engaged in acts of political activism for a long time, much of it related to issues that were most relevant to women, such as education, literacy, and health, given the gendered social and cultural expectations of women's positions and roles in society. Again, this is similar to what we saw in Northern Ireland where women were motivated initially to work with their own group on issues of greatest importance to them, as these issues reflected their lived experiences and they had to contend with them on a daily basis. Through the 1970s and 1980s, women's committees were created in the Palestine Liberation Organization (PLO) to address the needs of Palestinian women and to bring pressure on issues regarding the Israeli occupation. However, it should be noted that these activities were nonviolent and designed specifically to address the plight of Palestinian women. Here too we see parallels with Northern Ireland.

Second, although Palestinian women technically have the same political rights as men, the reality is they are underrepresented at the local and national levels of government and in the judiciary. Many of the women who did get involved politically were related to men, and this is not an atypical pattern for a patriarchal society (we see this again in chapter 5 on Sri Lanka). What makes many of these women successful is that often they were related to men (either as wives or mothers) who were either assassinated by Israelis or who were suicide bombers or martyrs. In these cases, it was the relationship to men that helped the women succeed in a patriarchal structure. For example, in the February 2006 election that brought Hamas to power, 6 of the party's 74 seats were won by women. Typically, Hamas and these women followed a conservative form of Islam that includes social segregation from men and wearing head scarves. Although the women drew on their traditional roles as wives or mothers as the basis for their political success, they also gained notoriety because one was "the mother of three Hamas supporters who were all killed by Israelis, and who was later quoted as saying that 'she wished she had 100 sons to sacrifice that way.'"[3] She subsequently became known as the mother of martyrs.[4] Another woman elected at that time was the widow of an assassinated leader of Hamas. In both cases, these women, who chose to work within the formal political system to achieve their desired ends of a Palestinian state, also demonstrated a determination in their support for the nationalist cause rather than a willingness to compromise in the name of peace.[5] But their decision to work within the system in and of itself shows some defiance of the expected role for women. They are also clearly not representative of the norm. These cases are the exception, and these women were able to achieve political office in no small part because of their relationships to men. This clearly has implications for the success of policies designed to protect and advance the status of women.

As was the case in Northern Ireland, the Palestinian example is one of women in a patriarchal society governed by religious tradition as well as secular political issues. For women to gain acceptance in this milieu would require them to breach a clearly male-dominated system. Some women were quite successful politically working within this structure; Palestinian spokeswoman Hanan Ashrawi stands as one example. The first woman to be elected to the PLO executive committee, Ashrawi emerged as the voice of reason and legitimacy for that organization. It is also important to note that she is a Palestinian Christian, not a Muslim, and an educated woman who spent time in and received much of her education in the West.[6] This sets her apart from the majority of Palestinian women who are Muslim and have not had the benefits that Ashrawi had.

Except for Ashrawi, however, few women are visible representatives of the Palestinians beyond those who have engaged in acts of violence. Unlike Northern Ireland, where women such as those in the Northern Ireland Women's Coalition served as high-profile symbols of peacemaking, Palestinian women's visibility often has been tied to acts of nonviolent struggle and, more often, violence. In this case we explore why that is so, the reasons women have taken on this role, and we look at examples of women who worked for peace.

Brief Historical Overview

A brief history is necessary to put the role of Palestinian women into perspective.[7] While the fight for a Palestinian state originated with the founding of the state of Israel in 1948, in reality it goes back further than that. Even before formal statehood was declared, virtually every step leading to the creation of the state of Israel was fraught with controversy and conflict as far back as the Balfour Declaration of 1917. As we noted in an earlier work, "The declaration was issued by the British government, the colonial power of the region, calling for the establishment of a Jewish homeland in what was then-called Palestine. While this was important symbolically, it would be up to the Jewish people who lived in or immigrated to that area to create a country."[8] According to the Palestinian perspective, the creation of a Jewish homeland was made at their expense, thus creating the call for Palestinian statehood and setting the stage for ongoing conflict.

As Jewish immigration to Palestine increased in the 1920s and 1930s, so did Arab resistance. To address the violence, the Peel Commission, convened by the British government to investigate the unrest, recognized that "a unitary state could not be created out of the contradictory obligations contained in the Balfour Declaration."[9] Instead, the Peel Commission recommended "that the mandate be terminated and that Palestine be partitioned into separate Jewish and Arab states."[10] The commission report also included the admonition that "partition means that neither will get all it wants."[11]

The partition plan was ultimately adopted by the United Nations in November 1947, and Britain withdrew from the region. However, the partition led to even more violence, culminating in what the Israelis call the War of Independence, which began immediately following the acceptance of the partition plan and as the British were preparing to leave. The Palestinians refer to this period as the Nakba (collective catastrophe). It is estimated that about 750,000 Arabs either fled or were expelled from Palestine.[12] In effect, this made the Palestinians a stateless people. To many of the Arab leaders, the displacement and treatment of the Palestinian people became symbols of the larger fight for Arab nationalism and against the state of Israel.

The 1967 war, which lasted six days before Israel defeated Egypt, Jordan, and Syria, provided an impetus for the growth of the nascent PLO, initially created in 1964. After the war, the PLO started to become a resistance organization designed to serve the interests of the Palestinians, in part by "making it clear that the world could no longer ignore the plight of the Palestinian people."[13] Yasser Arafat became head of the PLO in 1969 with a goal of uniting the various factions and bringing world attention to the Palestinian cause.

As the Israeli occupation of the West Bank expanded, and Israeli settlements began to take root over the next two decades, Palestinian frustration grew. Ultimately, this led to violence between Israeli forces and Palestinian youths that became known as the intifada (uprising) of 1987. The intifada was an important coalescing point for Palestinians and helped spur the Palestinian women's movement.

Attempts at peace between the two sides in the late 1980s and early 1990s culminated in the 1993 Oslo Accords (formally, the Declaration of Principles on Interim Self-Government Arrangements) in Washington, DC. U.S. president Bill Clinton, Israeli prime minister Yitzhak Rabin, and PLO leader Arafat shook hands on the White House lawn. At this time a transitional period of Palestinian self-rule in the West Bank and Gaza began, as well as the transfer of some powers from Israel to the Palestinian Authority (PA), which had political authority in the West Bank and Gaza (until Hamas's electoral win in 2006).[14] As of today, the political party Fatah controls the West Bank in its dominant role in the PA, while Gaza is controlled by Hamas following its violent takeover of the area in 2007. The two factions remain at odds with each other. Meanwhile, the Israelis continue to build settlements in the West Bank, the territory the Palestinians seek as their state.[15] Peace between Israelis and Palestinians remains elusive (see map, figure 4.1).

Figure 4.1 Map of Israel

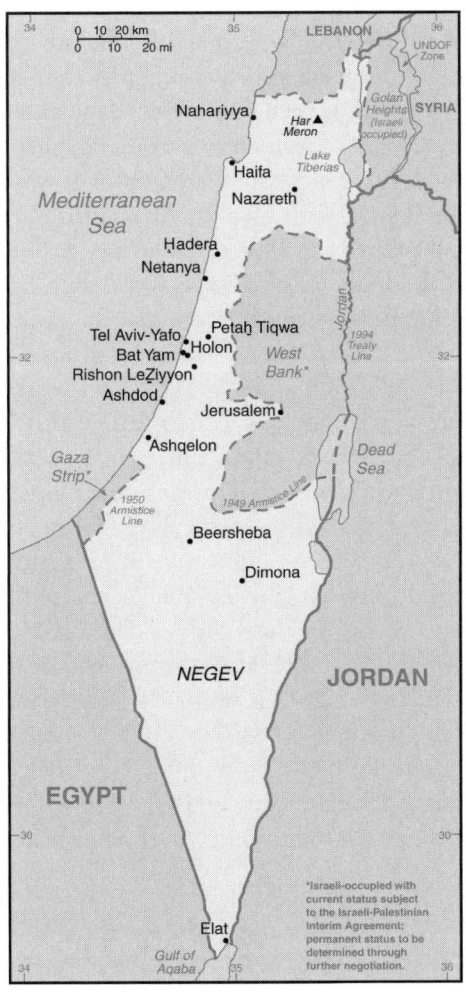

From World Factbook 2009 (Washington, DC: Central Intelligence Agency, 2009). https://www.cia.gov/library/publications/the-world-factbook/index.html.

Palestinian Women's Political Activism

As difficult as the conditions were for men in the occupied territories, they were as bad or worse for women, especially during the period subsequent to the 1967 war. As Sharoni avers, "The Israeli occupation confronted Palestinian women with at least three interlocking systems of oppression—as Palestinians, as women, and as workers. They were forced to simultaneously struggle against this triple oppression and at the same time explore new ways of coping with the overwhelming pressures and responsibilities imposed by the occupation."[16] Although Palestinian women had a long history of political involvement, Sharoni contends that the 1987 intifada helped further politicize Palestinian women. In her words, "The massive political mobilization of women in the West Bank and Gaza Strip called into question passive images of women as dutiful, daughterly, maternal and chaste."[17] Or, as noted by Leila Khaled, a Palestinian woman who was an active member of the Popular Front for the Liberation of Palestine (PFLP), "Women cannot be liberated until the entire nation is liberated."[18] This in turn suggests that Palestinian women were aware there was a relationship between the status of their state and their own future.

The result was the emergence of women's groups, some of which worked to better the plight of women, while others worked to establish a sovereign Palestinian state through peaceful means, often by working with Israeli women who shared their goals. Other groups also emerged that had a place for women who chose to become combatants and to fight and even die for their cause either with—or in spite of—male leaders. On the whole, these women were also very effective, in part because they played upon gendered assumptions that allowed them access to places men would not have been able to access. In the words of Frances Hasso, the women militants "challenged Israeli gendered assumptions that it is the Palestinian male and not female bodies that militarily threatened their racialized social order."[19] Furthermore, as Hasso also notes, these women "viewed themselves as legitimate militant actors."[20] In fact, they recognized their actions would be more dramatic because they were women. Importantly, Palestinian women expressed their agency in their political activism.

Women and Peace Activism

Palestinian women have not gained prominence for their work for peace but for their emergence as combatants, especially suicide bombers. But this does not mean women were not involved in working for peace. We contend that because the general assumption of women working for peace is the gender norm, less attention has been paid to that form of women's activism in this case than to women who were engaged in acts of nonviolent resistance and political violence, which challenges gendered assumptions. In fact, far more Palestinian women over the course of the struggles for statehood have been engaged in working with Israeli women for peace. Yet these cases are not widely known because they are not as sensational in general.

According to Elizabeth Fernea, "Feminists or women's activists, both Israeli and Palestinian, have tended to organize separately, creating women's centers in their own communities, establishing societies to aid the poor, helping women deal with legal and employment problems."[21] For example, Palestinian women created the Jerusalem Center for Women (JCW) in 1991 following a series of meetings with Palestinian and Israeli activists and political figures in Brussels in 1989. The goal of the JCW is to empower "Palestinian women's position in civil society, politics, and within the peace process."[22] Further, the organization "continues to support women's participation in the peace process and believes women's ideas for a just peace must be included in final status negotiations."[23] The JCW is also feminist in its orientation, as it "continues to increase women's skills and confidence to prepare them to become agents of change and powerful advocates for their communities and against Israeli occupation. Likewise JCW considers significant to support Palestinian women in apprehending, addressing, and altering the male societal patriarchy."[24] It is clear that the goals of the JCW demonstrate the blurring of the public/private divide in its work to empower women in their communities (e.g., provide legal advice for families whose houses are at risk of being demolished by the Israeli authorities) as well as to change the patriarchal system (e.g., training women as community leaders and politicians).[25]

Another example of Palestinian women's activism in promoting peace is the Women's Affairs Technical Committee (WATC). Established in 1992 in Jerusalem, the WATC is "one of the technical teams formed to support the peace negotiations."[26] But more than that, according to its website, the WATC also sees itself as playing a vital role in the infrastructure necessary to build a future Palestinian state. In doing so, the organization seeks "to integrate gender into all preparatory work in support of the peace process, to build state institutions in a manner that would fulfill the Declaration of Independence (1988) which affirms the principle of equality among Palestinians regardless of sex, religion or race."[27] The organization brought together women's organizations engaged in peace activism and supported the peace process (e.g., Union of Social Work Committees, Women's Action Union). For the WATC, increasing women's representation in the negotiating teams would be a way to integrate gender into the various "policies and plans being prepared by these [negotiating] teams."[28] Although the organization was not successful in institutionalizing its work as ministries in the PA, the WATC continued as a coalition of several women's groups working toward achieving women's equal rights and a role for women in decision making in the formal political structures, and also to promote "effective local leaderships" at the grassroots level.[29]

While these examples show Palestinian women's activism in the Palestinian territories, women peace activists have had a difficult time engaging in cross-communal activism. One of the major issues that kept Jewish and Arab/Palestinian women from working together for peace, a concept that would appear to benefit everyone, was a difference in perspective on exactly what peace meant. Did peace mean that the Israeli government would accept the Palestinian claim for statehood and sovereignty? Did it mean that the Palestinians would recognize the existence of Israel and its right to exist? These things were codified in the Oslo Peace Accords. Yet *peace*, as defined at its most basic level as an absence of armed hostility or conflict, did not result. Nor did any agreement resolve the issue of the right of return for Palestinian refugees, nor determine what to do with the occupied territories in establishing the borders of a Palestinian state. These issues remain real today and continue to divide the groups, thereby making it very difficult to address the conflict, let alone arrive at a situation of peace.

Despite the extent of the issues that divided Israeli and Palestinian women, it did not mean it was impossible for them to work for peace. As we saw in Northern Ireland, admittedly some of the work was done in the women's own community. The plight of the Palestinian women helped bring Israeli and Palestinian women together. As Ayala Emmett wrote, "Justice for Palestinians is at the center of women's understanding of peace and coexistence."[30] Thus, for women, "issues of human rights, including the treatment of Palestinians, were part of what they started to fight for."[31] From the 1980s into the early 1990s, some Israeli and Palestinian women came together in pursuit of issues to benefit all women.[32] For example, Women in Black, an explicitly feminist organization and one of the best known and most enduring of all women's organizations, began in January 1988, one month after the first intifada broke out, when ten Israeli women held a vigil in Jerusalem to protest Israel's occupation of the West Bank and Gaza (the weekly silent vigil continues today). The movement quickly spread throughout Israel, incorporating Israeli Palestinian women as well as Jewish women. However, it should also be noted that all the women who were part of this group were

Israeli citizens; it would have been too dangerous for Palestinian women who were not citizens to be involved in this kind of public protest.

This is another point that must be considered when looking at Palestinian women, specifically, the differences between those who lived in Israel or were Israeli citizens, versus those who lived in the occupied territories. Clearly Palestinian women who live in Israel and are citizens are more privileged than Palestinian women who are refugees or living in the occupied territories. This further divides even Palestinian women, making it more difficult for them to work together in pursuit of any single principle. Women in Northern Ireland did not have to face this issue. Even though their loyalty might have been divided, the women in Northern Ireland were British citizens and were entitled to participate in the formal political process should they have chosen to. However, many did not. And, as becomes clear in the next chapter, the women in Sri Lanka also did not face the dilemmas of citizenship and participation that so affected Palestinian women.

In the West Bank Palestinian women did (and continue to) act for peace. For example, in December 1998 the Palestinian Initiative for the Promotion of Global Dialogue and Democracy (MIFTAH) was created with Hanan Ashrawi as a primary founder and secretary-general. For Ashrawi, this followed two years (1996–1998) in which she served as the Palestinian minister of higher education, a position she resigned from in 1998 in protest against political corruption and Arafat's handling of the peace talks. She then helped found MIFTAH, which was designed "to promote the principles of democracy and good governance with various components of Palestinian society; it further seeks to engage local and international public opinion and official circles on the Palestinian cause."[33] The method to achieve this is through "an active and in-depth dialogue, the free flow of information and ideas, as well as local and international networking."[34] One of the programs of MIFTAH was specifically dedicated to the Empowerment of Palestinian Women Leadership. Funded by the Ford Foundation, this was a two-year project (2005–2007) to respond to the needs identified by women, one of which was "to enhance women's political participation in peace building and the negotiation process through networking, capacity building and simulated negotiations with Israelis," in the Women in the Peace Negotiations phase of the work.[35]

As part of capacity building, and with the goal of preparing the women who participated to take more action, the group held sessions on the main negotiation topics. MIFTAH conducted a three-day training course in negotiation skills, and the Palestinian Center for Israeli Studies was contacted to map Israeli peace organizations.[36] This was accompanied by another program specifically to address "the gender deficit in local politics and governance by developing a support network for Palestinian women interested in assuming a more prominent role in public life."[37] And a final and related program sought to build on the goals of United Nations Security Council Resolution 1325, which calls for women's participation in peace negotiations and postconflict reconstruction, specifically to strengthen networks of nongovernmental organizations and disseminate information.[38]

By the time of the publication of the 2009 *MIFTAH Annual Activities Report* in 2010, virtually no mention was made of the Women in the Peace Negotiations phase. Rather, the parts of the report that dealt with women continued to stress the need to support Palestinian women in assuming a role in political life, with a focus on Local Councils, which were parts of the government. There was a section titled Gender, Peace and Security, but the goals identified were "gender equality and the human rights of women and adolescent girls, particularly their reproductive rights, integrated in national policies, developmental framework and laws."[39] This represents an apparent change in priorities consistent with the pattern for the majority of Palestinian women who were activists, where their work was focused less on working to build peace, per se, either from their side or by working with Israeli women, as much as it was designed to improve the plight of Palestinian women, especially those in the occupied territories. This enabled the women to build on their roles as women while also furthering the cause of all Palestinian women, which was their priority.

This is not to suggest that Palestinian women abandoned the cause of working for peace, some of which was facilitated by outside groups or organizations. For example, in June 2010 the government of Spain, in conjunction with the UN Development Fund for Women and the International Women's Commission for a Just and Sustainable Israeli-Palestinian Peace (IWC), sponsored a two-day conference that brought together government leaders and experts on women's political and human rights as well as on the Israeli-Palestinian conflict. The IWC, which was formed in 2005 specifically to strengthen the implementation of UN Security Council Resolution 1325, was made up of Palestinian and Israeli women "living different realities on both sides of the conflict to speak with one voice on the most difficult political issues."[40]

Since 2005 the IWC worked with decision makers globally, from European Union and U.S. leaders to UN Security Council and Middle East Quartet members (the United Nations, Russian Federation, United

States, and European Union—which promote diplomatic solutions to the Israeli-Palestinian conflict), as well as in these officials' own countries to highlight the critical need to recognize civil society women leaders as participants in resolving the Israeli-Palestinian conflict, ensure that women have a place in all processes to negotiate peace, and take concrete steps to protect women from the specific ways conflict affects them. The IWC took a different approach to bringing Israeli and Palestinian women together by recognizing that sometimes in intractable conflict situations, outside mediators can be effective at bringing the groups together and has called for active third-party involvement in resolving the conflict, in addressing the asymmetrical power relations between Israelis and Palestinians, and in stopping evictions in East Jerusalem, dismantling settlements and the separation wall, and ending the siege in Gaza. The IWC appealed to the European Union to play a leading proactive role at the political level and for the United Nations to serve as the main referee of any peace process. An Israeli member of the IWC wryly noted, "We have 43 years of occupation, check points and humiliation. So many road maps and so few results."[41]

In 2008 the IWC issued "Political Vision: Paper of Understanding," which begins with the acknowledgment that the formal negotiations to end the conflict "are, once again, stagnated."[42] It stressed the fact that "in order to revisit the conflict in an innovative and constructive manner and move forward towards its resolution, as women we firmly believe that *it is no longer possible to ignore its roots*" (italics added).[43] The IWC also provided a cogent summary of the situation:

> These conditions are exacerbated by a pervasive sense of despondency and loss of hope. The tightening vise on Palestinian existence has generated either despair or escapism as a response to the prevalent feeling of personal and national victimization. Israelis, in turn, suffering from an ongoing sense of vulnerability despite their superior might, are fast forfeiting their belief in the possibility of a solution and, where possible, disengaging from its realities. *Women, more than others, continue to suffer its ramifications.* These differential effects on the minds and physical existence resulting from the prolonged conflict make the quest for gender parity an integral part of the solution to the conflict, just as the resolution of the conflict is key to gender equity in both communities.[44] (italics added)

It is apparent that as the formal peace negotiations between Israelis and Palestinians have stalemated, the situation for women in the Palestinian territories has not advanced either, despite reports to the contrary.

It is also important to note that with the exception of Hanan Ashrawi, women were largely omitted from leadership positions in the peace process and negotiations on both sides (Israeli women did participate in formal peace talks in the 1990s, although they were in secondary positions, such as midlevel negotiators, legal advisers, and secretaries, all still based on gender roles and stereotypes).[45] Thus, any attempts at communication across groups that could lead to peace negotiations, such as the facilitation described previously in the MIFTAH programs, are more in line with informal diplomatic initiatives than government-to-government formal negotiations as prescribed in UN Security Council Resolution 1325. One of the roles of the IWC was "to provide analysis about and solutions to the ongoing conflict with a unified voice. Yet its demands for inclusion in the peace talks have been rebuffed."[46] While the IWC had attempted "to present a unified Palestinian and Israeli women's perspective on peace, . . . the IWC disbanded" in 2011.[47] In light of continued Israeli military actions, including the 2008 military incursion into Gaza (Operation Cast Lead), it was increasingly difficult for Palestinian women to work with their Israeli counterparts. "Shared gender oppression" was not sufficient enough to bring the two groups together and present "a unified influence on larger peace processes."[48]

Despite the many issues that divide the Israelis and Palestinians, the height of the women's peace movement between the two sides did have some important and long-term consequences for Palestinian women working for peace. It started a dialogue between Israeli Jewish women, Israeli Arab women, and women in the occupied Palestinian territories. It helped raise women's voices in Israel and Palestine, and similar to what we saw in Northern Ireland, it helped provide a forum for and ongoing contact among women on issues common to women, including peace. Nonetheless, a great deal of suspicion and skepticism impedes any real dialogue or understanding across the two groups of women. As one Palestinian woman is quoted as saying "I see it from a *national perspective*. . . . How can I say these Israeli women soldiers at the checkpoint are my sisters?" (italics added).[49] Or, put another way, would it be possible to have real and authentic discussions of peace and conflict resolution between two groups of women where there are vastly different—asymmetric—power relationships, not to mention perspectives? Or do such differences point out another fallacy in addressing issues of women and peace, in that there are not enough bonds among women to bridge the gaps nor to assume that the quest for peace is enough to bring them together. What of the perception of Palestinians that they are engaged in a struggle against occupation and their resistance to Israeli state-sanctioned violence?[50] As Vanessa Farr concludes in her assessment of three Palestinian women's organizations dedicated to peace activism: "The degree of asymmetry between what Palestinians can negotiate for and how Israelis can choose to react is so severe that a meaningful and durable solution does not seem imaginable. Within this imbalanced arena, the powerlessness and marginality of women are extreme.... Palestinian women are trying to organize a response to a process that clearly does not prioritize or value women's voices for peace."[51]

Here the work of Sophie Richter-Devroe is especially helpful at pointing out the problems with trying to initiate a dialogue across these groups of women. She writes, "With resistance to the occupation (in its various forms) having rightly been identified as the 'overall guiding meta-frame for Palestinian politics'—but also as concerns social practices—the majority of Palestinian women not only construct their identity and choose their agency in line with this resistance discourse, they are also *expected* to do so" (italics in the original). And then she continues that Palestinian women are expected to "view themselves, first of all, as Palestinians resisting the occupation, before their status as women in patriarchal society can be discussed."[52] Thus, national identity supersedes gender identity, which in turn impedes the possibility of women engaging in "dialogue across difference" with Israeli women.[53] But there can be no discussion or dialogue if there are no opportunities to meet and to determine areas of commonality.

Cynthia Cockburn points out another challenge facing the Palestinian women who choose to pursue any kind of discussion across groups: "There are women enacting disloyalty by refusing an enmity proclaimed by politicians and militarists."[54] Cockburn also reminds us that for Palestinian women "it remains a continually open question whether and when the contact with Israeli women is beneficial and advisable" because of their different, and unequal, situations and that each group has very different reasons for talking, or wanting to talk.[55] Cockburn quotes a JWC board member, Amal Kreishe Barghouti: "It's a method of survival for us, for me. For the Israelis, it's more an ethical issue, an expression of political commitment."[56] The difference in perspective between the two groups is so profound it renders dialogue virtually impossible. Again, in the words of Cockburn, who interviewed Israeli and Palestinian women: "In talking with these women I saw clearly how the profound asymmetry between Israelis and Palestinians, those who have a state and 'rights' and those whom they deprive of both, undermine projects of cooperation."[57]

This also translates into questions about what is meant by peace, or in the words of one Palestinian woman, "What does it mean to be a 'peace activist' in Palestine? We can only *resist oppression*. Justice necessarily comes first. Peace is a second step" (italics in the original).[58]

Women, Nonviolent Struggle, and Political Violence

In his book *Contested Lands*, which includes case studies of divided societies including Israel and Palestine, Sumatra Bose describes the two versions of the story of the creation of the state of Israel and its impact on the Palestinian people: "One people's quest for emancipation has generated the other's unending oppression; they are two sides of the same coin, just as the Palestinians' 'freedom fighter' is Israel's 'terrorist.'"[59] Each of the two sides was fighting for self-determination: in Israel's case, for a Jewish state in the wake of the Holocaust, and for the Palestinians, for recognition of the land they had lived on and claimed for centuries as theirs. Palestinian women were not immune to the conflict. As discussed in chapter 2, women's gender identities become vulnerable to redefinition, and along with that, a change in their roles in the society, especially in patriarchal societies. In effect, as groups fight for their independence, recognition, self-determination, or sovereignty, every available person becomes necessary to fight for the cause. Thus, women become an essential part of the struggle, and the Palestinian case stands as an example of that. In other words, when it comes to the role of women engaging in nonviolent struggle and political violence, achieving the end becomes the most important goal, superseding social or cultural norms.[60]

In the late 1960s and early 1970s Palestinian women participated in the resistance movement, primarily recruited by their families, especially if their fathers or brothers were already involved. For example, the PFLP had a policy that brothers were to recruit their sisters. For the most part, women's resistance activities focused on "small-scale production, literacy and schooling and health education."[61] As the conflict continued, so too did women's political activism. The Democratic Front for the Liberation of Palestine (DFLP), a leftist-nationalist organization that split from the PFLP, was created in 1969. It was affiliated with the Palestinian Federation of Women's Action Committees (PFWAC), a nationalist-feminist women's organization located in the West Bank and Gaza, and created in 1978 by women in the DFLP.[62] As Frances Hasso notes, "Unlike most 'women's auxiliaries' of nationalist, revolutionary, or labor movements, the PFWAC remained relatively independent of the DFLP—charting a course that successfully combined a nationalist and feminist agenda for a 10-year period."[63] PFWAC members focused on empowering women in their daily lives at the grassroots level through literacy projects, training projects, and preschools.[64] In combining feminist and nationalist liberation, PFWAC members "viewed women's *active participation* in the national liberation struggle as a prerequisite for women's liberation" (italics in the original).[65] Interestingly, the DFLP had many women in its leadership ranks, women who were also members of the PFWAC. Women were recruited into the organization and then encouraged to pursue leadership roles in the DFLP.[66]

During the first intifada in 1987, women engaged in a variety of ways along the continuum of political activism, including nonviolent resistance through demonstrations, protests, visits to prisoners and support for martyrs' families, boycotting Israeli imports, and establishing a secret education system after the Israeli government closed the universities.[67] Since around 2007, Palestinian women's nonviolent resistance has moved beyond only boycotts to civil protest. For example, women engage in women-only protests next to the wall that divides Israel proper from the West Bank. Organizations focused on civil protest include local groups, nongovernmental organizations, and political parties.[68] In her interviews with Palestinian women activists ("peace, resistance and day-to-day activists") in the West Bank and East Jerusalem, Richter-Devroe found the restrictions on women's ability to mobilize to protest the occupation resulted from Israeli policies, such as "harsh military repression, spatial fragmentation, and mobility restrictions, but also indirectly through heightening insecurity (thus enforcing patriarchal restrictions on women's mobility as 'necessary' protection from gender-specific violence and potential sexual harassment) and increasing poverty (thus forcing women's preoccupation with issues of survival rather than resistance)."[69] Thus, while they are motivated to act against the continued Israeli occupation and to push for national liberation, Palestinian women's political activism is restricted.

Importantly, the maternal/motherist image is used by many Palestinian women in their resistance activism, not as "peaceful" but as resisters: the domestic sphere is politicized when women "present their domestic duties and reproductive roles as a form of political activism."[70] At the same time, women also "domesticate the public sphere by basing their political activities and entry into the public sphere on their domestic role as mothers."[71] Concerns about youth radicalization and survival of the family and community motivate women to engage in resistance activities (the why question of our research). Richter-Devroe quotes one of her interviewees, Ilham, who spoke of defending her land: "If the soldiers come and take my land that means I have nowhere to live. I have no home. So what can I do? I have to go out and defend my land."[72] Through motivation to defend their land, women challenge existing traditional gender norms by acting as the providers for their family (a traditionally male role) and also as protectors of the Palestinian people (again, a traditionally male role).[73] Richter-Devroe makes clear that such activism, as defined by the interviewees, is not intended to change "gender regimes and ideologies," and thus is not a "strategic feminist agenda."[74] What the activism is, however, is an opportunity for women to express their agency as political actors motivated to end the occupation and gain independence for Palestinians and Palestine.

Women's motivations to engage in nonviolent resistance and political violence have been and are personal and political. As Gentry shows in her study of Leila Khaled (a member of the PLFP), "By justifying political violence and by being able to defend her choices she portrays herself as an intelligent woman who made a choice forty years ago."[75] Women were not duped or tricked by men into becoming combatants engaging in acts of political violence. Rather, they made choices for a host of reasons, some broadly political, some personal, and in some cases, for feminist reasons.

But what also must be recognized is the role women were willing to play, in part because of the assumption that as women they were less suspicious, and as was the case with Northern Ireland, "men often under-endow women with violent or political intent," thereby putting women into a unique position to act.[76] As Hasso also notes in her study of four Palestinian women suicide bombers/martyrs, the women "contrasted their attacks to the perceived weakness and silence of Arab men leaders and castigated them for failing their duties."[77] Their actions challenged "gender-sexualized norms of duty and responsibility with respect to who protects the community and who is protected within it."[78] Thus, for many Arab women and girls, when the community is under attack, the response was "women's militant political action in defense of community."[79] This offers a different, but nonetheless important, context for understanding women's actions in this case. Women have suffered as much as men because of Israeli aggression, and women can respond to defend their community, and by extension, their role in it. Palestinian women have played another important role that cannot be overlooked. In addition to challenging Israeli gendered assumptions, "They concurrently called [Palestinian] men to arms in defense of community, and participated in that defense themselves, destabilizing the construct of men as defenders of community and women as the protected."[80] Thus, as women responded to the call from their leaders, they prompted men to do the same.

As with other cases of women's involvement in nationalist movements, however, women's liberation has been subordinated to Palestinian liberation.[81] Women never achieved the politically or socially prominent roles they were promised during the first intifada, and in the subsequent intifada, they tended to perform more stereotypical gender roles. As Anat Berko and Edna Eerez assert, "Palestinian women have been called to fight the occupying forces but at the same time to accept and obey patriarchal hegemony, presenting a paradox for women who respond to the call."[82]

Karla J. Cunningham notes that "Palestinian secular leaders have historically been willing to include women in an array of roles to gain strategic advantage and for operational reasons."[83] Consistent with the literature noted earlier, "Women have mobilized for several purposes that include, but are certainly not limited to, nationalism, to fill personnel requirements as their male counterparts are killed or arrested, because of the individual and collective impact of occupation, and political activism."[84]

One End of the Continuum of Political Activism: Suicide Bombers/Martyrs

Western media coverage and much of the mainstream academic work on the Israeli-Palestinian conflict is focused on Palestinian terrorism, including suicide bombing. Because of the fact that women have also participated in this type of activism, the media has covered these instances extensively. For example, in May 2007, *Time* magazine ran a story titled "Palestinian Moms Becoming Martyrs."[85] As a magazine for popular consumption in the United States, as opposed to an academic or scholarly journal, *Time* featured this story about Palestinian women who have chosen to become suicide bombers or martyrs for the cause. Geared to inform the general public about this phenomenon, the article is fairly straightforward and offers a range of explanations on why some Palestinian women have chosen this path: revenge, despair, religious fervor, honor, victims, to name but a few reasons given. The story was published shortly after Hamas broadcast a reenactment of the life of Reem Riyashi, age twenty-two, "a Palestinian mother of two who blew herself up in a suicide attack against Israeli soldiers at a Gaza border crossing in January 2004."[86]

The story itself depicts and in many ways sensationalizes the role of Palestinian women as suicide bombers. But it also summarizes in relatively simple terms the many reasons Palestinian women choose this option. In the case of Reem Riyashi, the woman highlighted in the story, those who studied her background learned that her husband found out she was having an affair with a senior Hamas commander. "Among conservative Palestinians, as in other parts of the Islamic world, an adulterous woman is often punished with death. Riyashi was given a second option: she could become a martyr."[87] The story then documents some of the reasons women choose this option while also suggesting that such incidents will continue: "The longer the stalemate [between Israel and Palestinians] persists and living conditions for the Palestinians continue to deteriorate, the more likely it is that slaughter will return to Israel's streets."[88] In the five years between 2002 and the time of publication of this story, eighty-eight Palestinian women attempted suicide bombings; eight of those were successful. And the author speculates that more will continue to do so as long as the Palestinian situation remains unresolved.

Another story, aired on CBS News in January 2009, was titled "Hamas TV Pictures Promotes Female Suicide Bombers Squad." In a photograph that was posted on a video-sharing website along with brief statements, three women are seen posing in front of a Hamas banner, their arms resting on Kalashnikov rifles. In their statements, one woman had pledged to "turn her body into a fire" that would burn Israeli soldiers. The second woman said that she was a mother of two "martyrs," and noted that Palestinian women are ready to "make the ultimate sacrifice" to stop Israel from moving into Gaza. The third woman made similar threats.[89] These testimonials of women suicide bombers/martyrs indicate women's political agency while also highlighting the gender-defying norms of their actions.

In trying to ascertain why some women, who would not otherwise kill themselves, would be willing to die for a cause, one can argue that women engage in this action as a feminist statement. In such a feminist statement, women gain access to the political, public sphere that would normally be closed to them in an otherwise patriarchal society; women can also prove themselves and their worth to the organization and to its goals.[90] One woman interviewed by Berko and Eerez said, "If you want to do something, you just believe in yourself and do it. Men respect me; they ought to respect me. Men and women ought to respect what I did. I did not do it for myself."[91] Another woman said, "I see myself as a Palestinian woman fighting for my rights; equality between men and women is the thing I fight about the most."⁹² Thus, engaging in acts of violence can be a form of empowerment for women, especially in traditional societies.

From this, Yoram Schweitzer's important conclusion is that "those sending the women may be exploiting the modern cry for emancipation of women: proving that women are equally eligible to die alongside men for a nationalist or religious cause ostensibly indicates an equivalency of value."⁹³ For the women, then, accepting this type of mission was seen as a step forward, not only for them but for all other women who follow them, a point that echoes one made by Bloom. As Bloom asserts, women's militancy affected the traditional gender norms that limited women's roles within Palestinian society in which women remain in the private sphere.⁹⁴ Women's political activism changed their gender roles in society and enabled them to profess their contributions toward reaching the political goals of the society and group. Yet, as Claudia Brunner asks, "Do these women, who have challenged the world at so many levels also substantially challenge the gender order through their participation in suicide bombings? Do women transgress more than traditional gender roles when resorting to arms?"⁹⁵ She answers her questions: "As far as the Israeli-Palestinian conflict is concerned, not really. . . . One can at a maximum speak of suspension of gender identities, even though gender roles might be transformed for a certain period of time."⁹⁶

But this leads to another question that is important to address, that is, whether the willingness to become suicide bombers actually furthers a feminist agenda. In the Palestinian case, data show that women "are rarely *portrayed* as committing suicide due to political motivations. However, the same holds true for many of the male suicides" (italics added).⁹⁷ From this we might conclude that political motives are secondary for men and women. Instead, the women "are portrayed as divorced, barren, influenced by brothers, uncles or other family members. Or, they are grief-stricken over the death of a relative or a friend. They fulfill the ultimate maternal-sacrificial code in that they want to give their own life on behalf of others' pain, grief or suffering."⁹⁸

The problem with this explanation is that others are interpreting women's motivations for engaging in suicide bombing rather than the women themselves and the agency they have. The gendered discourse permeates the accounting for women's political activism, including political violence. What we need instead is to hear women's voices, their reasons and motivations for activism. In short, once women were permitted to serve as combatants and even suicide bombers, they did so for a range of reasons, not unlike men. Berko and Eerez interviewed fourteen Palestinian women incarcerated in Israeli prisons for a range of security-related offenses and found that they ranged in age from eighteen to twenty-nine, and all, except one, were single and had no children. And despite the restrictions they felt were placed on them as women, they felt honored to be Palestinian and Muslim. But perhaps most important, the women "closely identified with the Palestinian national struggle; some were willing to risk their lives for 'the Palestinian people,' other national causes or *Jihad*."[99] And Hasso notes the way a writer in the Hamas newspaper defended Reem Riyashi, the longtime Hamas activist mentioned earlier in this chapter, who killed herself and four Israelis at the Erez border crossing in January 2004 by arguing that "with the final kiss to her two children, '*she was giving them power as a fighter and a martyr, which is higher than the quality of maternity*'" (italics added).[100]

In reviewing final testimonials by some Palestinian (and other) suicide bombers/martyrs, Tanya Narozhna argues that they show it is not "excessive personal grief" that motivates some women to engage in martyrdom/suicide bombings.[101] What these testimonials show instead is that the women's "private lives and individual identities" are closely linked to their national group's "destiny."[102] Instead of considering the personal and political as separate spheres, as well as the individual and the collective, they are intertwined.[103]

In another instance, Victor interviewed the director of a UN school in the Jabaliya refugee camp in Gaza, who said,

> I understand why children want to die defending their homeland. . . . How can I tell them that they can ignore what is happening all around them? How can I guarantee them that their fathers or brothers will not be shot just because they are on the street? . . . The Koran tells us that if we die as martyrs, we will have a better life in Paradise. . . . How can I ask them to live a life under occupation that gives them nothing and then forbid them to talk of achieving martyrdom and living for eternity in Paradise?[104]

In talking to a class of girls, Victor specifically asked how many wanted to be martyrs, and when she asked why, one responded, "To have everything in Paradise."[105] Once Islamic law was reinterpreted to allow women to become martyrs and enter paradise with all the advantages and wonder that came with it, one of the major strictures prohibiting women from serving in this role was removed, and women, like men, were finally allowed to achieve this goal.

This, then, reinforces the idea that personal and political motives are factors for women's decisions as they are for men, and women made choices to engage in acts of resistance and political violence or to work for peace, but they were clear choices and an expression of their agency.

Acceptance of Women in the Struggle: Women, Political Violence, and Islam

The case of Palestinian women engaging in political violence is an interesting one in that it crosses secular and religious lines. It is secular in its resemblance to a nationalist movement tied to self-determination and the desire to secure territory and freedom for its people leading to the creation of a Palestinian state. But it is also a religious struggle in that it is embedded in Islam and often a conservative interpretation of the religion that limits the role of women. It is this latter interpretation that had to be revised to allow for the active involvement of women. Thus, Palestinian women are not only fighting alongside men for the creation of a state but are often fighting those same men for the right to fight—and die—with and for them.

The history of Palestinian women's roles as combatants can be correlated with the two intifadas and the various wars with Israel, all of which served as important coalescing forces.[106] As we have seen in other cases, initially women mobilized as *either* mothers or warriors, with divisions emerging between the women in part because of questions about their roles. Cunningham writes, "The result was that the young 'warrior' women, whose public but usually non-violent activities challenged social norms of appropriate female behavior, were pushed out of the visible ('unveiled') public ('warrior') realm. In turn, mothers expanded their symbolic and support roles."[107] Initially, although there were religious overtones to the Palestinian struggle, the focus of the conflict with Israel and its allies was secular and tied to issues of statehood. Yet, the strictures of Islam were relevant factors constraining the role of women.

These factors started to change, as did women's roles, with the second intifada in 2000 and into 2001, when "women were increasingly visible participants in a range of violent activities that presaged their role as suicide attackers."[108] Most of these women were tied to or supported by the more extremist Islamic organizations, such as Hamas, which justified the new roles for women because of Israel's occupation of the Palestinian territories. The role of women combatants in Palestinian organizations thus changed from a more moderate and traditional one, tied to their role as mothers, to a more radical one culminating in the emergence of women suicide bombers. This was the result of the changing nature of the conflict and the concomitant need for more people to continue to fight these wars. Ness also writes, "Every militant group must similarly find a way to expand the definition of feminist *to include the conduct of violence*" (italics added).[109] We certainly see this to be true in the case of Palestinian women, especially with the rise of the more militant factions, secular and religious.

In January 2002 Yasser Arafat addressed more than a thousand women in his compound in Ramallah. According to Victor, "Flanked by his ever-present loyal guards and advisors, he made it clear that women were not only welcome but expected to participate in armed resistance against Israeli occupation. 'Women and men are equal,' he proclaimed with his hands raised above his head and his fingers forked in a sign of victory. 'You are my army of roses that will crush Israeli tanks.'"[110] He then encouraged them by telling them, "[You] are the hope of Palestine" who will "liberate your husbands, fathers, and sons from oppression. You will sacrifice the way you, women, have always sacrificed for your family."[111] That afternoon, the first Palestinian woman suicide bomber, Wafa Idris, blew herself up in a Jerusalem shopping mall killing one Israeli man and injuring 131 bystanders. In fact, the Al-Aqsa Martyrs Brigade, which was part of Arafat's secular Fatah faction, "began recruiting females for suicide missions at the beginning of the Second Intifada" in 2000 and claimed credit for the first four suicide bombings between January and May 2002.[112] This reflects a reversal about the role of women as combatants in general and their eligibility as suicide bombers, thereby giving them martyr status. Doing this required "redrawing" otherwise forbidden acts in a number of ways: "First, they were rationalized as desperate measures for desperate times. . . . Second, the bombings were historicized in the context of women militants in the past, with the recent militants seen as completing their path. . . . Lastly, the female suicide bomber was elevated to a level in which she was in some way made awe-inspiring—there was talk of the purity and beauty that Wafa Idris exuded with her bomb strapped to her body."[113]

While Palestinian women engaged in the liberation struggle inside secular Palestinian organizations, so too were they involved in primarily Islamic religious organizations. Whereas Islamic tradition glorifies women as wives and mothers and limits their role in the public sphere, these functions have been elevated to support the cause of national self-determination and independence. Thus, we have women as "the mothers of martyrs," whose role was to procreate for the state and to raise offspring willing to fight and die for the cause. Similarly, the rise of feelings of nationalism and opposition to the Israeli occupation and state violence encouraged women to participate, which they could do because of changing interpretations of those same traditions that limited women's involvement initially. The confluence of these factors allowed women to take a more active role in the struggle and also encouraged them to do so. This changed the image of women, glorifying them for their sacrifice. Thus, "with the inclusion of women as perpetrators of suicide bombing, women were no longer praised only for their support role, but also for becoming men's presumed equal partner in the national struggle."[114]

Women were gradually integrated into combat roles as Islamic fundamentalist groups revised or redefined their own norms so that women were then permitted to take on the role of combatant or even suicide bomber. Muslim women have indeed participated in nationalist conflicts.[115] It became necessary to find a way to reconcile women's participation with the well-defined doctrine and limitations regarding the role of women. Part of the reason for the expanded role of women can be explained by the ways religious leaders reinterpreted jihad. As Cunningham notes, interpreting jihad as a total war necessitates "that every man, woman and child mobilize for conflict, as opposed to limited war involving only adult males, often within a narrow age range."[116] By 2003 the Palestinian Islamic Jihad announced a shift to include women "largely in an effort to upgrade the operational capabilities of the organization."[117] This was followed by a number of other changes further legitimizing women's roles in these various Islamic organizations. Cunningham writes that "religious symbolism and terminology becomes a potent ideological force to mobilize society to support violence by arms groups. Women's mobilization, including violent mobilization, within this context is made consistent with cultural norms, mainly by emphasizing mothering and sacrifice, in the same manner as in non-Islamic settings such as Nicaragua and Colombia. . . . While the use of Islam in this context is a potent symbolic and ideological tool, it is more instrumental and ideological than truly religious."[118]

In articles 17 and 18 of its charter, Hamas addresses the role of women based on the Qur'an and Shari'a Law. Article 18 especially "recites the importance of both men and women surrendering to Allah" and reminding them that those men and women who do remember Allah are promised forgiveness and vast rewards.[119] Ultimately, these changes led the Palestinian clerics as well as political leaders to sanctify suicide bombings as part of a legitimate struggle women could not be excluded from.

As Kelly Oliver states, in using and justifying the use of female suicide bombers, several Islamic clerics declared that women too "can reach paradise as martyrs" even though previously it was claimed that only men could become holy martyrs.[120] Thus, it can be argued that women's politically violent roles were possible only because the male leaders, secular and religious, allowed this change because of their need for women to take on more roles and because of women's willingness to contribute to the nationalist struggle.

Conclusion

Palestinian women have a long history of political activism that predates the establishment of the state of Israel but has continued as Palestinians seek to end Israel's occupation. Women's motivations for such activism are personal and political. This political activism challenges prevailing gender norms of women's expected roles and behavior. A great deal of women's activism has been directed at ways to help and empower women, including increasing their numbers and roles in the formal political process. Women's activism also seeks to improve conditions in their communities as they seek to prevent the expropriation of their land and the demolition of their homes by the Israeli government, and also to challenge the patriarchal structure of Palestinian society. The violence that women experience is structural violence—the continued occupation of Palestinian lands by Israel as well as the violence committed against them when their land is taken or their houses demolished. These policies affect women's ability to provide for their families and their community. Consequently, their motivations to engage in political activism are a function of their transcending the private and public spheres and the concerns for their security.

It is also important to note here that many of the initiatives designed to improve the plight of Palestinian women have been generated and funded by outside groups, with the IWC as a prime example. While clearly groups such as this bring together Palestinian and Israeli women, unless there is acceptance at the grassroots level, they will not succeed. Rather, the very nature of the conflict (the asymmetry of power between Israel and the Palestinians), as well as the plight of Palestinian women in the occupied territories, suggests that the women's first priority will be to fight for their own welfare, including the creation of a state. In this case, the bonds of women cannot transcend the power differences that exist between Israeli and Palestinian women. In studying Palestinian women, Cockburn raises an important point that cannot be overlooked: "Women are disadvantaged and marginalized in Israel and the Occupied Territories, whether in Jewish,

Christian or Muslim cultures. They all experience the armed conflict in a gender-specific way. Is this enough to validate dialogue? Not necessarily."[121]

Increasingly, what we have seen is the radicalization of some Palestinian women, leading them to become armed combatants or even suicide bombers willing to die for the cause. But it is also important to note that this change in women's roles was only made possible because the men in power *allowed* women to take on those roles, and the society at large supported women's engaging in political violence. Thus, in this case, we see the interrelationship of two important factors: women's willingness to fight and die for the cause, and men's (and society's) willingness to allow them to do so, even if that meant altering the interpretation of social, cultural, and even basic religious tenets. Political expediency trumped social and cultural conventions. And women, for personal and political reasons, were willing to oblige, even in an environment of constrained agency.

Notes

1. "Palestinian Moms Becoming Martyrs," *Time* magazine, May 3, 2007, http://www.time.com/time/magazine/article/0,9171,1617542,00.html

2. Simona Sharoni, *Gender and the Israeli-Palestinian Conflict* (Syracuse, NY: Syracuse University Press, 1995), 58–59.

3. Ian Fisher, "Women, Secret Hamas Strength, Win Votes at Polls and New Role," *New York Times*, February 3, 2006, http://www.nytimes.com/2006/02/03/international/middleeast/03women.html?_r=1&oref=sloginl.

4. Ibid.

5. Kaufman and Williams, *Women, the State, and War*, 39.

6. Ashrawi received her PhD in medieval and comparative literature from the University of Virginia.

7. There are a number of good and very detailed histories of the region. For the sake of parsimony, some of this history is drawn from Kaufman and Williams, "Israel and Palestine: Two Peoples, One Land," in Kaufman and Williams, *Women, the State, and War*, 115–55, which already synthesizes some of the histories and includes bibliographic references.

8. Kaufman and Williams, *Women, the State, and War*, 117.

9. William Cleveland, *A History of the Modern Middle East*, 2nd ed. (Boulder, CO: Westview Press, 2000), 252.

10. Ibid.

11. Ibid.

12. Dennis Ross, *The Missing Peace: The Inside Story of the Fight for Middle East Peace* (New York: Farrar, Straus and Giroux, 2004), 36.

13. Ross, *Missing Peace*, 37.

14. Neal G. Jesse and Kristen P. Williams, *Ethnic Conflict: A Systematic Approach to Cases of Conflict* (Washington, DC: Congressional Quarterly Press, 2011), 289.

15. Central Intelligence Agency, *World Factbook*, https://www.cia.gov/library/publications/the-world-factbook/geos/we.html.

16. Sharoni, *Gender and the Israel-Palestinian Conflict*, 63.

17. Ibid., 38–39.

18. Caron E. Gentry, "The Committed Revolutionary: Reflections on a Conversation with Leila Khaled," in *Women, Gender and Terrorism*, ed. Laura Sjoberg and Caron E. Gentry (Athens: University of Georgia Press, 2011), 128. Leila Khaled became famous, or infamous, for her part in two aircraft highjackings that she carried out for the PFLP in 1969 and 1970. The PFLP was founded in 1967 as an alternative to the Fatah organization. "While both movements advocated Arab unity [a] prerequisite for the liberation of Palestine, [the] PFLP, under the influence of national liberation movements worldwide, adopted a Marxist-Leninist ideology to attract members," Victor, *Army of Roses*, 61.

19. Frances S. Hasso, "Discursive and Political Deployments by/of the 2002 Palestinian Women Suicide Bombers/Martyrs," *Feminist Review* 81(2005): 24.

20. Ibid., 28.

21. Elizabeth Warnock Fernea, *In Search of Islamic Feminism* (New York: Anchor Books, 1998), 345.

22. "History." Jerusalem Center for Women, 2012, http://www.j-c-w.org/index.php?option=com_content&task=view&id=22&Itemid=9.

23. Ibid.

24. Ibid.

25. Ibid.

26. "WATC's Beginnings," n.d., http://www.watcpal.org/english/display.asp?DocID=7.

27. Ibid.

28. Ibid.

29. Ibid.

30. Ayala Emmett, *Our Sisters' Promised Land: Women, Politics, and Israeli Palestinian Coexistence* (Ann Arbor: University of Michigan Press, 2003), 183.

31. Kaufman and Williams, *Women, the State, and War*, 141.

32. The JCW and Bat Shalom (an Israeli women's feminist organization of Israeli Jewish and Israeli Palestinian women established at the same time as the JCW), formed Jerusalem Link in 1994 as a coordinating body to work together and "to form a platform for women's voices to influence the peace process." With the Israeli attack on Gaza in December 2008, the two organizations found it difficult to work together on joint projects and activities and "decided that the priority lies in working separately on their own constituency to prepare the ground for future peace work . . . where each organization works to strengthening the respect

for human rights and democracy within their own society." As a result of these difficulties, Jerusalem Link was dissolved. "History."

33. "About Us: The Palestinian Initiative for the Promotion of Global Dialogue and Democracy: MIFTAH," 2010, accessed July 7, 2010, http://www.miftah.org/AboutUs.cfm.

34. Ibid.

35. *MIFTAH's Ninth Annual Activities Report 2009*, "Empowerment of Palestinian Women Leadership," 2010, http://www.miftah.org/Mact/MiftahActivityReport2009.pdf, p. 18. According to the previous Miftah report, this phase was designed "to enhance women's political participation in peacebuilding and the negotiations process through networking, capacity building and simulated talks with Israelis," 18. (http://www.miftah.org/Mact/MiftahActivityReport2007.pdf).

36. *Annual Activities Report 2009*, 19–20.

37. Ibid., 21.

38. United Nations Security Council Resolution 1325, October 31, 2000, http://www.un.org/events/res_1325e.pdf.

39. *Annual Activities Report 2009*, 16.

40. UN Women, "Women Share a Vision for Israeli-Palestinian Peace," news release, June 3, 2010, http://unifem.org/news_events/story_detail.php?StoryID=1095.

41. Ibid.

42. International Women's Commission, "Political Vision: Paper of Understanding," August 30, 2008, http://unispal.un.org/UNISPAL.NSF/0/A83B4CCC93BAE9E185257737006F78AB

43. International Women's Commission, "Political Vision."

44. Ibid.

45. Sarai Aharoni conducted an empirical study of Israeli women's participation in the negotiations of the Oslo peace process (1993–2000). She interviewed thirty-one Israeli women who participated in several roles, "midlevel negotiators, professional and legal advisors, spokeswomen and secretaries." She found that "women's incorporation in the formal peace negotiations was based on traditional definitions of gender roles and stereotypes." Sarai Aharoni, "Gender and 'Peace Work': An Unofficial History of Israeli-Palestinian Negotiations," *Politics & Gender* 7, no. 3 (2011): 392, 414.

46. Sanam Anderlini, "Translating Global Agreement into National and Local Commitments," in *Women and War: Power and Protection in the 21st Century*, ed. Kathleen Kuehnast, Chantal de Jonge Oudraat, and Helga Hernes (Washington, DC: USIP Press, 2011): 29–30.

47. Vanessa Farr, "UNSCR 1325 and Women's Peace Activism in the Occupied Palestinian Territory," *International Feminist Journal of Politics* 13, no. 4 (December 2011): 547.

48. Ibid.

49. Richter-Devroe, "Gender, Culture, and Conflict Resolution," 35.

50. In an informal presentation by Kristen P. Williams in January 2012 at the Arab World for Research and Development in Ramallah, Palestine, attendees made it very clear that to focus only on Palestinian violence omitted an acknowledgment and recognition of the violence committed by Israel against Palestinians.

51. Farr, "UNSCR 1325," 550.

52. Richter-Devroe, "Gender, Culture, and Conflict Resolution," 36.

53. Porter, "Participatory Democracy," 158.

54. Cockburn, *From Where We Stand*, 106.

55. Ibid., 116

56. Ibid.

57. Ibid., 117.

58. As quoted in Cockburn, *From Where We Stand*, 118.

59. Bose, *Contested Lands*, 214.

60. See Ness, "Rise in Female Violence."

61. Caron E. Gentry, "Twisted Maternalism: From Peace to Violence," *International Feminist Journal of Politics* 11, no. 2 (June 2009): 242.

62. Francis S. Hasso, "The 'Women's Front': Nationalism, Feminism, and Modernity in Palestine," *Gender & Society* 12, no. 4 (August 1998): 442–43, 445.

63. Ibid., 445.

64. Ibid., 446.

65. Ibid., 449.

66. Ibid., 452–53. Hasso writes that following the rise of Hamas in 1988 and the splintering of leftist-nationalist political organizations following the first intifada, "Women's very presence in public space was severely regulated," making it difficult for women to remain politically active in the nationalist struggle. In 1990 the DFLP and PFWAC split into two separate organizations. Ibid., 460.

67. Sophie Richter-Devroe, "Defending Their Land, Protecting Their Men: Palestinian Women's Popular Resistance after the Second Intifada," *International Feminist Journal of Politics* 14, no. 2 (June 2012): 185.

68. Ibid., 187.

69. Ibid., 191.

70. Ibid., 193.

71. Ibid.

72. Ibid.

73. Ibid.

74. Ibid.

75. Gentry, "The Committed Revolutionary," 129.

76. Hasso, "Discursive and Political Deployments," 26.

77. Ibid., 30.

78. Ibid.

79. Ibid.

80. Ibid., 28.
81. Skaine, *Female Suicide Bombers*, 32.
82. Anat Berko and Edna Eerez, "Gender, Palestinian Women, and Terrorism: Women's Liberation or Oppression?" *Studies in Conflict & Terrorism* 30, no. 6 (June 2007): 495.
83. Cunningham, "Evolving Participation of Muslim Women," 88.
84. Ibid.
85. McGirk, "Palestinian Moms."
86. Ibid.
87. Ibid.
88. Ibid.
89. CBS News, "Hamas TV Pictures Promotes Female Suicide Bombers Squad," January 14, 2009, http://www.cbsnews.com/8301-502684_162-4722620-502684.html.
90. Bloom, "Mother. Daughter." 57.
91. Berko and Eerez, "Gender, Palestinian Women, and Terrorism," 502.
92. Ibid., 501.
93. Yoram Schweitzer, "Introduction," in *Female Suicide Bombers: Dying for Equality?* ed. Yoram Schweitzer (Tel Aviv: Jaffee Center for Strategic Studies, 2006), 10, http://www.e-prism.org/images/memo84_Female_suicide_bombers_-Jaffee_Center_-_Aug06.pdf.
94. Bloom, "Mother. Daughter." 57.
95. Claudia Brunner, "Female Suicide Bombers—Male Suicide Bombing? Looking for Gender in Reporting the Suicide Bombings of the Israeli-Palestinian Conflict," *Global Society* 19, no. 1 (January 2005): 47.
96. Ibid.
97. Eager, *From Freedom Fighters to Terrorists*, 187.
98. Ibid.
99. Berko and Eerez, "Gender, Palestinian Women, and Terrorism," 500.
100. Hasso, "Discursive and Political Deployments," 34.
101. Narozhna, "Power and Gendered Rationality," 90.
102. Ibid.
103. Ibid.
104. As quoted in Victor, *Army of Roses*, 183.
105. Ibid., 185.
106. It can be noted that these events also served to spur Palestinian and Israeli women to work for peace. See Kaufman and Williams, "Israel and Palestine," *Women, the State and War*, 115–55.
107. Cunningham, "Evolving Participation," 88–89.
108. Ibid., 89.
109. Ness, "In the Name of the Cause," 24–25.
110. Victor, *Army of Roses*, 19.
111. Ibid., 20.

112. Ness, "In the Name of the Cause," 26. See also Hasso, "Discursive and Political Deployments."

113. Ness, "In the Name of the Cause," 27.

114. Berko and Eerez, "Gender, Palestinian Women, and Terrorism," 494.

115. Cunningham, "Evolving Participation," 84.

116. Ibid., 85.

117. Davis, "Women and Radical Islamic Terrorism," 2.

118. Cunningham, "Evolving Participation," 85.

119. Skaine, *Female Suicide Bombers*, 37.

120. Kelly Oliver, *Women As Weapons of War: Iraq, Sex and the Media* (New York: Columbia University Press, 2007), 33.

121. Cockburn, *From Where We Stand*, 120.

5

Women's Political Activism in Sri Lanka: Tamil Tigers

> *December 23 1987 was a warm, clear day, and I was hiding under a lantana bush with eight of my comrades in a village north of Jaffna. With our rifles cocked and our cyanide capsules clenched between our teeth, we awaited the soldiers who had been scouring the area for us for several hours. Our orders were to empty our magazines into them before biting into the glass capsules we called "kuppies" that hung on a thread around our necks. As a Tamil Tiger guerrilla, there was no honour in being caught alive.*[1]

THE CONFLICT IN SRI LANKA (THE ISLAND FORMERLY KNOWN AS CEYLON) IS NOT given to easy classification. Sri Lanka is a multiethnic, multireligious, multicultural island, which, in 2007, while in the midst of violent conflict, "had the highest score on the Human Development Index in South Asia."[2] Sri Lanka has also become known for its lengthy and vicious civil war, which turned the country into "one of the most dangerous places on earth."[3] Between 1983 and 2009, an estimated seventy thousand people died as a result of the conflict, and it is possible that the number is actually higher.[4] According to Monique Skidmore and Patricia Lawrence, "British colonial policies resulted in the transformation and hardening of ethnic identity in Sri Lanka," with the peoples of the island categorized into "races" on the basis of their spoken language.[5] These categories were then formally recognized in legal procedures with political power linked to racial criteria. Today, Sri Lanka's ethnic identities, categorized generally as Tamil speakers versus Sinhala speakers, are "a recent historical development resulting from the failure of British policy to establish protective provisions for minorities in the multi-ethnic society."[6]

Adding to that general understanding of the roots of the conflict attributable directly to British colonial history, Alison notes that the conflict can also be attributed in part "to the impact of mass media and state education, which were likewise developed under British colonial rule."[7] Thus, although the conflict itself was a civil war between two groups vying for power, the roots of the conflict are a legacy of the British colonial period. As we see in this chapter, that has affected numerous aspects of the society.

Sumantra Bose, while similarly attributing part of the causes of the civil war to British policies, puts it slightly differently when he describes Sri Lanka's fate as it descended into conflict as "a lesson in the consequences of the *concept* of democracy as majority rule—where majorities and minorities are understood to be fluid and shifting—becoming deformed in *practice* to denote the entrenched supremacy of an ethnic, linguistic, and religious majority" (italics in the original).[8] According to his interpretation, when the colony gained its independence in 1948, the British bequeathed a system of government modeled on their own with a strong central parliamentary structure. Ultimately, this led to the growth of nationalism, with the majority group (Sinhalese) taking away rights of citizenship from the minority Tamil population. Thus, the "mass-based nationalism conspicuous by its absence in colonial Ceylon was ready to erupt, once the country became a sovereign state and a democracy."[9] By that interpretation, the violence, while rooted in the legacy of British colonialism, was homegrown.

Eventually, the country descended into a civil war that pitted the Sri Lankan Tamil minority, who were largely concentrated in the north and east of the country and are generally Hindu, against the ethnic Sinhalese majority, who are primarily Buddhist.[10] This was not a religious or even an ethnic war but a political one in which the Tamils were fighting for independence and self-determination against the majority Sinhalese Sri Lankan government, which sought to preserve the island's integrity as a whole. The Sri Lankan government proclaimed an end to the war in May 2009 after the army took control of the island and killed Velupillai Prabhakaran, the leader of the Liberation Tigers of Tamil Eelam (LTTE). Throughout the civil war, members of the LTTE became the major actors fighting for Tamil self-determination.

Despite the fact that this is a fairly traditional and patriarchal society, women played an active role throughout the conflict, not only as combatants and suicide bombers for the LTTE, which is the popular depiction, but as political and social activists at all levels and on both sides, including serving as leaders of the country. One of the unique characteristics of the LTTE, however, as opposed to other instances in which women were involved as combatants such as with the Palestinians, was its overtly feminist orientation. The cadres of the LTTE "are the ultimate symbol of women's liberation" and "are said to achieve liberation from oppressive gender roles through active combat."[11] But perhaps even more important than that is the finding that women said they "had not been aware of issues pertaining to women's social conditions, women's rights or equality before they joined the movement. . . . All of them have had this awareness raised since being with the movement and many of them now seem to have a clear commitment for wanting to improve life for Tamil women."[12] Thus, while most women did not join the LTTE for feminist reasons, after becoming part of it they saw the relationship between fighting for the liberation of their country and fighting for women. What this case clearly demonstrates is that women challenged existing gender norms as women engaged in political activism for a variety of reasons; they were accepted as part of the formal political process but also as combatants and fighters in the struggle for national liberation and self-determination.

In this chapter, although we look at both sides of the conflict, we focus primarily on the Tamil women, since they were the ones who tended to be most active politically as they contributed to what they saw as a fight for self-determination. Not only are their roles the most clearly documented but so is their transformation as they became more actively involved in the struggle, moving from "non-violent politics into armed struggle,"[13] and from warriors to feminists along the continuum of political activism.

Brief Historical Overview

As noted in the previous section, the outbreak of the civil war in Sri Lanka can be attributed to its British colonial history. This is not a new story—a colonial power creating a political structure that results in privileging one group at the expense of another. For example, Rwanda, which had been a colony of Belgium, erupted into a brutal civil war between the Hutu and Tutsi tribes after Belgian rule ended, and the Hutus, encouraged by the departing Belgian military, overthrew the Tutsi monarchy. The British partition of what had been the territory of India into two countries, Hindu India and Muslim Pakistan in 1947, resulted in conflict and the deaths of one million in the fighting and riots that erupted in the immediate aftermath of the decision to partition. Kashmir, the territory between the two countries, has been the focal point of much of the conflict, which has resulted in armed warfare at various points. And of course, the partition of what had been Palestine to create the state of Israel, while leaving the Palestinian people formally stateless, serves as yet another example, discussed in chapter 4.

In the case of Sri Lanka, however, what made the situation unusual was that precolonial Ceylon "was characterized by ethno-religious pluralism and co-existence over antagonism and conflict," as well as by religious diversity and group intermingling.[14] And "the connections among ethnic difference, conflict, terrorism, and secessionism are not automatic. Narrow interpretations of cultural identity and models of conflict resolution built on ethnic dualism contribute to ethnic polarization and inhibit sustainable peace."[15] Also, in contrast to the situation with India and Pakistan, for example, initially the transition from colony to independent nation was peaceful and orderly. Around the time of Ceylon's independence from Britain in 1948, the ethnic Sinhalese were the majority group (about 70 percent of the total population) with the minority Tamils (about 11 percent of the population) concentrated in the north or eastern parts of the country.[16] (See map, figure 5.1.)

Despite their religious differences, the two groups "share many parallel features of traditional caste, kinship, popular religious cults, and customs."[17] Thus, this was not a country with deep-seated ethnic or religious hatreds. Rather, it was only after independence when the Sinhalese-dominated parliament took away the rights of the Tamil minority that the seeds of conflict were planted.

Following independence and the creation of a new state, the emergence of Solomon Wes Ridgeway Dias Bandaranaike, a British-educated member of the majority Sinhalese elite group, helped spark the divisions with his campaign slogan "Sinhalese Only!" and his commitment to make Sinhalese the national language of the new state. The elections of 1956 became a turning point growing from this Sinhalese nationalism. At the same time, the Tamil Federal Party (FP) declared "the Tamil people's unchallengeable title to nationhood, their rights to political autonomy and desire for federal union with the Sinhalese."[18] In 1957 the leaders of the two groups agreed to a Tamil-led regional authority in the north and east, with Tamil as the primary language. One year later Bandaranaike abrogated the pact, which ultimately led to rebellion among the Sinhalese and the emergence of another Sinhalese leader, Junius Richard Jayewardene, who started mobilizing Sinhalese public opinion against Bandaranaike's apparent capitulation to the Tamils. This further fueled feelings of Sinhalese nationalism and sparked competition between the two groups. Bandaranaike was assassinated in 1959.[19]

In response to the abrogation of the pact and promises broken, the FP began a campaign of civil disobedience that was met by repressive police action. Growing tensions exploded into violent riots in 1958 directed

Figure 5.1 Map of Sri Lanka

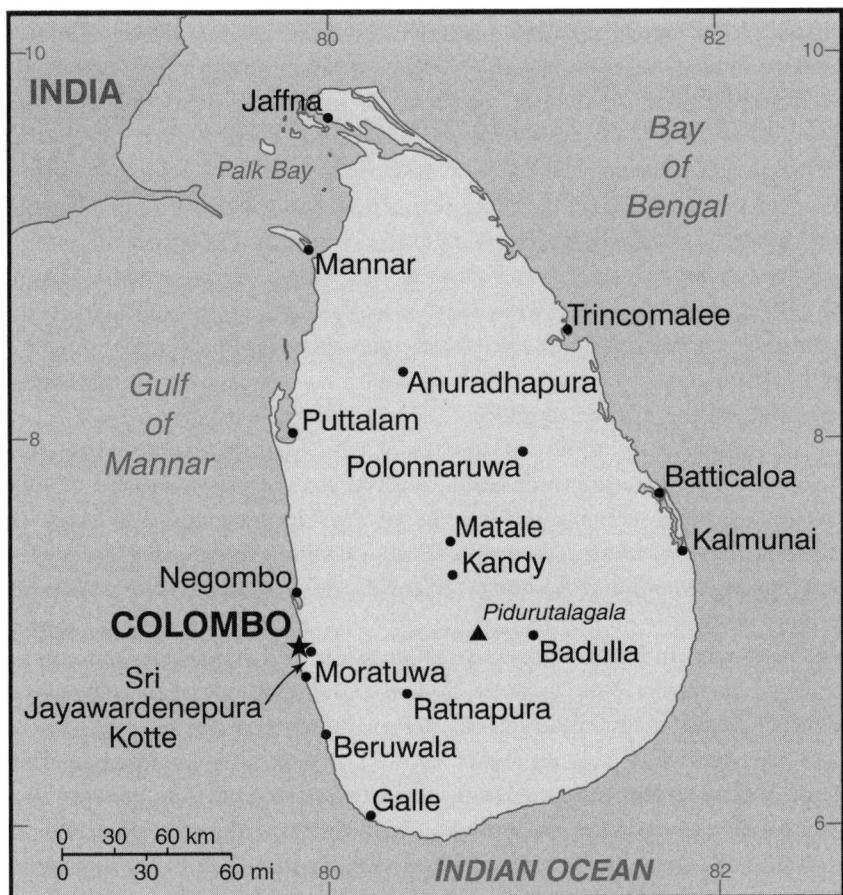

Courtesy University of Texas Libraries.

especially against the Tamils living in primarily Sinhalese areas. This violence proved to be a precursor to the violence that would intensify in the 1970s and 1980s, ultimately leading to civil war.

In 1965 a Sinhalese prime minister again attempted to negotiate a compromise with the Tamils. This resulted in yet another pact with the FP leadership, but like the previous one, it was never implemented, thereby creating even more tensions between the two communities. What was emerging was a dynamic "of *intra*ethnic competitive chauvinism among the

Sinhalese, which had the effect of growing *inter*ethnic polarization with the Tamils"(emphasis in original).[20] The British type of electoral system gave the benefit to those who win by even a narrow plurality, which contributed to competition between the two major Sinhalese groups, each of which tried to build support by adopting more intransigent positions on the Tamil issues. Because of the structure of the system and the concentration of Tamils in a relatively small area of the country, they were relatively unrepresented in the parliament, while the Sinhalese were assured the majority.[21]

A new Sri Lankan constitution written in 1972 codified the Sinhalese-only policy as well as the centrality of Buddhism. Although the Tamils protested, their objections were brushed aside. As Bose notes, "By the time of the 1977 general election, the divide between the Tamils and Sinhalese had become critical, and radical ideas of national liberation through armed struggle were beginning to take root among Tamil youth."[22]

Although a slew of reforms were instituted, by then it was too late, and the situation continued to deteriorate. By the end of the 1980s, Sri Lanka was engaged in a violent and bloody civil war. But by that time, there was also a significant change in the attitude of the Tamils, which had serious repercussions for the country. Many Tamils "no longer saw their goal as constitutional equality of the majority and minority languages; *instead they sought security and collective ethnonational rights—self-determination—in a separate state*" (italics added). This was particularly true for the younger generation of Tamils.[23] By the late 1970s, as the country was moving toward civil war, the LTTE was emerging as the leading Tamil insurgent group. After an LTTE ambush in 1983 in which thirteen Sinhalese government soldiers died, a massacre of Tamils resulted in the deaths of between 2,000 and 3,000 with another 150,000 Tamils made homeless.[24] This incident proved to be the flashpoint that led to the violent civil war that followed. Between 1983 and 2009 attempts were made to end the conflict and find a political settlement, but the failure of each of these attempts only contributed to escalating violence and an increasingly militarized society.

The civil war in Sri Lanka is the story of cycles of violence punctuated by failed cease-fire and peace agreements. During the duration of the conflict, thousands were killed and displaced, and as in other war-torn countries, women had to make choices about their lives. According to Patricia Lawrence, "In Sri Lanka war has provided the ground for reshaping women's lives and relationships." And she also says about women in Sri Lanka that some "have chosen to take up weapons with the LTTE to fight against the GOSL [Government of Sri Lanka] for Tamil self-governance, other women view the violence of war as the enemy, and still others have experienced such severe personal disabilities and loss that a sense of agency in relation to the war is unavailable to them."[25]

Role of Muslims in Sri Lanka

In looking at Sri Lanka as a whole, it is also important to remember that groups other than the Sinhalese and the Tamils are on the island, although these two emerged as the primary actors during the war. July 2011 statistics indicate that 7.6 percent of the population was Muslim, about the same number as Tamil.[26] Interestingly, most Muslims in Sri Lanka were Tamil speakers, but as a community they were treated separately. Because of education reforms in the 1970s and the imposition of a quota system that benefited the Muslims, the economic status of Muslims as a whole rose. The result was that "the improved competitiveness of Muslims threatened the traditional advantages of the Sri Lankan Tamil minority, as well as separatist claims to the north and east, where Muslims are a significant population."[27] Looking at the Muslim group offers a different perspective on Sri Lanka, one in which a minority could live peacefully and thrive as opposed to the Tamils, partly because of the difference in the way the groups were treated. According to one analysis, "The divergence in the experiences of the two minorities lies in two contrasting approaches to success: advancement within the Sri Lankan political system on the part of the Muslims and secession on the part of the Sri Lankan Tamils."[28] The sense of Muslim identity deepened with the growth of Islamic economic and social organizations and as aid to the mosques and other Islamic-based organizations came in from the oil-rich Middle East. Thus, this group was able to remain largely outside the conflict.[29]

As the violence intensified, though, the Tamils sought to pull the Muslim group into their camp on the basis of their common language, while the Muslims resisted, fearing they would be known as Muslim Tamil.[30] Ultimately, a Tamil-Muslim rift emerged, and along with that, the fear of further bloodshed between these two groups. While many of the Muslims were and continue to be poor, a thriving "Muslim economy" also emerged in the eastern parts of the country where the wealthy Muslims were able to buy land from the Tamils and the Sinhalese while these two groups were at war with each other.[31]

From a gender analysis, one can ask whether the Islamic women in Sri Lanka, "since they suffer a patriarchal oppression comparable to that experienced by women in other Sri Lankan social formations, have more in common with other Sri Lankan women than Muslim men?"[32] Or, put another way, what is the basis for these women's identities and actions as opposed to the Tamil or Sinhalese women during the conflict? One answer to that question can be seen in the creation of the Muslim Women's Research and Action Forum, which was founded in 1986 to recognize the specific socioeconomic and legal problems of Muslim women in Sri Lanka. The organization grew from informal gatherings of Muslim women beginning in 1976 "to discuss critical issues facing *Muslim* women in Sri Lanka" (italics added).[33] Rather than being inclusive in addressing issues that women in Sri Lanka were facing, the group identified its objectives as to create "a Sri Lankan identity where there is no concept of majority and all citizens are of equal status [and] to ensure the rights of women in Muslim communities are not subsumed under the collective rights of the community."[34] In this case their identity as Muslim women superseded their identity as women in Sri Lanka facing common problems, and because of this they were able to choose to remain aloof from the political violence.

The example of Muslim women once again reinforces the idea that the issues underlying this war were neither simple nor easy to solve despite the many attempts to do both, nor is it easy to understand the gendered dimensions of it.

Women Political Leaders in Sri Lanka

Despite the traditional expectations for women inherent in a patriarchal society, and in contrast to the other cases discussed in this book, women emerged to serve as the country's political leaders a number of times. According to Malathi de Alwis, "In Sri Lanka, where much of the nationalist rhetoric was, and continues to be phrased in terms of a Motherland and mother tongue, the idealization of womanhood signified through the construction of the 'respectable lady,' the repository of tradition and domesticity is based on the valorization of motherhood: as the creator and protector of the home, as the chaste and industrious wife and as the iconic representation of the nation."[35] In addition to serving as the signifiers of community, culture, and tradition, they were "the upholders of morality and spirituality, but even more importantly, as the protectors and disseminators of [these values] through their primary responsibility as the progenitors and nurturers of future generations of middle class, Sinhala Buddhist nationalists."[36]

Sirimavo Bandaranaike, widow of the Sinhalese nationalist leader Solomon Bandaranaike, served as prime minister from 1970 to 1977 as the country was descending into civil war. But unlike her successor, Hema Premadasa, Bandaranaike was from an upper-class family, who after her marriage became an active member in one of the largest social service organizations in Sri Lanka, thereby continuing the image of the traditional woman. An astute politician, she was, as her political platform suggested, merely carrying out the political pledges made by her husband to his voters, "like any dutiful wife."[37] She often spoke not only as head of government, "but even more as a woman and mother."[38] But this identity was used against her, for example, when she did not keep her election pledge to increase the free rice subsidy allowed. And when her government "brutally put down a popular youth uprising in 1971, the opposition came out [with statements] that referred to the 'mother who shot her own children.'"[39]

In 1993, while the country was in the midst of war following the assassination of her husband, president Ranasinghe Premadasa, Hema Premadasa took the opportunity to seek higher formal political office as opposed to the informal role she had played under his presidency. Premadasa had also built her reputation as first lady by developing an identity of a nurturing "Mother of the Nation,"[40] delivering lunches to soldiers and distributing materials to those who needed such goods. Because of her position as first lady, she also became head of the Seva Vanitha Movement (SVM), founded in 1983 as a nongovernmental organization (NGO) whose main objective was "to harness the support of Sri Lankan women in National Development projects through service."[41] An astute politician herself, while serving as president of the SVM, Premadasa "hijacked" the SVM International Women's Day celebrations, "which until then, had been the preserve of a few feminist groups and left parties in the country."[42] By cultivating this separate identity for herself, which put her very much in the public eye, she also opened herself up to public scrutiny and criticism. Seen as coming from the lower class and a lower status, she was antithetical to the notion of the "respectable lady" that was exemplified by the British model. Or as de Alwis describes it, "In the patriarchal gaze of the nation, the 'public woman' simultaneously exists as a signifier of respectability i.e., as wife, mother, etc. but also of degradation and debasement."[43]

This legacy of women who became leaders because of their family connections and husbands' deaths continued in 1994 with the election of Chandrika Bandaranaike Kumaratunga. Chandrika was the daughter of former prime ministers Solomon and Sirimavo Bandaranaike and wife of a popular movie actor who advocated conciliation with the Tamils and was murdered by an ultranationalist. Chandrika took over the leadership of the Sinhalese party founded by her father and promised to end the civil war and start peace talks with the LTTE. Once elected, "Chandrika spoke eloquently of rebuilding Sri Lanka as 'a country where people can live without fear, a vibrant living democracy of new systems and new institutions.'"[44] And she spoke of being inspired "by 'what has been possible in South Africa and between the Israelis and Palestinians.'"[45]

Chandrika Kumaratunga ran for president in 1994, winning a landslide victory. In January 1995 the government and the LTTE reached a short-lived cease-fire agreement that ended in April with an LTTE suicide attack on a government naval base. The government retaliation that followed resulted in civilian deaths and an acceleration of the war. During 1995–1996, the president moved from being a dove to a hawk. She pledged "to wage a 'war for peace'" to defeat the LTTE.[46] Thus, it appears that Kumaratunga was deeply affected by the deaths of the civilians and authorized an acceleration of military strikes. However, Adele Balasingham, who was married to Anton Balasingham, both of whom were deeply involved with the LTTE, had a different interpretation of Kumaratunga's position. She writes, "Though Chandrika assumed power as Head of State with a mandate for peace, she swung towards the side of hard-line militarists under the *façade* of a strategy of 'war for peace'" (italics added).[47] And she argues that the Sri Lankan military as well as the Sinhala Buddhist nationalist forces "that formed the backbone of Kumaratunga's government were opposed to peace and to any rational political settlement that might provide for regional autonomy or self rule to the Tamil people."[48] Thus, her real intentions could be subject to interpretation. What is undeniable is that she authorized an escalation of the conflict. In 1999 Kumaratunga was the victim of a suicide bombing. Although she survived the attack, she lost an eye.

The stories of these three women leaders are interesting and provide some insight into the role of women in Sri Lanka as well as a counterpoint to the cases of Northern Ireland and the Palestinians. All three were Sinhalese, and all came to power because of their ties to men. Nonetheless, all were able to get elected in their own right, partly because of their appeal to Sinhalese nationalists either on their own or because of their spouse's position. Yet, they also relied upon traditional female roles (as wives, mothers, peacemakers) to consolidate their own political power in a patriarchal society. All were astute politicians who learned from their family experiences. And despite the apparent skepticism many had of Premadasa, who did not fit the image of the respectable lady, she was able to assume a major political role. Further, all three presided over some part of the escalation of the civil war. At the same time, the story of these three unusual women does not begin to capture the political activism of women in Sri Lanka in general. What it does suggest is that women in this country could achieve high political office deespite the patriarchal nature of the political system and social structure.

Women's Political Activism: Challenging Gender Norms

Sri Lanka is a case in which "local female activists place themselves at risk as they challenge asymmetrical relations and publicly protest unspeakable violence through collective acts of conscious intentions."[49] While much of what is popularly known about women's political activism in this country is tied to the LTTE and the high profile of the women perpetrating acts of resistance and political violence, even serving as suicide bombers, the reality is that women have been active politically in a number of ways. Asoka Bandarage notes what she calls "the privatization of conflict resolution," which contributed to the proliferation of national and international NGOs in Sri Lanka as far back as the early 1970s and played a prominent role in defining the conflict as an "ethnic conflict."[50] The NGOs and various women's organizations also helped provide support as well as a source of economic and political strength for women on both sides of the conflict. These organizations became especially important in a militarized society.

As noted earlier in the discussion of the MWRAF, women's groups emerged based on common interest and often tied to social issues, as we have seen in the two other cases in this book. In the case of Sri Lanka specifically, just as Muslim women came together through organizations in which they could pursue common interests, so did Tamil and Sinhalese women. Lawrence asserted that

> Tamil women living in this warscape are forming organizations and convening meetings where they speak confidently about overcoming discriminatory relationships. Whether they are speaking out about social reforms as members of the LTTE, as members of women's civil society organizations, or as oracles in local Tamil Hindu temples who borrow the agency of the Amman (a divine epithet meaning "Mother" and a term of address for Tamil goddesses), women in Batticola [in the northeast] have replaced earlier networks shattered in the course of war and are empowering women's agency as a social force in both the secular and religious spheres.[51]

The patriarchal nature of the society and the worship of local goddesses elevated the image of women. Especially prior to the war, there were strong familial and kinship ties, often anchored by the woman. Many of these were disrupted or displaced during the war; "nevertheless, Tamil women's networking is resilient."[52] The social networks and strong bonds among women in this otherwise patriarchal society helped get women through the violence. (Interestingly, it was also used to help recruit women to the LTTE as combatants—the how question we posed in chapter 1.) For example, in 2002 the World Bank funded a project to rehabilitate irrigation systems. Networks of mothers were used "to create women's village development councils parallel to the existing councils dominated by men."[53] While men resisted in the beginning, recognition that the women's contributions were beneficial for the entire community led to a change in "the dynamics of gender relations and won the men's respect."[54] In addition, the project provided economic support to two other groups of women: "widows and women who did not benefit from the original irrigation program."[55]

A point that Balasingham makes about the women also bears noting as we continue the discussion of women's political activism: "Historically, the women of Tamil Eelam have been politically conscious and participated actively in the Tamil national struggle for self-determination. They were the active forces in the *non-violent* political struggles of the sixties and seventies" (italics added).[56] She continues that thought with words that parallel what we saw in the case of Palestinian women: "The women's participation in the armed struggle . . . was an extension of their participation in the national struggle for liberation."[57] This was a struggle "of the people" that required the participation of *all* the people. Part of that process, which she described in an earlier piece, is one of the women moving "from non-violent politics into armed struggle," which she also depicts as "the inevitable extension of their [women's] long contribution to national political campaigns against State oppression."[58] And she acknowledges that this change required a concomitant change in the cultural images of women. "Parliamentary politics and non-violent struggle remain within the acceptable domain of women's behavior. The history of women in combat in the armed struggle is a chronicle of a fundamentally different order."[59] In all these ways, women's agency is expressed along the continuum of political activism.

Women Working for Peace

Contrary to the popularly held image, women in Sri Lanka were politically active in ways besides serving as combatants and suicide bombers, discussed in more detail later in this chapter. As noted in the case of Palestinian women (chapter 4), it is far easier to focus on the cases of women who were engaged in political violence because that is antithetical to the gendered assumption about women, especially in patriarchal societies.

In her study of Tamil nationalism and the construction of woman, Maunaguru addresses the role of women "positioning themselves as mothers," who organized to protest human rights abuses "since they thought it was their legitimate and moral responsibility to do so."[60] In her depiction of "the Social Mother," Maunaguru draws on the work of others who studied the region to note that "by accepting this responsibility to nurture and preserve life, which is valorized by the Sri Lankan state," women, especially those who positioned themselves based on their roles as mothers, revealed the "'transgression' of the state," including its resorting to violent repression.[61] "It was this contradiction that the women in the North who organized themselves as mothers, forming groups such as the Mothers' Front, and the Association of Missing Youth, operated to use their 'motherhood' as a political force."[62] As Alison reminds us, there was also a parallel southern Sinhalese Mothers' Front, "with the same attendant benefits and costs of using motherhood as a site of political protest."[63]

Regarding the Tamil case, Maunaguru continues: "It is also important to note the peaceful, non-violent tone that was embodied in the activities of these mothers. Furthermore, these groups tried to link themselves with women's organizations in the South, and in many instances called for a political settlement to the ethnic conflict."[64] Importantly, this leads Maunaguru to conclude that "this construction of motherhood—appealing for peace—represents an important moment of protest which contradicted the image of the mother calling for war,"[65] which was an important political symbol. This further suggests that women were able and willing to construct images and interests that empowered women, even within the more traditional framework of motherhood.

Although far less known than the women combatants, it is also clear that women in Sri Lanka have made attempts to reach out across communities. As is often the case, some of this effort was prompted by personal loss. For example, Visaka Dharmadasa's son disappeared in 1998. A Sinhalese woman, she reached out to other families and formed the Association of Servicemen Missing in Action, an organization that "advocates on behalf of missing servicemen and offers counseling and advice to families." Importantly, she extended her work in connecting with "Tamil mothers on 'the other side'" recognizing the losses Tamils also experienced during the conflict.[66] Since forming the association, "she has led a public rally of Sinhalese and Tamil mothers, 12,000 of them, as a reminder to the government and public on the plight of the missing."⁶⁷ In 1999 she led a group of five mothers into Tamil territory to meet with members of the LTTE. Anderlini writes of Dharmadasa, "She has been tireless in her efforts to bring about peace talks and at the forefront of demanding women's participation in the peace process."⁶⁸ When subsequent peace talks stalled, in 2003 the LTTE "called on her to convey their messages to the government. . . . [She] is widely recognized and trusted for her commitment to ending the violence through negotiations."⁶⁹

In 2002 Sinhalese and Tamil women held a rally for the missing, drawing on the work of Dharmadasa's organization and the Association of War Affected Women, both of which built upon a grassroots desire for peace. These women "lobby the government to reciprocate the LTTE's actions of releasing soldiers and civilians, mobilize cross-community dialogue, and design workshops on rehabilitation, reintegration and reconciliation."⁷⁰ According to a background paper for an event highlighting Dharmadasa, cosponsored by the Wilson Center's Asia Program and Project on Leadership and Building State Capacity and by the Initiative for Inclusive Security, "Both communities [Tamil Hindu and Sinhalese Buddhist] realized that, as mothers, they felt the same emotions and 'could really make bonds and build a common ground.'"⁷¹ Dharmadasa added to that in saying, "A resolution to the national problem calls for all Sri Lankans to address embedded ethnic prejudices and the need for both Sinhalese Buddhist and Tamil Hindu communities to feel that they are treated with dignity and equality by each other."⁷²

In designing and facilitating the informal dialogue process between the LTTE and the government, Dharmadasa has worked to bring together influential civil society leaders, particularly women. She contended that the inclusion of women in the peace negotiations brings the attention of the national authorities to the long-term humanitarian component of the cease-fire, a broad approach often taken by women, rather than merely the short-term aspects, such as disarmament. However, she also stated that women need to consider their security issues as well when interacting with the authorities, as "addressing the humanitarian content alone by talking of 'our dying sons' is not effective when dealing with authorities."⁷³

This highlights what we have seen and learned in the other cases in this volume: women often are successful at working across communities, drawing on their roles as mothers; regardless of their differences, women are often drawn together by common tragedy; and informal diplomacy is often a more effective tool to bridge gaps between groups in conflict than going through formal political channels. But it also underscores the important role women can play, even in more patriarchal societies.

An important caveat needs to be added here as well. Despite the peaceful and nonviolent tone Dharmadasa and her organization tried to take, especially by drawing on their role as mothers, Maunaguru also notes that "the possibilities of 'motherhood' being mobilized in a peace movement were near impossible within the Tamil context which was, and continues to be, dominated by warmongering and violence. . . . Nevertheless, this construction of 'motherhood'—appealing for peace—represents an important moment of protest which contradicted the image of the mother calling for war."[74]

Clearly, the informal attempts to end the conflict were not totally successful, although they did help bring the groups together in some ways. A UNIFEM (UN Development Fund for Women, now part of UN Women) report, however, also notes that only men attended the first round of formal peace talks facilitated by the Norwegian government in September 2002 with representatives from the Sri Lankan government and the LTTE. In the five subsequent rounds of talks, one woman, representing the LTTE, participated.[75] A Subcommittee on Gender Issues created as part of the negotiations "acknowledged the widespread and profound suffering of women as a consequence of war, especially in the most affected areas. It was decided to focus their [committee members'] efforts on: the equal representation of women in politics, educational structures and gender bias, violence against women and allegations of sexual harassment, . . . political representation and decision-making and reconciliation."[76] The document also states that after the session held on March 2003, no agenda was set for further talks. The conflict formally ended in May 2009, when the forces of the government of Sri Lanka prevailed over the Tamils.

Women: Nonviolent Resistance and Political Violence

In the words of the editors of the book *Women and the Contested State*, "Tamil women must live with what they cannot control, yet find ways to mediate and protest violence in a terrain where violence is most immediate and difficult; the everyday lived reality of the war zone."[77] On the whole, women who engaged in the nationalist conflict in Sri Lanka gained fame and notoriety not because of what they did to work for peace, although clearly there were women who did so, as previously noted, but because of how active and visible they were as combatants and how effective they were as suicide bombers. Since the country was engaged in conflict almost from the time of its independence, it was also a highly militarized state. The majority Sinhalese population dominated the membership of the security forces. Moreover, the actual number of people in these forces grew significantly; in the early 1980s about 12,000 people were members. By the 1990s the number grew to more than 175,000.[78] Interestingly, the Sri Lankan Women's Army Corps was created in 1980 "as an unarmed, non-combatant support unit. Set up with the assistance of the British Women's Reserve Army Corps, it was identical in structure to its parent organization, and its first generation of officer cadets was trained in Britain."[79] This role primarily for Sinhalese women was consistent with the British approach to "respectability" and the stereotyped perception of women, and it stands in marked contrast to the approach taken by the LTTE.

According to a history of the LTTE, which was formed in 1976, "The integration of women and girls into fighting proceeded slowly so as not to offend the cultural values and sensibility of the society at large."[80] Alison describes the ways women were recruited into the LTTE in the 1980s (another answer to the how question) but women did not engage in combat for a number of years (until the mid-1980s). Rather, in the beginning, women's duties included "propaganda work, medical care, information collection, fundraising and recruitment"; in short, women were relegated to the roles traditionally associated with women along the continuum of activism.[81] The LTTE then moved to give women a combat role, first with the creation in 1983 of "a special section for women," the Women's Front of the Liberation Tigers, with formal combat training in 1985.[82] And two years after that (in 1987), the LTTE leader set up the first all-women training camp.[83] (Men and women generally trained in separate camps.)

According to Paige Whaley Eager, the change in the LTTE's policy regarding the recruitment and the role of women was because of a number of reasons. With more men dying in the fighting as well as the increased number of refugees, the LTTE recognized that it needed more bodies. So, as we saw in the cases of Northern Ireland and Palestine, the very nature of the conflict and the concomitant deaths of young men made the need to recruit women all the more pressing. Second, there was an ideological need "to demonstrate that the LTTE was in fact an all-encompassing social movement, and not only concerned with military battles."[84] The third reason to account for the recruitment of women is that the women convinced the group to let them participate.[85] And, finally, the leader of the LTTE, Velupillai Prabhakaran, "was confident that women had the potential for military training and combat. . . . [He] was determined that women should have equal opportunity for participation in all aspects of the armed struggle."[86] However, this also meant that Prabhakaran had to persuade the other men, "many of whom were more resistant to the idea, to accept and encourage women."[87]

Even though Tamil society is patriarchal, "The LTTE stood out in comparison to other insurgent groups because of the large number of women it has on its rolls." From 1983 to 1984, when young women joined the LTTE, and thereafter, "women combatants have taken part in almost all military offensives, in varying degrees, at times displaying ferocious courage."[88]

According to Lawrence, an increasing number of Tamil women were recruited into the LTTE starting in the 1990s following massacres in Tamil villages.[89] Most of the women were between the ages of fifteen and thirty-seven, and many were young widows or heads of households. Women made up about 35 percent of the LTTE fighting ranks, in part because of intense recruitment drives that included the rule "that each Tamil family must either give one child to the organization for military training or support the LTTE financially."[90] Thus, women were always considered an important part of the national liberation struggle.

Women in the LTTE became part of a disciplined, militarized culture that required complete commitment. The women also adhered to a modified version of the "four virtues" of Tamil women in which the traditional virtues of "modesty, charm, coyness and fear" were replaced by the new notions of "courage, confidence, and thirst for liberation."[91] These ideals conform to the rules imposed on the women by the male military command. But it is also important to note the need "to glorify and emphasize the nurturing role of Tamil women," including reconstructing old myths.[92] Thus, especially in the early phases of the conflict, Tamil leaders referred to these mythological heroines as "Brave Mothers," "and appealed to women to follow those characters as their ideals."[93]

Fighting for the cause (the why question) is clearly a powerful motivator for women as well as for men. Alison, who interviewed LTTE female combatants in Sri Lanka, concurs with the conclusion drawn in an earlier work by Bose that "LTTE women, like LTTE men, are primarily motivated by 'nationalist fervor.'" Alison found that among the reasons women chose to join the fight was that they were committed to the ideas of "freedom for the Tamil nation, self-determination, land and rights for Tamils."[94] Lawrence similarly found that "Female LTTE cadres have unshakable confidence in the rightness of their struggle for liberation."[95]

However, Alison contends that nationalist sentiment is a "meta-reason" for joining the group and argues that other more personal factors are involved as well.[96] Here Alison provides insights into some of the other motivations women have for being combatants. She draws on her interviews as well as research to identify a range of factors that include "communal perception of suffering, oppression and injustice" and personal experiences, such as anger over the deaths of loved ones, which lead women to look to and take up arms.[97] The notion of revenge is cited by men and women as a motivating factor in becoming combatants.

Ness makes another point about the women in the LTTE who chose the combatant path specifically because of the combination of their being celebrated for their valor and courage while maintaining their image "as caring and soft outside of combat. . . . LTTE female combatants are constructed not as abandoning their femininity but, rather, as suspending it on a situational basis—they maintain the innate qualities of femininity as recognized by the culture that surrounds them, even as they kill."[98]

As we discussed in chapter 2, another factor that must be considered when trying to understand women who choose to become combatants is that often the notion of "fighting for the cause," specifically liberating the country, is tied to women's liberation as well, a point that has come up in the other cases. According to Alison, "The LTTE has an official ideological commitment to women's liberation, and its female cadres are seen to symbolize this. One potentially problematic element of this is that the independence struggle invariably frames the struggle for women's rights: the Tamil struggle is prioritized, and women's emancipation is seen as depending on the struggle."[99] As a result, "many LTTE women have come to be committed to women's rights and advancing women's status and position in Tamil society."[100] Lawrence quotes a speech by the head of the LTTE women's political wing that also reinforces this link between the struggle for national liberation and the liberation of women: "Our liberation struggle has brought women's struggle to the forefront. We are successfully expelling superstitions ensconced in the dark recesses of our mind that portray women as secondary citizens. The women's liberation movement is forging ahead as an integral part of our greater struggle. *The ideal of women's liberation is core to our national liberation movement*" (italics added).[101]

Or, as Bouta et al. describe it, "Men and women in armies tend to share danger, living conditions, and roles, and often have access to training and education that is not gender stereotyped."[102] No wonder women choose to fight for the cause rather than work for peace. Their very future existence is bound up with the struggle for and success of that cause.

Balasingham also points out the cultural changes offered to women as being part of the LTTE that would otherwise not have been possible. Not only does being part of the LTTE represent a departure from the norm in a patriarchal society where "male control follows them throughout their lives," but the decision to join "makes a social statement about the characters of the young women. It tells society that they are not satisfied with the social status quo; it means they are young women capable of defying authority; it means they are women with independent thoughts . . . [prepared] to fly in the face of tradition . . . the women who are the catalysts for change."[103]

But M. R. Narayan Swamy, Eager, and others warn about the dangers of assuming that the increasing role of women combatants in the LTTE should be equated *solely* with women's liberation or the improvement of the plight of women in Sri Lanka in general. Swamy writes, "The women's role in the Tamil Eelam war should not be taken to mean—as some believe—that the LTTE emancipated or elevated the status of women by making them fighters and killers. Aid workers who saw the LTTE from close quarters, post 2002, say that many in the women's wing would slip away or stand back when male cadres passed by."[104] Eager also makes this point by questioning whether women's participation in the LTTE "has brought about improvements for Tamil women as a whole."[105] Even Balasingham, who writes with great reverence of the women fighters of the LTTE, notes the difficulties facing women "struggling to find a new identity in a society heavily influenced and manipulated by reactionary conceptions of women."[106]

Where women in the LTTE gained fame and notoriety for their involvement as combatants, Lawrence brings in another dimension of their work when she writes that the creation of women's networks is "to mobilize women for social change, to choose a life with purpose, and to serve in a movement dedicated to a better life for the Tamil majority."[107] She also notes that "LTTE female cadres have developed new interests in women's education and liberation."[108] Lawrence also offers an insight about women and conflict that is worth repeating: "As women's agency is reshaped by the shared experiences of war and its consequences, women are increasingly overcoming political silencing and speaking out in both religious gatherings and secular public meetings."[109] This point resonates especially in more patriarchal societies, like Sri Lanka, where women's roles are defined traditionally, and where the conflict forced women to make choices.

LTTE Suicide Bombers

It should also be noted that despite their high profile, in general, women suicide bombers/martyrs played only a marginal role in their organizations. Women did not plan the operations, nor did they determine the targets or the timing of when they would detonate their bombs.[110] This leads Schweitzer to speculate still further about women's motivations:

> Female suicide bombers appear almost exclusively in societies that are heavily traditionalist and conservative, where women lack equal rights and their status in society is much lower than that of their male counterparts. In some of the dispatching organizations such as the Kurdish PKK [Kurdistan Workers Party] and the Sri Lankan LTTE, leaders promised that women participating in such operations would pave the way for other women to enjoy an equal status and to be emancipated. Although women were already integrated into the army, they did not earn commanding positions, and hence the promise—ultimately empty—of gender advancement for their colleagues if they volunteered for suicide operations.[111]

For the women, then, accepting this mission may have been seen as a step forward, not only for them but for all other women who follow them, although one could question the motives of the male leaders who sent them out as suicide bombers.

Giving life for the cause is the greatest sacrifice any woman—or man—can make. Balasingham, in her (admittedly biased) history of Tamil resistance, writes that the members of the LTTE are "freedom fighters who are prepared to sacrifice their lives to save and protect the community. Here one finds an extraordinary phenomenon of self-sacrifice, the renunciation of individual life for the redemption of the collective life, which is a supreme humanist ideal. It is in this context that martyrs are honored."[112] Drawing on the work of Balasingham, Ness describes women suicide bombers in the LTTE as "a wholly willing subject."[113] Women in the LTTE were driven by "the act of defending Tamil life against its perceived enemies," as opposed to women in Islamic fundamentalist groups who are drawn, at least in part, by "the promise of a blissful afterlife."[114] For Ness, then, the act of defending Tamil life and community becomes the critical factor.

The LTTE began suicide attacks in 1987 and, according to Skaine, "is the only organization that has succeeded in assassinating two heads of state by suicide bombings: former Indian prime minister Rajiv Gandhi in May 1991 and president Ranaginghe Premadasa of Sri Lanka in May 1993."[115] She also claims, "It is the most active group in the use of suicide terrorism," yet it was unsuccessful at achieving its goal of an independent Tamil state.[116] Of the more than 200 suicide attacks perpetrated by the LTTE, 30 percent to 40 percent involved women who "are trained and go on suicide missions like men."[117] Furthermore, as Ness notes, unlike radical Islamic groups, such as the Palestinians described in chapter 4, "martyrdom has not been differently scripted for male and female cadres."[118] Women are not refused the distinction of "martyr," and after their deaths, "the honorific title of '*ma-virar*,' or 'Great Hero, would be applied to both equally."[119] Male and female suicide bombers alike would have their last meal with the LTTE leader Prabhakaran. For purposes of this type of mission, men and women were treated no differently. In fact, as Ness concludes, "It could be argued that the motivation of LTTE females to embrace killing and death, compared to other militant groups, is, for these reasons, most fully constructed in political terms."[120]

Robert Pape, in his study of suicide bombers, asserts that community support is vitally important for Tamils who "are willing to commit suicide for the Tamil Tigers."[121] These individuals were concerned with "how the community would interpret and remember their actions."[122] And then he describes the ways that support is generated by venerating the individuals who killed themselves in the name of the cause, such as "displaying their pictures on posters and holding public processions with pomp and pageantry (singing is common) in their honor."[123] There is a "Heroes Day" in memory of the first Black Tiger (suicide) attack, and monuments are built in Tamil towns memorializing Black Tigers. While such public ceremonies demonstrate community support for suicide bombers, Pape also argues that "there is evidence of broad Tamil support [and respect] for martyrdom in the context of national resistance. . . . there are no visible signs of public disaffection with the Black Tigers or any other Tigers who voluntarily died for the cause."[124] And it should be noted that this is true of male and female suicide bombers.

In considering characteristics of the suicide bombers, the female Black Tigers were neither mothers nor married. According to Gunawardena, "The female suicide bomber in the context of the Tamil Tigers has more than political and organizational underpinnings."[125] Rather, "The self-sacrifice of the female bombers is almost an extension of the idea of motherhood in the Tamil culture, [as] in this strongly patriarchal society, Tamil mothers make great sacrifices for their sons on a daily basis. . . . Acting as a human bomb is an understood and accepted offering for a woman who will never be a mother."[126]

On the one hand, the veneration of motherhood is an important symbol for the Tamil movement and, as noted previously, an important coalescing force for peace. On the other hand, in the LTTE, women were not allowed to be married before the age of twenty-five.[127] The leader of the Tamil Tigers, Velupillai Prabhakaran, personally chose which women could join the women's suicide wing; the ratio for females to males was three to two. He also chose children between the ages of fourteen and sixteen because of concerns about the limitations on movement as well as body searches, and thus young boys and women, rather than men, were preferred.[128] But this also means women who were selected as suicide bombers were those who were not, and would never be, mothers, which challenges the gender norm of women's roles as bearers of children and nurturers.

The case of LTTE women as combatants and as suicide bombers shows that women are not only as fierce as men, but that in many instances the existing gender roles provided them with the opportunity to engage in resistance and political violence in ways that were not open to men. For example, Dhanu, the suicide bomber who blew herself up to kill Rajiv Gandhi in 1991, was successful in part because she was "a remarkably beautiful woman in her late twenties"[129] and wore a suicide belt under her clothing so that she looked pregnant. Her beauty and alleged condition (pregnancy) gave her access to Gandhi in a way that would have been more difficult for a man. One account of the assassination revealed that "a policewoman had attempted to prevent Dhanu . . . from reaching the prime minister. But Gandhi intervened." In fact, according to Bloom, "Gandhi may have been blinded by gender."[130]

Preparing for Peace?

The end of the conflict in 2009 was facilitated partly by the success of the Sri Lankan army in taking some of the LTTE strongholds, especially the Elephant Pass, a strategic piece of land between the Jaffna Peninsula and the main island, and the death of LTTE leader Prabhakaran. Sri Lanka's president Mahinda Rajapakse declared the conflict to be over with the government prevailing. But, as noted in a report produced by the British government on the situation, "The humanitarian cost has been very high and both parties to the conflict stand accused of war crimes. Sri Lanka now faces the twin challenges of reconstruction and, if peace is to be sustainable, implementing political and constitutional reforms that will give genuine autonomy to the north and east, where Tamils are in the majority."[131] Thus, the formal end of the conflict is not enough. The challenge is preparing for peace—a lasting one.

At the end of the conflict in 2009, the British House of Commons issued a research paper, "War and Peace in Sri Lanka." This document states clearly that unlike earlier cases, "Future negotiations, under whatever auspices, must fully include *all* Sri Lanka's groups, including the multiple voices that exist within each of the communities, if they are to have a chance of success; civil society should also be represented" (italics added).[132] The document also warns of the dangers of marginalizing any group because of its links to the LTTE, stating that "many analysts would argue that such groups ultimately have to be brought into negotiating processes if there is to be a successful outcome."[133]

It is easy and tempting to exclude the group that can be seen as the cause of the conflict, just as women are often excluded from negotiations because they were not in positions of leadership. Yet, as the Sri Lanka case illustrates, women were an important force on both sides, working for peace but also as hawks advocating for and actively engaged in the conflict. One of the questions Alison raises about the role of women in Sri Lanka postconflict, and an especially important one in this case, is "whether this public sphere activity was temporary and transitory, ending with the war, or 'whether the gains they made in times of war' can be 'consolidated in terms of gender equity in times of peace.'"[134] And while women's participation in the armed struggle is no guarantee of future equality, Alison also writes that "the expressed ideological commitment to women's equality in Tamil nationalism are significant sociopolitical changes."[135] The question really is, how enduring are these changes? Clearly, the role that LTTE women played during the conflict raised the consciousness of society on the range of actions women are capable of, often in defiance of cultural norms. "Many LTTE women were very actively involved in a wide variety of women's development and community development programs."[136] And it seems that the LTTE left an important legacy for women.

One news story gives the example of Shereen Xavier, a human rights activist, who can wear trousers (pants) as opposed to the traditional sari. While this might seem trivial, this "is among the indicators that thanks to the efforts of the Tamil Tiger rebels who were defeated by the government last year after nearly three decades of armed conflict, women here are slowly being freed from the strict roles and ways imposed on them by tradition. Although the Tigers failed in their military conflict to create a separate state for minority Tamils—a conflict that took the lives of more than 70,000 soldiers, rebels and civilians—they helped women here take a closer look at themselves and take on roles and ways other than those dictated by society."[137]

But in Sri Lanka, as is the case with many societies making the transition from conflict, women have been only minimally involved. In fact, as shown in a piece by the Center for Humanitarian Dialogue, an NGO based in Geneva, Switzerland, "Being absent from key decision making in the legislature and local government had implications for the peace process. Women Parliamentarians were not present at any of the formal peace negotiations, which were conducted entirely by male politicians."[138] And the author also states that "Sri Lanka needs to make the transition from a post-war to a post-conflict society. Conflicts inevitably produce structural transformations for some women, opening up new social, economic and political opportunities which challenge and reframe gender hierarchies and roles. One way to consolidate such positive gains is to ensure women's participation and representation in post war decision making processes." South Africa, Rwanda, and Liberia are used as examples of the ways post-conflict policy and legal reforms "can contribute to women's empowerment in post-war contexts."[139]

At this point, with the conflict barely over, but clearly with women once again in the background, it will be instructive to see what lessons have been learned as the country begins to knit itself together.

Conclusion

Balasingham argues that "women's participation in armed struggle is for both national and social emancipation. Their participation itself constitutes a step towards their emancipation, a step towards their empowerment. When women start to struggle against oppression then we have to accept that women have begun to move towards their emancipation."[140] The case of Sri Lanka supports the idea that even in a traditional, patriarchal society, women can be empowered and can play an important role not only as insurgents fighting against the mainstream but even within the male hierarchy. Their agency is constrained, but these women do have agency.

In this case, we saw examples of women who were able to achieve positions of leadership, attaining the rank of president—in this way challenging gender norms of women's behavior and roles in society as participants in the formal political (public) sphere. At the same time, we also saw that these women's policies were antithetical to the gendered assumptions of women working for peace. Rather, not only did they not bring an end to the conflict—in one case despite election promises to the contrary—but they each contributed to the escalation of the conflict to some degree.

Further, we also saw that all three women were able to rise to their positions largely because of their spouses. Yet, it also cannot be denied that these women were astute politicians in their own right who were able to get elected to high office on their own. In this traditional society, it might have required a man to get them access to the position, but it was up to each of them to find a way to maintain her position.

It is also important to point out that all three of these women were members of the Sinhalese majority. Minority women, whether Tamil or Muslim, did not have the same options. Muslim women were able to succeed on the whole because they took advantage of the educational opportunities available to them. They also stayed largely removed from the conflict, preferring instead to come together as Muslim women. The Tamils took a different approach, particularly through their participation in the anti-state movement, the LTTE. The LTTE served almost as family, accepting and absorbing women into their ranks, taking advantage of what women would bring to the conflict. And the Tamil women who joined the LTTE did so in no small part because it offered opportunities they were largely barred from and a sense of belonging and empowerment they did not have otherwise. Participation in an organization involved in political violence also challenged gender norms of women as peaceful. Throughout the conflict, the symbolism of women was a powerful motivator on both sides.

To understand all aspects of women's political activism in Sri Lanka, we need to look at the full range of their involvement, which, as discussed previously, goes far beyond simply women as combatants but is rather a continuum of political activism in which women take advantage of their agency as political actors motivated by political factors. In doing this, it is also important to remember that because of its duration, the civil war became all encompassing, which, in effect, meant that the country was operating on a "war footing."[141] As a document from the World Bank notes, that has had an impact on women especially, and as the country makes the transition from war to peace, special attention must be paid to the needs of women. For example, the "government of Sri Lanka estimates some 50,000 war widows are living on the east coast. . . . Most of these women are now heads of households without a proper income or relevant skills to find a profitable source of employment. They are also burdened with a number of dependents including husbands/sons/others disabled by war."[142]

Finally, if we are to truly draw lessons from the cases of Sri Lanka, Northern Ireland, and the Palestinians, we will need to better understand the role of women, especially ex-combatants, in the postconflict demobilization, disarmament, and reconciliation process. Alison reminds us, "Ways of utilizing the confidence and abilities of ex-combatant women in projects to rebuild war-torn societies in more gender equal ways must be found, rather than re-marginalizing these women or expecting them, metaphorically and literally, to return to the kitchen."[143] As we see in the next chapter, however, where rebuilding a war-torn country is a challenge in and of itself, finding a meaningful role for women, especially ex-combatants, provides another whole set of issues.

Notes

1. "Life as a Female Tamil Tiger Guerrilla Relived by One of First Female Soldiers," *Telegraph*, May 8, 2009, http://www.telegraph.co.uk/news/worldnews/asia/srilanka/5283438/Life-as-a-female-Tamil-Tiger-guerilla-relived-by-one-of-first-female-soldiers.html.

2. Asoka Bandarage, *The Separatist Conflict in Sri Lanka: Terrorism, Ethnicity, Political Economy* (Bloomington, IN: iUniverse, 2009), 1. The Human Development Index was developed by the United Nations specifically to offer comparative data about the well-being of countries based on a number of indicators, including life expectancy, years of schooling, and gross national income per capita. United Nations, "Human Development Reports," http://hdr.undp.org/en/statistics/hdi/.

3. Cecile Van de Voorde, "Sri Lankan Terrorism: Assessing and Responding to the Threat of the LTTE," *Policy Practice and Research* 6, no. 2 (May 2005): 195.

4. Bandarage, *Separatist Conflict*, 1.

5. Monique Skidmore and Patricia Lawrence, "Resisting Terror: Women, Agency, and the Micropolitics of Sri Lankan Life," in *Women and the Contested State: Religion, Violence, and Agency in South and Southeast Asia*, ed. Monique Skidmore and Patricia Lawrence (Notre Dame, IN: University of Notre Dame Press, 2007), 85.

6. Ibid.

8. Bose, *Contested Lands*, 13.

9. Ibid., 15.

10. Ibid., 13.

11. As quoted in Alison, *Women and Political Violence*, 138.

12. Ibid.

13. Adele Ann Balasingham, *Women Fighters of Liberation Tigers* (Thasan Printers, 1993), 1, accessed July 29, 2012, http://www.tamilnation.co/books/Eelam/adeleann.htm.

14. Bandarage, *Separatist Conflict*, 5.

15. Ibid., 5.

16. Ibid., 3.

17. Bose, *Contested Lands*, 14.

18. Ibid., 18.

19. The historical background in this section is drawn from Bose, *Contested Lands*, chapter 1, "Sri Lanka," 6–54; and Bandarage, *Separatist Conflict*, chapter 2, "Prelude: The British Colonial Period and Early Years of Independence," 29–52.

20. Bose, *Contested Lands*, 22.

21. Ibid.

22. Ibid., 24.

23. Ibid., 26.

24. Ibid., 28.

25. Patricia Lawrence, "The Watch of Tamil Women: Women's Acts in a Transitional Warscape," in *Women and the Contested State: Religion, Violence, and Agency in South and Southeast Asia*, ed. Monique Skidmore and Patricia Lawrence (Notre Dame, IN: University of Notre Dame Press, 2007), 90–91.

26. Central Intelligence Agency, "Sri Lanka," *World Factbook*, modified November 14, 2012, https://www.cia.gov/library/publications/the-world-factbook/geos/ce.html, updated Nov. 14, 2012.

27. Bandarage, *Separatist Conflict*, 59

28. Ibid.

29. For more details about Muslim identity, see Qadri Ismail, "Unmooring Identity: The Antinomies of Elite Muslim Self-Representation in Modern Sri Lanka," in *Unmaking the Nation: The Politics of Identity & History in Modern Sri Lanka*, ed. Pradeem Jeganathan and Qadri Ismail (New York: South Focus Press, 1995), 62–107.

30. Bandarage, *Separatist Conflict*, 138.

31. Ibid.

32. Ismail, "Unmooring Identity," 65.

33. Muslim Women's Research and Action Forum, "Our History," http://www.mwraf.org/history.php?menutab=abtus.

34. Ibid.

35. Malathi de Alwis, "Gender, Politics and the 'Respectable Lady,'" in *Unmaking the Nation: The Politics of Identity & History in Modern Sri Lanka*, ed. Pradeem Jeganathan and Qadri Ismail (New York: South Focus Press, 1995), 140.

36. Ibid., 140–41.

37. Ibid., 148.

38. Ibid.

39. Ibid., 149.

40. Ibid., 146.

41. Ibid., 145. The SVM was formally incorporated in March 1987. "Among the objectives of the Movement are the following: a) to maintain a record of current public affairs with particular reference to the interests of women, children and youths so as to ensure their physical, mental, moral, religious and social development and to protect them from exploitation and discrimination; b) to promote cooperation and mutual confidence among all members irrespective of race, religion, language, occupation and political opinion to enable women to act as a single

group interested in National Development; c) to ensure that the women actively participate in development activities outside their homes; and d) to conduct surveys and studies and collect data on problems relating to women and children in collaboration with the Women's Bureau, Children's Secretariat and Governmental and nongovernmental agencies." Seva Vanitha Movement of Sri Lanka (Incorporation) Act (No. 10 of 1987), 10 March 1987, National Center for Biotechnology Information, http://www.ncbi.nlm.nih.gov/pubmed/12346608.

42. de Alwis, "Gender, Politics," 147.
43. Ibid., 151.
44. Bose, *Contested Lands*, 37.
45. Ibid. Bose writes, "In 1994 South Africa had just completed its transition from apartheid to multiracial democracy, while the Oslo process in the Middle East seemed to most to be a viable route to forging peace between Israel and the Palestinians."
46. Ibid., 38.
47. Adele Balasingham, *The Will to Freedom: An Inside View of Tamil Resistance* (Mitcham, England: Fairmax, 2001), 308.
48. Ibid.
49. Skidmore and Lawrence, "Resisting Terror," 86.
50. Bandarage, *Separatist Conflict*, 136.
51. Lawrence, "Watch of Tamil Women," 89–90.
52. Ibid., 93.
53. Anderlini, "Translating Global Agreement," 32.
54. Ibid.
55. Ibid.
56. Balasingham, *Will to Freedom*, 278.
57. Ibid.
58. Balasingham, *Women Fighters*, 1.
59. Ibid.
60. Sitralega Maunaguru, "Gendering Tamil Nationalism: The Construction of 'Woman' in Projects of Protest and Control," in *Unmaking the Nation: The Politics of Identity & History in Modern Sri Lanka*, ed., Pradeem Jeganathan and Qadri Ismail (New York: South Focus Press, 1995), 165.
61. Ibid., 166.
62. Ibid.
63. Alison, *Women and Political Violence*, 171.
64. Maunaguru, "Gendering Tamil Nationalism," 166.
65. Ibid., 166.
66. Anderlini, *Women Building Peace*, 64.
67. Ibid.
68. Ibid., 65.
69. Ibid.

70. Beena Sarwar, "Some Mother's Son," Countercurrents, June 24, 2004, http://www.countercurrents.org/hr-sarwar210604.htm.

71. "Negotiating for Peace in Sri Lanka: A Behind-the-Scenes Perspective on Mediating Conflict Resolution," Wilson Center, April 20, 2006, http://www.wilsoncenter.org/event/negotiating-for-peace-sri-lanka-behind-the-scenes-perspective-mediating-conflict-resolution.

72. Ibid.

73. Ibid.

74. Maunaguru, "Gendering Tamil Nationalism," 166.

75. "Sri Lanka: UNIFEM Report: Gender Profile of the Conflict in Sri Lanka," Women Living under Muslim Laws, August 23, 2009, http://www.wluml.org/node/5489.

76. Ibid.

77. Skidmore and Lawrence, "Resisting Terror," 86.

78. Lawrence, "Watch of Tamil Women," 91.

79. "Women's History: Sri Lankan Army Women's Corps," October 1988, http://womenshistory.about.com/library/ency/blwh_sri_lanka_women_military.htm. It is very difficult to find references to this unit, as opposed to all that has been written about women combatants in the LTTE.

80. Ness, "In the Name of the Cause," 23.

81. Alison, "Cogs in the Wheel?" 38–39.

82. Ibid.

83. Ibid., 39.

84. Eager, *From Freedom Fighters to Terrorists*, 138.

85. Ibid.

86. Balasingham, *Women Fighters*, 4.

87. Alison, *Women and Political Violence*, 125.

88. M. R. Narayan Swamy, *The Tiger Vanquished: LTTE's Story* (New Delhi, India: Sage, 2010), lxxiii.

89. Lawrence, "Watch of Tamil Women," 98.

90. Ibid.

91. Ibid., 99.

92. Maunaguru, "Gendering Tamil Nationalism," 160.

93. Ibid.

94. Alison, "Cogs in the Wheel?" 40.

95. Lawrence, "Watch of Tamil Women," 100.

96. Alison, "Cogs in the Wheel?" 40.

97. Ibid.

98. Ness, "In the Name of the Cause," 24–25.

99. Alison, "Women as Agents of Political Violence," 455.

100. Ibid.

101. Lawrence, "Watch of Tamil Women," 100.

102. Bouta et al., *Gender, Conflict, and Development*, 16.
103. Balasingham, *Women Fighters*, 5.
104. Swamy, *Tiger Vanquished*, lxxiii.
105. Eager, *From Freedom Fighters to Terrorists*, 140.
106. Balasingham, *Women Fighters*, 5.
107. Lawrence, "Watch of Tamil Women," 115.
108. Ibid.
109. Ibid.
110. Schweitzer, "Introduction," 10.
111. Ibid.
112. Balasingham, *Will to Freedom*, 289.
113. Ness, "In the Name of the Cause," 24.
114. Ibid., 24.
115. Skaine, *Female Suicide Bombers*, 87.
116. Ibid., 87–88.
117. Ibid., 88.
118. Ness, "In the Name of the Cause," 24.
119. Ibid.
120. Ibid.
121. Pape, *Dying to Win*, 143.
122. Ibid.
123. Ibid., 144.
124. Ibid., 145–46.
125. Gunawardena, "Female Black Tigers?" 84.
126. Ibid.
127. Ness, "In the Name of the Cause," 23.
128. Joshi, "Sri Lanka: Suicide Bombers."
129. Pape, *Dying to Win*, 226.
130. Bloom, "Mother. Daughter." 54.
131. Jon Lunn, Claire Taylor, and Ian Townsend, "War and Peace in Sri Lanka" (research paper 09/51), June 5, 2009, 3, http://www.parliament.uk/briefing-papers/RP09-51.pdf.
132. Lunn et al., "War and Peace," 70.
133. Ibid., 70.
134. Alison, "In the War Front," 143.
135. Ibid.
136. Ibid., 145.
137. Feizal Samath, "Rights—Sri Lanka: How the War Gave Tamil Women More Space," Inter Press Service News Agency, April 20, 2010, http://www.ipsnews.net/2010/04/rights-sri-lanka-how-the-war-gave-tamil-women-more-space/.
138. Samuel Kumudini, "Sri Lanka: The Link between Women's Political Representation and the Peace Process," Center for Humanitarian Dialogue, Febru-

ary 8, 2011, http://www.hdcentre.org/files/Sri%20Lank-%20a%20the%20link%20 between%20women%E2%80%99s%20political%20representation%20and%20 the%20peace%20process%20-%208%20February%202011.pdf.

139. Ibid.
140. Balasingham, *Will to Freedom*, 291.
141. See Bouta et al., *Gender, Conflict, and Development*.
142. "World Bank Civil Society Fund 2011: Theme: Gender and Demographic Transition in Sri Lanka," http://siteresources.worldbank.org/SRILANKAEXTN/Resources/233046-1298393467535/FINAL04042011Theme.pdf.
143. Alison, *Women and Political Violence*, 219.

6

Imagined Peace

AS WE ATTEMPT TO BRING TOGETHER WHAT WE HAVE LEARNED IN THIS RESEARCH and what our findings suggest for women's political activism in situations of violent political conflict, it becomes clear that men and women often have very different approaches to and understandings of issues of war and peace, political activism, and the roles they can—and do—play during conflict and after. While these are broad generalizations, they often unfold in the political sphere, not only during conflict but as countries begin the process of making the transition from war or conflict to peace. It is important to remember that this is a process, and the way it is handled, specifically who is involved and how inclusive the process is, has implications for the society that emerges at the end of the conflict. Just as men and women are affected differently by the social and political changes prior to and during the conflict in light of the gendered social and political realities of their societies, so too peace can mean different things and affect them differently. This is especially true of male combatants and female combatants who had different experiences during the conflict and who need to be integrated into the social structure after the conflict ends but who also have different relationships to their societies and often different problems with reintegration.

We have titled this chapter "Imagined Peace," a phrase that was used by Jane Parpart at a session at the joint meetings of the British International Studies Association and the International Studies Association in Edinburgh, Scotland, in June 2012. Her point, which is very relevant here, suggests that when we envision the situation that will exist after a conflict ends, what does that peace look like? Does that peace reflect a society in which the traditional roles that existed prior to the conflict return? Is that the norm? Do we envision a peace in which men and women alike are active participants in the social and political structure of the nation? Is the expectation that all the wrongs that contributed to the conflict in the first place have been corrected and addressed? And are we imbuing the concept of peace with characteristics that are impossible to attain? Just as men's and women's understandings of and involvement during conflict varies, it can also be said that different expectations about what the society *should* look like after the conflict ends affect the ways men and women approach peacemaking, postconflict transformation, and rebuilding, which in turn makes it more difficult for the state/nation/society to be knitted together after the conflict ends. We have focused this research on the impact of conflict on women and ways women responded to situations of conflict. But if we are really to understand the whole picture, it is equally important to gain some sense of the postconflict situation for the role women play and the impact of postconflict decisions on women as well as men.

As we assert throughout this book, women's political actions during conflict fall along a continuum of activism that runs from working for peace to nonviolent resistance to becoming engaged as combatants and suicide bombers, although these are neither mutually exclusive nor binary categories. Rather, what we tried to stress is the dynamic that women's political activism, and women's decisions to become politically involved in some way, is the result of conscious choice and agency. As the cases we include here and others demonstrate clearly, women engage in nonviolent protests and working for peace, but they also engage in actions that support conflict and war, whether through tacit approval or through explicit action (conducting surveillance, storing weapons, fighting, and blowing themselves up and others with them). And as we saw in the preceding chapters and the specific cases, women have political and personal motives for their decisions.

In addition to reviewing the results of these cases, we conclude with a discussion of women's roles in conflict resolution and the postconflict period, particularly women's roles in peace negotiations and in programs that attempt to reintegrate combatants into society. These issues become especially relevant in light of UN Security Council Resolution 1325 and the prescription—or hope—that women need to be part of the rebuilding that might actually start during a conflict but certainly after the formal conflict ends if the country is truly going to recover and rebuild.[1]

This chapter provides a review of the main findings from the cases in chapters 3, 4, and 5 as we seek to answer the overriding research questions with regard to women's political activism during conflict: Why do some women become involved in political activism? How did they become involved? And so what—why does studying women and women's political activism matter? A final question we start to address in this chapter, which is the logical next step of this research, is what role or roles, if any, did women play in postconflict reconstruction, and what roles *should* they play if peace is to prevail?

Women and Political Activism: Challenging Gender Norms

When a state moves toward intrastate or interstate war, "the social and political structure changes, as do the economic priorities, all of which have a direct effect on women."[2] In making the trade-off between "guns and butter," a trade-off that is necessary for a country to go to war, states invariably remove the social safety net so many women are depending on for their everyday lives.[3] In making that trade-off, women are increasingly vulnerable as well as politically powerless.[4] Thus, the costs of war are borne by women in many ways, even before the war escalates and certainly during the conflict. Similarly, as women work in the community or talk with neighbors, they might be especially sensitive to changes in attitudes or feelings between or among groups that could be the precursor to conflict. And once armed conflict actually breaks out, it is often women who are especially vulnerable to the violence (not only because of the political violence associated with the conflict but because domestic violence is often linked to state violence), and whose lives are disrupted as they make choices to stay and deal with the conflict or flee. The symbolism of women, manifested in how nationalism is gendered, also spurs the group to violence, and women, as wives/mothers/sisters/daughters, feel the effects as they watch the men who are closest to them fight and die for the cause. Women are protected, while men are the protectors.

At the same time, of course, women heed the call for self-determination. Nationalist sentiment and demands for national liberation are made by women as well as men through their political activism, as seen in Sri Lanka and Palestine. This can be seen even in the case of Northern Ireland, where the Catholics/Republicans saw themselves as fighting to defend and protect themselves from what they perceived to be the tyranny of the British state, while the Protestants/Loyalists saw themselves as protecting the sanctity of their state. As this research also demonstrates, women increasingly have become engaged with the political violence of civil conflict, not only by supporting the cause indirectly but by making the decision to pick up arms and become involved directly, especially as the number of men is depleted through death or imprisonment. When they do so decide, as we have seen in all three cases, generally women are "permitted" to take on these roles because male leaders allow them to, sometimes even modifying the dominant cultural or religious norms to make a place for women's participation. We have also seen it is necessary that the community supports and accepts women in these overtly political roles. What this suggests is that allowing women to fight for the nation or the national cause trumps social or cultural gender norms when more bodies are needed.

Consequently, women's political activism challenges gender norms of women's appropriate behavior and roles in society. It is our contention throughout this book that gender norms are challenged in a number of ways when women engage overtly in political activism associated with conflict, although women as peace activists in many ways reinforce the existing gender stereotypes of women as peaceful and nurturing. This argument has been made by any number of feminist authors and is not a terribly new finding.[5] Nonetheless, it is important to restate the point.

Even political activism working for peace is a challenge to gender norms, as women often were drawn into the conflict at the community level or, in some cases, in their homes, moving them from what would otherwise be the private sphere into the public one. Often in spite of their own desire to stay removed from the conflict, as the political violence touched women directly they made a decision to take action of some kind, where working for peace is one form of political activism. In some cases, this might involve working with women from the other side of the conflict to begin to build trust and understanding. However, in other cases, the impact of the conflict might have prompted women to pick up arms and engage in acts of political resistance and violence themselves.

We found ample evidence in all three cases studied here that support the contention that women were involved at the private level, that is, not at the level of big P politics, but at the level of the community or even the family. Thus, that political activism and empowerment of women is another challenge to gender norms, as it removes women from the domain in which they are often assumed to be located (i.e., home and family) and inserts them into the conflict, either working for peace, albeit on a microlevel, or supporting the political violence overtly or as a combatant, both of which are generally considered the public sphere, which is the domain of men.

What this research also points out then is the artificiality of the distinction that is often made between *public* and *private*, since in the case of conflict there is a confluence or overlap between the two rather than a dichotomy. Yet, the move to the public sphere, that is, the active participation of women whether working for peace in nonviolent ways, such as engaging in street protests or discussions within the community or running for political office, is a challenge to gender norms even when the actions are in support of what are assumed to be women's issues.

Finally, women clearly challenge gender norms of behavior when they engage in acts of political resistance and violence by overtly acting in the public sphere and especially by engaging in behavior that is not peaceful or nurturing but violent. This leads us to ask the question, why do women choose the path of supporting violence as a way to achieve their political goals, and specifically what motivates them to do so?

Motivations for Women's Political Activism: Why Women Become Involved

In this research, we looked at three cases in which women were involved across the continuum of political activism. In all three cases we found women played active roles at all points; of the three cases, only Northern Ireland had no examples of women suicide bombers, but in general this was not a tactic that was used during this conflict. The point here is that in three cases of civil conflict we can find examples of women who worked for peace at the community and national levels, women who also supported one side of a conflict, and some who engaged in acts of political violence.

Women, Men, and Peace

Significant differences underscore our understanding of why and how some women choose to work for peace and try to knit the society together, as opposed to those who opt to pick up arms and become combatants. It is clear that once conflict does start, women are often at the forefront of pushing for resolution. Our research has shown that women work for peace at the local and community levels as well as at the national level of politics, although far less so at the national level. In fact, as we have seen in all three cases, women's involvement in working for peace is generally at the community level and tied to issues common to women, such as working together to improve access to health care or education. Here we see women building on their common bonds and location within society at the community level, sometimes drawing on their roles as mothers. But another important finding is that in many of those cases, they do not term their own work as big P politics. Whether this is because women are co-opted, as noted in chapter 2, or simply because it allows them to work within the sphere in which they are most comfortable—and effective—is a matter for speculation. What we have seen in all three of our cases is that once women are engaged at the community level, they remain engaged even after the conflict ends, generally continuing to work for social or political reform that especially benefits women and their communities.

That said, we also found very few examples of women who worked for peace at the community level and then used that experience to seek higher (national) office. This confirms what the literature and our examples show, that is, that women can make a difference and can see the impact of their work at the community level. In general, given the patriarchal structure of most countries, which does not change after a conflict ends, women often opt out of working in that structure in the belief that they can have a greater impact at the community level. Their decision to work at the community level is also a function of the structural barriers to women's participation in formal politics. After the Troubles in Northern Ireland ended, women went back to "doing what [they] do best," that is "trying to change society from the bottom up," according to Jane Morrice.[6] But as she also stated, that does not mean that women should not keep pushing for a "space at the top. Nothing should stop pushing for that."[7] In fact, the implication, which was repeated by others in Northern Ireland, was that unless or until the patriarchal structure of the political parties and the political system changed, women would and could be more effective working *outside* the formal process. Margaret Ward described the political party structure as so patriarchal and male dominated that there is little to encourage women to participate. Rather, women could be more involved and have a greater impact by pursuing other routes, such as serving on public boards and commissions.[8] Thus, despite the myriad roles played by women in Northern Ireland during the Troubles, working for peace and engaging in political violence on both sides, after the conflict ended, the formal political structure was no more welcoming to women.

We did find exceptions to that generalization, however. As stated in chapter 4, following the 2006 Palestinian election 6 of the 74 seats won by Hamas were held by women. Interestingly, all of them came to office at least in part because of their relationship to a male (husband or son) who had been killed or martyred in the conflict with Israel. This put them into a privileged position vis-à-vis other women and gave them access that others did not have, an important finding. Also important is that all of them supported the Palestinian cause of fighting for self-determination, rather than any kind of reconciliation or peace with Israel.

The research also shows that for many women who work for peace, their desire is not just an end to the conflict itself. Rather, they see the issue in far broader terms where postconflict reconstruction becomes a way to address the structural issues that were contributing factors to the conflict in the first place. As we and others have argued, for women peace is much broader than the absence of violence. It is also about social justice and equality for all members of society, which means an end to what Galtung referred to as "structural violence."[9] It is the difference between addressing the social and political structure of society as a way to minimize the possibility of conflict arising in the future versus bringing about a surrender of the rebel group, as we saw in Sri Lanka, or decommissioning the militias, as was the case in Northern Ireland. Or, put another way, it is the difference in approach between addressing the underlying causes of the conflict or the symptoms of it. The need to end the cycle of violence, referred to in chapter 1, becomes all the more important for a society in the postconflict period.

This represents a significant difference in men's and women's approaches that has affected various women's groups that have worked for peace, such as the Northern Ireland Women's Coalition (NIWC), versus the approach taken in official formal negotiations. Here the case of Northern Ireland is illustrative. When the talks that led to the Good Friday Agreement started, and the NIWC was created specifically as a way to give women a voice in the negotiations, the approach that group took was that the talks needed to be inclusive and all major actors needed to be represented. This approach, the inclusion of all parties at the negotiating table, differed from that of their male counterparts. For the NIWC members, the core values of equality, human rights, and inclusion were part and parcel of their approach. There was an inherent difference in understanding regarding *who* should be at the table and why. They also had a different approach to the negotiation process itself. Unlike the men, the women in the NIWC wanted to ensure that all positions and points of view were discussed and considered. In this way, the talks could move forward.[10] This stands in contrast to the approach taken by most of the men at the table, all of whom were political or party leaders and many of whom were directly involved with the violence of the Troubles. The men advocated for decommissioning weapons as an indicator of the end of conflict rather than looking at some of the underlying issues, which is what the women wanted. And the case of Northern Ireland is not unique, as other cases demonstrate.

Just as war and violent conflict affect women differently than men, women bring to the negotiating table different perspectives to negotiations and to ending the conflict. This argues for the important role women play in ending a conflict and in the postconflict disarmament, demobilization, and reintegration (DDR) process, a point that is explored in detail below.

Women, Men, and War
One of the issues we explored in this book was whether women's decisions to engage in acts of resistance and political violence can be a feminist statement, although the women might not label it as such. In some cases, our research supports that assertion. For example, as we saw in chapter 5 in the case of Sri Lanka, there was the perception of a direct relationship between the liberation of the country and the liberation of women, which certainly is a feminist statement. And while the symbolism of women and motherhood can be essential to the rationale for conflict and motivation for fighting, the reality is that women do not benefit directly from the status of being a mother. Thus, especially in patriarchal societies (which most are), women view the act of becoming combatants or even suicide bombers as a statement of equality, where they not only are equal members of the group but are also valorized in a way they would not be otherwise.

The cases explored here, as well as others that we did not study in depth in this research, such as Chechnya, the Kurds in Turkey, Nicaragua, Sierra Leone, and Liberia, to name but a few in which women were engaged as combatants, all support the conjecture that women are as committed as nationalists as men are and that they too will pick up arms and engage in acts of political violence in support of a cause they believe in. In that sense, there is little difference between men and women combatants in their rationale for fighting—and dying—in nationalist wars. Nonetheless, some key differences can be seen in other areas. Even in cases with all-female units or cadres, men were always in the leadership ranks. Women were permitted to play a role only because the men allowed them to. And, in most cases, men permitted this because they needed additional able bodies to fight. In other words, having women combatants would not necessarily be the first choice—it often became the only choice.

In addition, women were engaged as combatants, especially in these patriarchal social structures, often only because the rules or cultural or religious norms were reinterpreted by the men to enable women to play an important role, whether in direct support of the violence or by actually engaging in acts of violence. Sometimes this involved exploiting women's roles as mothers, whether for symbolic purposes or because it was a convenient subterfuge that gave women freedom and access. Women in Northern Ireland hiding explosives in baby carriages, or Dhanu, the Sri Lankan suicide bomber who hid explosives under her clothing so she looked pregnant, are examples of the ways women were uniquely positioned to take on these roles, provided the male leaders allowed them to.

Another major finding is that no clear-cut pattern exists regarding who the *typical* female combatant or suicide bomber is. She might be young or relatively old, well or poorly educated, married or single, a mother or childless. What we have found in our research is that the differences in age, marital status, and motherhood were more a function of the prevailing social and cultural norms than any other single factor. This speaks to the importance of understanding the particular cultural traditions rather than trying to generalize across all cases in order to understand the phenomenon of woman as combatant.

Another question we asked was whether men and women appeared to have different motivations in their actions during civil conflict, especially regarding their decision to become combatants and even suicide bombers. Here too our findings are instructive. In our research, we found fewer differences than the gendered assumptions might lead us to expect.

Robert Pape claims that contrary to popular belief most suicide attackers, male and female, are "rarely socially isolated, clinically insane, or economically destitute individuals, but are most often educated, socially integrated, and highly capable people who could be expected to have a good future."[11] And he makes the important distinction between understanding motives for suicide in general and suicide terrorists in particular. Suicide terrorists' motivations are very different from those who choose "ordinary suicide."[12] Suicide terrorists, he argues, "probably would not commit suicide absent the special circumstances that create these motives."[13] For example, an article in the *Far Eastern Economic Review* on suicide bombers in Sri Lanka features a seventeen-year-old boy named Vasantharaja. When asked why he was prepared to carry out this drastic action, he replied, "This is the most supreme sacrifice I can make. The only way we can get our eelam [homeland] is through arms. That is the only way anybody will listen to us. Even if we die."[14] In documenting other cases of members of the LTTE who chose this course, the article quotes another young man (age twenty-two) who lost three brothers that served with the Tamil Tigers, including one who was a suicide bomber. In discussions with him about his decision to join, his reasons were fairly clear: "'The harassment that I and my parents have suffered at the hands of the army makes me want to take *revenge*.' Mahendren [the young man] claims to have been arrested and kept in custody seven times—without reason and without evidence, he says. 'It is a question of Tamil pride, especially after so much sacrifice'" (italics added).[15]

In many ways, the assumption that women's reasons for acting as combatants are different from men's is in itself a gendered one. It assumes that engaging in acts of violence is inherently masculine and that doing so runs counter to women's proclivities. However, the data do not bear out this assumption. In fact, Bouta et al. claim that the reasons men and women support and participate in political violence are alike: they are forced to join, patriotic, and motivated by religion or ideology. People may have a lack of educational opportunities. People may choose to engage in violence because of economic reasons.[16] So men and women are motivated to join out of some necessity they think will be met if they participate actively as combatants.

One of Jessica Stern's conclusions in her study of religious terrorism is that "developing a single profile of suicide bombers is nearly impossible."[17] Clearly, serving as combatants, and even suicide bombers, is no longer the purview of men only. Rather, as we have seen in these case studies and other examples, women have become more involved in engaging in acts of political violence. Yet, ironically, they also remain largely barred from participating in the process of conflict resolution and peacemaking for reasons that are largely structural. While even fundamentalist Islamic clerics could bend or modify rules to allow women to fight and die for the cause, the dominant patriarchal political structure has been far less willing to allow women's participation in the political process. As a result, women can serve as combatants and even suicide bombers in nationalist struggles, but they cannot actively participate in ending the conflict. This in turn also means they can and do play only a limited role in the DDR processes that follow the end of formal hostilities.

Furthermore, even if they were to be part of the formal political process, the election of female political leaders is no guarantee of peace or the end to conflict. Sri Lanka stands as an example that women can be as nationalistic and militaristic as men; we saw three women politicians take actions to escalate the conflict despite the fact that one of them explicitly came into office proclaiming her desire for peace. While this flies in the face of gendered assumptions about women as peacemakers, it also is consistent with examples of other women leaders—Benazir Bhutto (Pakistan), Indira Gandhi (India), Margaret Thatcher (United Kingdom), Golda Meier (Israel)—who were not only unafraid to lead their countries into conflict but prided themselves on their ability to make such decisions.

This leads us to conclude that while the motivations for men and women who engage in combat might be the same, the structure in which they operate is significantly different. Even the process that gets them to this position of combatant differs significantly in that, in most cases, women had to wait for men to permit them to take on this role. Or, in the case of elected women leaders, they had to prove that they too could be as bellicose as any male leader, thus, as a gender analysis would reveal, reinforcing notions of masculinity being valued more than femininity.

In this research, one of our more interesting findings is that women often give similar responses when asked why they work for peace and why they choose to support a cause. As we showed in chapter 5, women in the LTTE interviewed by Miranda Alison stated that they joined the organization because of the perceived suffering of their community.[18] In comparison, activists who worked for peace in Northern Ireland also pointed to the desire to make their community a better place. Thus, there are some shared components of political activism between women who work for peace and those who become combatants, one of which is the desire to take action that will affect the course of the conflict, but especially will make their communities better. Whether working for peace or becoming combatants at the local or national levels, women have to establish a sense of legitimacy within the political structure, whether the formal political establishment or an informal structure tied to ethnic, religious, or nationalist goals.

Understanding How Women Become Involved

In addition to trying to better understand women's motivations for engaging politically, we asked how women become involved in political activism. Specifically, we were interested in learning *how* they became involved, whether working for peace or as combatants, because learning more about that also provides important information about women's political activism. Our cases show that family ties are especially important as are women's groups, even those that had been created for nonpolitical purposes. Women's groups tend to fall into two broad categories: those created to address issues common to women and those that were auxiliaries to men's groups and were often related to the conflict in some way. The latter, especially, became important recruiting grounds for women who supported the conflict initially, leading to their roles as combatants eventually.

In all three cases that we studied here, the evidence is clear that family ties play an integral role in encouraging women to become engaged politically. Especially in patriarchal societies, the family becomes an important bridge between the private and the public involvement of women. As we saw in the Palestinian case, relationship to a family member who had become a martyr to the cause gave a woman legitimacy as well as an impetus to act. In the case of Northern Ireland, the family was a safe place for the recruitment of women; in addition, it set certain norms and expectations for women's involvement. In Sri Lanka, women were actively recruited into the LTTE, but, more important, each Tamil family was asked to contribute one member.[19] Thus, the family was complicit in the recruitment of women, if not actively involved.

One of the most important ways women became involved, especially in working for peace, was through women's groups that emerged often to address particular social issues that affected women. For example, in Northern Ireland women worked together at the community level to try to address issues such as access to health care, education, domestic violence, and so on that were common to all women, whether Catholic/Republican or Protestant/Loyalist. We see this same pattern in Sri Lanka, where women within each group (Tamil, Sinhalese, and Muslim) initially came together to address social and economic issues pertaining to women. Eventually, what helped women cross the group divide was the recognition of common bonds, as mothers and as advocates for particular causes, such as the fate of servicemen who were missing in action. In that case, the women bonded as mothers and because of the common sense of loss. This helped build trust that contributed to women's desire to continue to work across the divide at the community level.

But we also see these women's groups, which might have started as a way to peacefully protest existing conditions, grow into ways to recruit and encourage women to take on more active roles, even violent ones. For example, in Sri Lanka, Tamil women's peaceful protests against the Sinhalese government mobilized women who eventually became part of the more militant and violent LTTE.[20] Thus, we cannot assume that a women's group that was created to work for social issues or for a cause common to all women would remain peaceful; rather, it can ultimately prove to be a significant recruiting ground for women combatants.

In all three cases, we also see the emergence of women's groups as auxiliaries to the major men's groups, whether political parties (as in Northern Ireland and Palestine) or militia/rebel groups (as with Sri Lanka). It was the women who ultimately pushed for more and greater roles in the struggles. This took persuading the male leaders to allow them to do so, but once the men were persuaded, these men trained and worked with the women, who as combatants proved to be a formidable force.

Finally, in Sri Lanka especially, we see the recruitment of women into the LTTE by other women for expressly feminist reasons, especially the promise of an improved role and situation for women. As an organization that was overtly feminist in its perspective, the LTTE offered Tamil women opportunities they saw as missing in Sri Lankan society as a whole.

From these cases we can conclude there are many paths to the recruitment of women. What this means is that ultimately women have a number of choices, starting with whether to become politically active and then on what course of action to take.

So What?

The third question we asked at the outset of this book was why does studying women and women's political activism matter? The answer to that question should be apparent: it matters because women *are* actively involved in conflict, from working for peace to engaging in acts of resistance and political violence, so if we are ever to really understand conflict, we must understand women's roles, motivations, and how they become involved. Since so much of the study of international relations is the study of war and conflict, omitting women would mean an incomplete picture of any war and conflict. Similarly, without including women in the study of peace and postconflict transitions, we are eliminating an important part of the process. Using a gender analysis to explore and analyze people's decisions to engage in political activism along the continuum reveals new ways of understanding war and peace, and how war and peace are gendered, and the gendered discourses that are present.

The End of War? Next Steps

We have asked and answered our three central research questions using our cases but also drawing on other examples as appropriate. We have also raised another question that grows from the other three and from the research, specifically, what role or roles, if any, did women play in postconflict reconstruction, and what roles should they play if peace is to prevail? While we cannot presume to answer that question now—that is a topic for further research—we think it should be raised in the context of this work.

Ample evidence suggests that society will benefit from the inclusion of women in all aspects of the peace process but that conversely women are often barred from participating for a host of reasons. Here we need to start with a very basic question: when is war actually over? As Ann Jones astutely remarks, "Long after treaties are signed, soldiers live with injuries, flashbacks, anguish, and remorse about things they saw and did during the war. Women live with consequences of what was done to them."[21] Violence against women continues and often gets worse; there is a direct correlation between an increase in domestic violence and conflict, a pattern that does not end once the conflict officially ends. And that is only one of a list of issues that a society—and women—face in dealing with the transition from conflict to peace. This also tells us much about how we need to redefine what we mean by security and peace when the formal hostilities end.

Cahn, Haynes, and Ní Aoláin list some of the pressures on societies that are trying to recover from conflict: displaced people, deterioration of schools, roads, health clinics, businesses, and so forth, all of which have to be rebuilt and strengthened.[22] They also note the ways "the transformation of a country from 'conflicted' to 'peaceful' is partial and exclusionary" for women.[23] They continue, "The term 'peaceful transition' is highly contested for women, as it assumes a linear movement from violence to non-violence, which is rarely the case for women in post-conflict societies."[24] And they provide an interesting warning call about postconflict reconstruction and transformation: "A post-conflict process will fail if it focuses only on separating the warring parties, on restoring earlier institutions, or even if only on rule of law reform along western democratic lines allied with market liberalization. Instead, the transition process must somehow manage the impact of social injustices that often helped cause or exacerbate the conflict, and the high levels of violence that may accompany the end of the 'official' war."[25]

Additionally, women feel the social disruptions that come from the conflict, having had to jump in and take over while the men were fighting, incarcerated, or after their deaths. After the conflict ends, they pay the price in any number of ways, such as an increase in domestic violence and assumptions that they would return to their traditional gender roles.

Thus, the difference in approach to ending the conflict and subsequent rebuilding suggests that women are deeply affected but also will often be omitted from the discussions, and then once decisions are made, they are often made by the men involved with the negotiations with little regard for women's priorities or needs. According to Donald Steinberg, deputy administrator of USAID, what this means is that "we face real challenges in how to translate our growing awareness and activism into concrete improvements on the ground, both by prioritizing these issues in the corridors of power and by assuring the adoption and implementation of effective programs and projects with rapid impact."[26] The situation for women is further complicated when they served as combatants during the conflict, as this strategy of political activism challenges gender norms about women's roles and behavior. The international community's slow and insufficient response to the role of women as combatants after the conflict ends demonstrates how this activism challenges gender norms, which is addressed in the next section.

UN Resolutions, DDR, and Women's Participation in the Peace Process

When the conflict is near its end or has ended, the hard work of peace negotiations, postconflict reconstruction, and peace building begins. As part of those efforts, the DDR of former combatants is vital. As a document from the United Nations makes clear, "DDR activities are crucial components of both the initial stabilization of war-torn societies as well as their long-term development. DDR must be integrated into the entire peace process from the peace negotiations through peacekeeping and follow-on peacebuilding activities."[27]

In this document, *disarmament* is defined as "the collection, documentation, control and disposal of small arms, ammunition, explosives and light and heavy weapons of combatants and often also of the civilian population." *Demobilization* refers to "the formal and controlled discharge of active combatants from armed forces or other armed groups." *Reinsertion* refers to "the assistance offered to ex-combatants during demobilization but prior to the longer-term process of reintegration." In essence, reinsertion is seen as "a form of transitional assistance to help cover the basic needs of ex-combatants and their families," including food, shelter, health services, training, and safety allowances. Finally, *reintegration* is defined as "the process by which ex-combatants acquire civilian status and gain sustainable employment and income."[28] A longer-term program, reintegration is considered to be "a social and economic process with an open timeframe, primarily taking place in communities at the local level."[29]

As defined by the United Nations, combatants include individuals who actually carried arms as well as those in supporting roles (such as cooks, sex slaves, and "war wives").[30] This definition includes women, as well as men, as individuals who meet the criteria for DDR assistance. In addition, the United Nations has specifically focused on gender in DDR programs, namely through "gender-aware interventions" and "female-specific actions" at all stages of the DDR process.[31] All DDR programs and policies are also to incorporate gender mainstreaming, as reflected in the guidelines of the United Nations' Integrated Disarmament, Demobilization and Reintegration Standards.[32]

On October 31, 2000, Resolution 1325 on Women, Peace and Security was adopted by the UN Security Council. Nongovernmental organizations and a number of sympathetic officials were instrumental in getting the Security Council resolution passed. The resolution marked an important milestone in the international community's recognition of the impact of war and conflict on women. In addition, the resolution recognized the contributions that women can make in the processes of conflict resolution, peace negotiations, and peace building. As Elisabeth Porter remarks, this was the first time the Security Council "discussed women in their own right in relation to peace and security. It is also the first time that the Security Council officially endorsed civil society groups, especially women in the peace process."[33] The document itself makes clear "the important role of women in the prevention and resolution of conflicts and in peace-building, . . . and the need to increase their role in decision-making with regard to conflict prevention and resolution."[34]

Although the resolution is considered to be a significant first step forward for women, the reality is otherwise. Implementation has proven to be far more problematic, according to Margaret Ward: "While Resolution 1325 provides for women's voices to be heard, it does not emphasize their role as agents of social change but merely reiterates the importance of their participation for the maintenance of peace and security. Therefore, while women are being included within organizations, they remain mere token presences. Increasingly, they are making it plain that much more will be necessary before women can effect meaningful change in society."[35]

In looking at this and other similar international resolutions, what seems to be ignored or overlooked is the fact that "many women are already involved in community groups. Their political skills are not recognized, and they are not harnessed in more formal political arenas."[36] While war is often thought of as the domain of men, and if peace is a woman's issue, then why are women not included more actively in working for peace at the formal level? In fact, women bring skills they have cultivated and developed from their work at the community and grassroots levels that can be of importance in the postconflict peace talks and the peace building that ensues after the fighting is over. However, those experiences are often not valued by the men who generally oversee the negotiation process and therefore downplay or diminish the role women could play, even if they were to be permitted to be included at all.

In addition to recognizing the importance of women's participation in the peace process and postconflict reconstruction, Resolution 1325 also explicitly acknowledges the need to include women and girls in DDR programs. In a study issued by the UN secretary-general in 2002, the importance of disarmament for women's security was highlighted: "Such disarmament activities are of great importance to women because of heightened threats to their personal security with the proliferation of weapons in post-conflict situations. For this reason, women and girls are actively involved in weapons collection programmes."[37] The study noted the role that women's groups and women in the community (civil society) play in terms of providing information about numbers of weapons and locations of weapons caches. Examples of countries where women played positive roles in disarmament efforts include Afghanistan, Albania, Democratic Republic of Congo, and Liberia.[38] With regard to demobilization, because women's and girls' roles as combatants or in supportive roles are not often considered, they are discriminated against throughout the process of demobilization. "Incentive programs have routinely favoured men and marginalized or excluded women and girls. At times, this has resulted in women and girls having few economic choices except to stay with their captors who have received money, material goods and training. There are often barriers to women and girls being granted training and resettlement allowances."[39]

The challenges women and girls face in the postconflict stage are significant. Since the UN secretary-general's report was published a decade ago, not much has changed in terms of women's successful participation in DDR programs. Scholars have documented the ways DDR programs fall short for women and girls.[40] For example, in the case of East Timor, more than ten thousand male ex-combatants registered for DDR programs. Female ex-combatants were not included.[41] In Sierra Leone, most girls were not demobilized through DDR programs as a result "of a gender-discriminatory framework which saw girls and women only as 'sex slaves', 'wives', and 'camp followers'." Susan McKay argues that this gender-discriminatory framework meant that women and girls were not perceived "as appropriate recipients of DDR benefits, such as skills training or schooling."[42] The vast majority of girls knew nothing about DDR programs. When the fighting ended, they returned home or "were taken in by friends, relatives, or helpful adults."[43]

In terms of actual financial assistance, while women are recognized as combatants and supporters of conflict, the criteria for the amount of financial benefit from DDR is related to rank. Because most women were of lower rank in the fighting forces than the men, they end up with fewer benefits. Further causing problems for women's participation in DDR programs is the decision of many women (and girls) not to enroll because of the social stigma they may face in their communities from having been a combatant or supporter of the conflict. As a result, women usually return to their communities without any involvement in DDR programs. This demonstrates how entrenched gender social norms remain in postconflict societies.[44] The long-term negative effects of such exclusion and entrenched gender norms on peace and stability are significant.

Yet, the inclusion of women significantly alters the dynamics of the peace process itself, as well as in preparing for the society that will follow. Porter also makes clear that the inclusion of women in peace negotiations matters for the "democratic legitimacy of the process."[45] Women's participation is necessary because the peace process is then "more responsive to the priorities of all affected citizens."[46] The challenge for women, and also the men involved, is how to include women and ensure their voices will be heard and their ideas taken seriously.

The challenge to gender norms is evident in the larger peace-building process as well as to DDR programs specifically. Women are not encouraged to participate, their voices are not heard (although they are speaking), and they are not consulted. Rather, prevailing gender norms of behavior, that women should remain in the private sphere of the home, hinders women's full equality in society, particularly when the conflict ends. Women are expected to fulfill their traditional roles once the fighting ends, even if they were fighters themselves.[47]

The future for long-term peace and stability is threatened when women do not have a seat at the negotiating table, do not have a voice about how the postconflict society should be structured, and do not have a role in the government. Invariably, gender equality and changing gender norms can only come about when expectations about women's and men's behavior and roles in society change.[48]

Lessons from the Cases

The lessons from the cases highlighted in this volume confirm the fact that women's participation in the formal peace process is far from the norm. In the Palestinian case, for example, despite the fact that the International Women's Commission for a Just and Sustainable Israeli-Palestinian Peace was formed specifically to provide input into the peace process, women's voices were not included. Although the literature supports the need for women to be included in the conflict resolution, peacemaking, and peace-building processes, the fact of the matter is that it remains within the purview of the political leaders to determine who is included, and that generally means the exclusion of women.

So what are the lessons, not only from these cases but from the countless others in which there is a transition from war to peace (or postconflict), especially for women, outside of stressing the obvious that women need to be involved at all stages of the peacemaking/peacekeeping/peace-building processes? It seems clear that investing in women at the community level will pay off, and there are lessons to support that conclusion and the contention that true peace will never occur unless, or until, the structural factors that contributed to war at all are changed or at least addressed, and while it would be ideal should this happen at the national level, working at the community or local levels provides an important starting point.

Those in communities know their own needs best. After the signing of the Good Friday Agreement and subsequent weapons decommissioning, when people in Northern Ireland spoke of how they saw the members of the paramilitaries turn into gangs involved with drugs and money laundering, they knew what they were speaking about since they saw these transitions firsthand. The perception was that the paramilitary units went from defending their communities, which brought with it a certain level of support, to undermining them. As a result, some of these community-based activists also noted an outpouring of anger toward those groups, with the communities turning against them. One woman also said that as a result more women started to get involved in support of their communities.[49]

And we can see the same pattern repeated in other places as paramilitary or rebel groups that had been militarized and often glorified during a conflict try to retain their status even after a conflict ends. However, after a conflict, those groups no longer get the support they had during the conflict, as they are seen as morphing from community saviors to criminals or thugs in the eyes of the community. This finding holds key implications for policymakers.

Women, children, and the elderly suffer during situations of conflict and have potentially the most to gain once the conflict ends and the situation stabilizes. They also have the greatest understanding of what their own needs are. Therefore, even if they are not included in the peace negotiations directly, they need to be consulted about the rebuilding process. Furthermore, because much of women's political activism is at the community level, providing funding for groups that work at that level could help stabilize the postconflict situation. But this in turn will require learning where the funding is needed most. Funding for education programs that enable women to take an active role in the political process would seem to be one fruitful avenue.

But it is important to address the social issues that not only contributed to the conflict in the first place but that need to be addressed if not resolved if the society is to continue to make its transition from conflict to peace. For example, given the correlation between political violence and domestic violence, it will be important to make sure there is funding for groups that work with women who have been victims of such violence. This also suggests the need to work with men to ensure their behavior will change, something that will be far more difficult but would play a major role in any imagined peace.

A way to ensure a safe space for the integration of former combatants, men and women, is also necessary, something that has been especially difficult for women, many of whom do not want to or cannot admit their roles in political violence. Unless they can step forward and acknowledge their roles, then their reintegration cannot be addressed. Similarly, it will be necessary to identify the skills that will enable those women to become self-sufficient and contributing members of society. If one of the reasons women give for participating in acts of political violence was because they saw few options, then those options will have to be made available to them. These might include access to education, job or work skills, and help in job placements.

One of the lessons of the cases, though, is that it is important not only to identify these issues but, ideally, to begin to address them before the conflict starts or at the very least during the conflict if at all possible. Waiting until after the conflict ends might be too late, as the patterns are already engrained. The lessons of ending the conflict successfully, therefore, are preparing for peace even while the conflict is still under way.

Finally, another lesson from the cases is the importance of working with women and encouraging them to participate actively within the formal political structure and not just through the informal process. Only by doing so will women's voices really be heard.

Conclusion

We asked three important questions in this research and then added a fourth, which grew from our findings. We began by asking why some women get involved in political activism; that is, what motivates them. By studying three cases and looking more generally at an array of others, we can conclude that there is no one answer to this question. Women choose to engage in some form of political activism for a range of reasons, as do men, and often the motivations for men's and women's political activism are the same: personal and political. Clearly, there were cases in which women chose to work for peace as mothers. Women also organized on the basis of feminist activism. Rather than essentializing any conclusion (i.e., women as peacemakers, nurturers, etc.), we conclude that the difference between women's and men's political activism is primarily about access and opportunity. Because of their expected gender roles in the community, women often have more access to other women. Especially in more patriarchal societies, those opportunities generally are confined to women who can then take advantage of them to work for peace across communities, drawing on commonalities but also recognizing that women are not a monolithic group—they are separated by class, ethnicity, race, and so forth—the intersectionality that feminist security theorists remind us to remember. Women do not speak with one voice.

The second question that we asked was how women become involved in political activism. Here our cases support the contention that women become involved through a variety of means, primarily close friends and family, but often because of other women. Often joining a women's organization that is auxiliary, and therefore secondary, to men's organizations becomes a catalyst for more and greater political activism.

Our third research question asked why studying women's political activism matters. Intrastate conflicts continue in the international system today, and while the reporting and analysis of these conflicts often omit women, women are not invisible in times of conflict or in times of peace. Moreover, gender norms and gender discourses matter in studying conflicts and peace. And women's political activism tells us much about those norms and discourses, as well as our understanding of violence and security. Women are political actors, they express their agency, and they are affected by—and have an impact on—war and peace.

We then asked a final question: What is the logical next step of this research? What role or roles, if any, did women play in postconflict reconstruction, and what roles *should* they play if peace is to prevail?

By answering this question we can get a more complete picture or understanding of conflict and conflict resolution. We provide the most cursory overview here, but clearly, this is a question that needs further research. This research provides important clues toward understanding women's political activism in situations of conflict. But it is only a starting point. As stated throughout this book, far more research is to be done before we can get a more complete picture and understanding of women's political activism.

Notes

1. United Nations Security Council, Resolution 1325, October 31, 2000, http://www.un.org/events/res_1325e.pdf.
2. Kaufman and Williams, *Women and War*, 2–3.
3. Ibid., 3.
4. Ibid.
5. See, for example, Tickner, *Gendering World Politics*; Peterson and Runyan, *Global Gender Issues*; and Kaufman and Williams, *Women and War*.
6. Jane Morrice, interview by Joyce Kaufman, Belfast, Northern Ireland, November 21, 2007.
7. Ibid.
8. Ward, interview.
9. Galtung, "Violence, Peace and Peace Research," 171.
10. Kaufman and Williams, *Women and War*, 109.
11. Pape, *Dying to Win*, 200.
12. See Pape, "Altruisum and Terrorism," in *Dying to Win*, 178–98.
13. Ibid., 172.
14. Joshi, "Sri Lanka: Suicide Bombers."
15. Ibid.
16. Bouta et. al., *Gender, Conflict, and Development*, 12.
17. Jessica Stern, *Terror in the Name of God: Why Religious Militants Kill* (New York: HarperCollins, 2003), 51.
18. Alison, "Cogs in the Wheel?" 41.
19. Ibid., 39.
20. Balasingham, *Women Fighters*.
21. Ann Jones, *War Is Not Over When It's Over: Women Speak Out from the Ruins of War* (New York: Metropolitan Books, 2010), 19.
22. Naomi Cahn, Dina Haynes, and Fionnuala Ní Aoláin, "Returning Home: Women in Post-Conflict Societies," *Baltimore Law Review 39*, 339, http://law.ubalt.edu/downloads/law_downloads/Cahn_After_First_EIC_Edit%5B1%5D1.pdf.
23. Ibid.

24. Ibid.

25. Ibid., 345.

26. Donald Steinberg, "Women and War: An Agenda for Action," in *Women and War: Power and Protection in the 21st Century*, eds. Kathleen Kuehnast, Chantal de Jonge Oudraat, and Helga Hernes (Washington, DC: United States Institute of Peace Press, 2011), 118.

27. "United Nations Peacekeeping: Disarmament, Demobilization and Reintegration," accessed March 7, 2011, http://www.un.org/en/peacekeeping/issues/ddr.shtml.

28. Ibid.

29. "What Is DDR?" United Nations Disarmament, Demobilization and Reintegration Resource Centre, accessed March 7, 2011, http://www.unddr.org/whatisddr.php.

30. Ibid.

31. Ibid.

32. Ibid. For a critique of gender mainstreaming, see Ní Aoláin et al., *On the Frontlines*, 10–15.

33. Elisabeth Porter, "Women, Political Decision-Making, and Peace-Building," *Global Change, Peace & Security* 15, no. 3 (October 2003), 253.

34. See the full text at United Nations Security Council Resolution 1325.

35. Margaret Ward, "Gender, Citizenship and the Future of the Northern Ireland Peace Process," *Irish Feminist Studies* 41, no. 1–2 (Spring/Summer 2006): 15.

36. Porter, "Women, Political Decision-Making, and Peace-Building," 255.

37. United Nations, "Women, Peace and Security," 2002, 129, http://www.un.org/womenwatch/daw/public/eWPS.pdf.

38. Ibid.

39. Ibid., 132–33.

40. See, for example, Mark Knight and Aplasian Ozerdem, "Guns, Camps and Cash: Disarmament, Demobilization and Reinsertion of Former Combatants in Transitions from War to Peace," *Journal of Peace Research* 41, no. 4 (July 2004): 499–516; Elaine Zuckerman and Marcia Greenberg, "The Gender Dimensions of Post-Conflict Reconstruction: An Analytical Framework for Policymakers," *Gender and Development* 12, no. 3 (November 2004): 70–82; Susan McKay, "Reconstructing Fragile Lives: Girls' Social Reintegration in Northern Uganda and Sierra Leone," *Gender and Development* 12, no. 3 (November 2004): 19–30; and Valerie Norville, "The Role of Women in Global Security," United States Institute of Peace Special Report 264 (January 2011), http://www.usip.org.

41. Zuckerman and Greenberg, "Gender Dimensions," 75.

42. McKay, "Reconstructing Fragile Lives," 23.

43. Ibid.

44. Katrin Planta, "The 'X' Factor," International Relations and Security Network, October 12, 2010, http://www.isn.ethz.ch/isn/Security-Watch/Articles/Detail/?id=122420.

45. Porter, "Women, Political Decision-Making," 251.

46. Ibid.

47. Knight and Ozerdem, "Guns, Camps and Cash," 503.

48. See Woodbury for a discussion on how reconstructing "masculine identities that are not tied to violence, but focused on more traditional ideas of males as providers of households and community leaders, has the potential to lay the foundation for more effective transitions to peaceful and flourishing post-conflict states." Laura Woodbury, "Reconstructing Gender Identity for Child Combatants in Post-Conflict African Societies," *Journal of International Service* 20, no. 1 (Spring 2011): 33.

49. Discussion with "Audrey," "Rab," and "Claire." Last names cannot be used because of the sensitivity of what these individuals were saying and the fact that they were making these observations. These are not politicians or activists, but average people living and working in the community. Their comments were made with the promise that their real full names would not be used. Belfast, November 2007.

Bibliography

"About CWP." Coalition of Women for Peace. Accessed January 30, 2010. http://www.coalitionofwomen.org/?page_id=340&lang=en.
"About Us: The Palestinian Initiative for the Promotion of Global Dialogue and Democracy: MIFTAH." 2010. http://www.miftah.org/AboutUs.cfm.
"About Women in Black." Women in Black. Accessed December 27, 2011. http://www.womeninblack.org/en/about.
Ackerly, Brooke A., Maria Stern, and Jaqui True, eds. *Feminist Methodologies for International Relations*. Cambridge: Cambridge University Press, 2006.
Agnes, Flavia. "Transgressing Boundaries of Gender and Identity." *Economic and Political Weekly* 37, no. 36 (2002): 3695–98.
Ahall, Linda, and Laura J. Shepherd, eds. *Gender, Agency and Political Violence*. Basingstoke, UK: Palgrave Macmillan, 2012.
Aharoni, Sarai. "Gender and 'Peace Work': An Unofficial History of Israeli-Palestinian Negotiations." *Politics & Gender* 7, no. 3 (2011): 391–416.
Alison, Miranda. "Cogs in the Wheel? Women in the Liberation Tigers of Tamil Eelam." *Civil Wars* 6, no. 4 (Winter 2003): 37–54.
———. "'In the War Front We Never Think That We Are Women': Women, Gender, and the Liberation Tamil Tigers of Eelam." In *Women, Gender, and Terrorism*, edited by Laura Sjoberg and Caron E. Gentry, 131–55. Athens: University of Georgia Press, 2011.
———. *Women and Political Violence: Female Combatants in Ethno-National Conflict*. New York: Routledge, 2009.
———. "Women as Agents of Political Violence: Gendering Security." *Security Dialogue* 35, no. 4 (December 2004): 447–63.

Anderlini, Sanam Naraghi. "Translating Global Agreement into National and Local Commitments." In *Women and War: Power and Protection in the 21st Century*, edited by Kathleen Kuehnast, Chantal de Jonge Oudraat, and Helga Hernes, 19–36. Washington, DC: USIP Press, 2011.

———. *Women Building Peace: What They Do, Why It Matters*. Boulder, CO: Lynne Rienner, 2007.

Anthias, Floya, and Nira Yuval-Davis. "Introduction." In *Woman-Nation-State*, edited by Nira Yuval-Davis and Floya Anthias, 1–15. London: Macmillan, 1989.

———. *Racialized Boundaries: Race, Nation, Gender, Colour and Class and the Anti-Racist Struggle*. London: Routledge, 1992.

Aretxaga, Begona. *Shattering Silence: Women, Nationalism, and Political Subjectivity in Northern Ireland*. Princeton, NJ: Princeton University Press, 1997.

Bailey, Alison. "Mothering, Diversity, and Peace Politics." *Hypatia* 9, no. 2 (Spring 1994): 188–98.

Balasingham, Adele. *The Will to Freedom: An Inside View of Tamil Resistance*. Mitcham, England: Fairmax, 2001.

———. *Women Fighters of Liberation Tigers*. Thasan Printers, 1993. http://www.tamilnation.co/books/Eelam/adeleann.htm.

Bandarage, Asoka. *The Separatist Conflict in Sri Lanka: Terrorism, Ethnicity, Political Economy*. Bloomington, IN: iUniverse, 2009.

Barnes, Ciaran. "Battered and Dumped in Stockman's Lane, Murder Still Has Power to Shock." July 7, 2008. http://saoirse32.blogsome.com/2008/07/24/p11157/.

"Battered to Death in UDA Club: Allegation." *Belfast Telegraph*. August 7, 1974.

Beckwith, Karen. "Beyond Compare? Women's Movements in Comparative Perspective." *European Journal of Political Research* 37, no. 4 (2000): 431–68.

———. "The Comparative Politics of Women's Movements." *Perspectives on Politics* 3, no. 3 (September 2005): 583–96.

Berko, Anat, and Edna Eerez. "Gender, Palestinian Women, and Terrorism: Women's Liberation or Oppression?" *Studies in Conflict & Terrorism* 30, no. 6 (June 2007): 493–519.

Beyler, Clara. "Messengers of Death—Female Suicide Bombers." Herzliya, Israel: International Institute for Counter-Terrorism, 2003.

Blanchard, Eric M. "Gender, International Relations, and the Development of Feminist Security Theory." *Signs* 28, no. 4 (Summer 2003): 1289–1312.

Blood, Baroness May. *Watch My Lips, I'm Speaking*. Dublin: Gill and Macmillan, 2007.

Bloom, Mia. *Dying to Kill: The Allure of Suicide Terror*. New York: Columbia University Press, 2007.

———. "Mother. Daughter. Sister. Bomber." *Bulletin of the Atomic Scientists* 61, no. 6 (November/December 2005): 54–62.

Bose, Sumantra. *Contested Lands: Israel-Palestine, Kashmir, Bosnia, Cyprus and Sri Lanka.* Cambridge, MA: Harvard University Press, 2007.

Bouta, Tsjeard, Georg Frerks, and Ian Bannon. *Gender, Conflict, and Development.* Washington, DC: World Bank, 2005.

Brunner, Claudia. "Female Suicide Bombers—Male Suicide Bombings? Looking for Gender in Reporting the Suicide Bombings of the Israeli-Palestinian Conflict." *Global Society* 19, no. 1 (January 2005): 29–48.

Cahn, Naomi, Dina Haynes, and Fionnuala Ní Aoláin. "Returning Home: Women in Post-Conflict Societies." *Baltimore Law Review* 39 (May 2010): 339–69. http://law.ubalt.edu/downloads/law_downloads/Cahn_After_First_EIC_Edit%5B1%5D1.pdf.

CBS News. "Hamas TV Pictures Promotes Female Suicide Bombers Squad." January 14, 2009. http://www.cbsnews.com/8301-502684_162-4722620-502684.html.

Central Intelligence Agency. "Introduction: West Bank." *World Factbook.* August 24, 2012. https://www.cia.gov/library/publications/the-world-factbook/geos/we.html.

Central Intelligence Agency. "Sri Lanka." *World Factbook.* Last modified November 14, 2012. https://www.cia.gov/library/publications/the-world-factbook/geos/ce.html.

Cleveland, William. *A History of the Modern Middle East*, 2nd ed. Boulder, CO: Westview Press, 2000.

Cockburn, Cynthia. *Antimilitarism: Political and Gender Dynamics of Peace Movements.* Basingstoke, UK: Palgrave Macmillan, 2012.

———. *From Where We Stand: War, Women's Activism and Feminist Analysis.* London: Zed Books, 2007.

———. "Gender Relations as Causal in Militarization and War." *International Feminist Journal of Politics* 12, no. 2 (June 2010): 139–57.

———. *The Space between Us: Negotiating Gender and Nationalist Identities in Conflict.* London: Zed Books, 1998.

Cohn, Carol. "'Feminist Security Studies': Toward a Reflexive Practice." *Politics & Gender* 7, no. 4 (2011): 581–86.

Confortini, Catia. "Feminist Critical Methodology, Decolonization and the Women's International League for Peace and Freedom (WILPF), 1945–75." *International Feminist Journal of Politics* 13, no. 3 (September 2011): 349–70.

———. "Galtung, Violence, and Gender: The Case for a Peace Studies/Feminism Alliance." *Peace and Change* 31, no. 3 (July 2006): 333–67.

Cunningham, Karla J. "The Evolving Participation of Muslim Women in Palestine, Chechnya, and the Global Jihadi Movement." In *Female Terrorism and Militancy: Agency, Utility, and Organization*, edited by Cindy D. Ness, 84–99. New York: Routledge, 2008.

Cuomo, Chris J. "War Is Not Just an Event: Reflections on the Significance of Everyday Violence." *Hypatia* 11, no. 4 (Fall 1996): 30–45.

Daily Mail. "IRA Send in the Girl Bombers." September 2, 1976.
Daily Mirror. "The Deadly Secret of Mum-to-Be." July 7, 1973.
Daily Mirror. "Pantie Bombers Blow Up Café." January 8, 1977.
Daily Telegraph. "Ten Women Held in Dawn Raids." April 13, 1974.
David, Hugh. "Threat by New Provo Leader." *Daily Telegraph.* January 8, 1973.
Davis, Jessica. "Women and Radical Islamic Terrorism: Planners, Perpetrators, Patrons?" Canadian Institute of Strategic Studies, Strategic Datalink #136. May 2006. http://www.opencanada.org/wp-content/uploads/2011/05/SD-136-Davis.pdf.
de Alwis, Malathi. "Gender, Politics and the 'Respectable Lady.'" In *Unmaking the Nation: The Politics of Identity & History in Modern Sri Lanka*, edited by Pradeep Jeganathan and Qadri Ismail, 138–56. New York: South Focus Press, 1995.
Disney, Jennifer Leigh. *Women's Activism and Feminist Agency in Mozambique and Nicaragua.* Philadelphia, PA: Temple University Press, 2008.
Dudouet, Veronique. *Nonviolent Resistance and Conflict Transformation in Power Asymmetries.* Berlin: Berghof Research Center for Constructive Conflict Management, 2008. http://www.berghof-handbook.net/documents/publications/dudouet_handbook.pdf.
Eager, Paige Whaley. *From Freedom Fighters to Terrorists: Women and Political Violence.* Burlington, VT: Ashgate, 2008.
Eduards, Maud L. "Women's Agency and Collective Action." *Women's Studies International Forum* 17, no. 2–3 (1994): 181–86.
Emmett, Ayala. *Our Sisters' Promised Land: Women, Politics, and Israeli-Palestinian Coexistence.* Ann Arbor: University of Michigan Press, 2003.
"Empowerment of Palestinian Women Leadership." MIFTAH's Ninth Annual Report (2008). http://www.miftah.org/Mact/MiftahActivityReport2007.pdf.
Enloe, Cynthia. *Bananas, Beaches and Bases: Making Feminist Sense of International Relations.* Berkeley: University of California Press, 1989.
Farr, Vanessa. "UNSCR 1325 and Women's Peace Activism in the Occupied Palestinian Territory." *International Feminist Journal of Politics* 13, no. 4 (December 2011): 539–56.
Fearon, Kate. *Women's Work: The Story of the Northern Ireland Women's Coalition.* Belfast: Blackstaff Press, 1999.
Fearon, Kate, and Monica McWilliams. "Swimming against the Mainstream: The Northern Ireland Women's Coalition." In *Gender, Democracy and Inclusion in Northern Ireland*, edited by Carmel Roulston and Celia Davies, 117–37. New York: Palgrave, 2000.
Fernea, Elizabeth Warnock. *In Search of Islamic Feminism.* New York: Anchor Books, 1998.
Galtung, Johann. "Violence, Peace and Peace Research." *Journal of Peace Research* 6, no. 3 (1969): 167–91.

Gaskell, Jane. "The Frightening Cult of the Violent Women." *Daily Mail*, March 26, 1973.
Gentry, Caron E. "The Committed Revolutionary: Reflections on a Conversation with Leila Khaled." In *Women, Gender and Terrorism*, edited by Laura Sjoberg and Caron E. Gentry, 120–30. Athens: University of Georgia Press, 2011.
———. "Twisted Maternalism: From Peace to Violence." *International Feminist Journal of Politics* 11, no. 2 (June 2009): 235–52.
Giles, Wenona, and Jennifer Hyndman, eds. *Sites of Violence: Gender and Conflict Zones*. Berkeley: University of California Press, 2004.
Giles, Wenona, Malathu de Alwais, Edith Klein, and Neluka Silva, eds. *Feminists Under Fire: Exchanges across War Zones*. Toronto, Canada: Between the Lines, 2003.
Goldstein, Joshua S. *War and Gender*. Cambridge: Cambridge University Press, 2001.
Greig, Stuart. "Women Join the Snipers and Bombers." *Daily Mail*. September 24, 1973.
Grylls, James. "New Jail for Women." *Daily Mail*, December 7, 1974.
Gunawardena, Arjuna. "Female Black Tigers: A Different Breed of Cat?" In *Female Suicide Bombers: Dying for Equality?* edited by Yoram Schweitzer, 81–90. Tel Aviv: Jaffee Center for Strategic Studies, Tel Aviv University, 2006. http://www.e-prism.org/images/memo84_Female_suicide_bombers_-_Jaffee_Center_-_Aug06.pdf.
Hamilton, Carrie. "The Gender Politics of Political Violence: Women Armed Activists in ETA." *Feminist Review* 86 (2007): 132–48.
Hasso, Frances S. "Discursive and Political Deployments by/of the 2002 Palestinian Women Suicide Bombers/Martyrs." *Feminist Review* 81 (2005): 23–51.
———. "The 'Women's Front': Nationalism, Feminism, and Modernity in Palestine." *Gender & Society* 12, no. 4 (August 1998): 441–65.
Helms, Elissa. "Gender Essentialisms and Women's Activism in Post-War Bosnia-Herzegovina." In *Feminists under Fire: Exchanges across War Zones*, edited by Wenona Giles, Malathi de Alwis, Edith Klein, and Neluka Silva. With the assistance of Maja Korac, Djurdja Knezevic, and Zarana Papic, 181–93. Toronto: Between the Lines, 2003.
"History." Jerusalem Center for Women. 2012. http://www.j-c-w.org/index.php?option=com_content&task=view&id=22&Itemid=9.
Hoggart, Simon. "Woman Nationalist Is New Leader of Provisional Sinn Fein." *Guardian*. January 8, 1973.
Hudson, Valerie M. "But Now Can See: One Academic's Journey to Feminist Security Studies." *Politics & Gender* 7, no. 4 (2011): 586–90.
Hunt, Swanee. "Moving Beyond Silence: Women Waging Peace." In *Listening to the Silences: Women and War*, edited by Helen Durham and Tracy Gurd, 251–71. The Netherlands: Koninklijke Brill BV, 2005.

Hunt, Swanee, and Cristina Posa. "Women Waging Peace." *Foreign Policy* 124 (May–June 2011): 38–47.
Hutchinson, Wesley. "Engendering Change in the UDA: Gary Mitchell's Loyal Women." *Estudios Irlandeses*, no. 0 (2005): 67–76. http://cain.ulst.ac.uk/estudiosirlandeses/hutchinson05.pdf.
International Women's Commission. "Political Vision: Paper of Understanding." August 30, 2008. http://unispal.un.org/UNISPAL.NSF/0/A83B4CCC93BAE9E185257737006F78AB.
Ismail, Qadri. "Unmooring Identity: The Antinomies of Elite Muslim Self-Representation in Modern Sri Lanka." In *Unmaking the Nation: The Politics of Identity & History in Modern Sri Lanka*, edited by Pradeep Jeganathan and Qadri Ismail, 62–107. New York: South Focus Press, 1995.
Jacobs, Susie, Ruth Jacobson, and Jennifer Marchbank, eds. *States of Conflict: Gender, Violence and Resistance*. London: Zed Books, 2000.
Jacobson, Ruth. "Women and Peace in Northern Ireland: A Complicated Relationship." In *States of Conflict: Gender, Violence and Resistance*, edited by Susie Jacobs, Ruth Jacobson, and Jennifer Marchbank, 179–98. London: Zed Books, 2000.
Jacoby, Tami Amanda. *Women in Zones of Conflict: Power and Resistance in Israel*. Quebec: McGill-Queen's University Press, 2005.
James, Paula. "Gunning to the Front." *Daily Mirror*, December 17, 1975.
Jesse, Neal G., and Kristen P. Williams. *Ethnic Conflict: A Systematic Approach to Cases of Conflict*. Washington, DC: Congressional Quarterly Press, 2011.
Jones, Ann. *War Is Not Over When It's Over: Women Speak Out from the Ruins of War*. New York: Metropolitan Books, 2010.
Jordan, Kim, and Myriam Denov. "Birds of Freedom? Perspectives on Female Emancipation and Sri Lanka's Liberation Tigers of Tamil Eelam." *Journal of International Women's Studies* 9, no. 1 (November 2007): 42–62.
Joshi, Charu Lata. "Sri Lanka: Suicide Bombers." *Far Eastern Economic Review*. June 1, 2000. http://www.essex.ac.uk/armedcon/Countries/Asia/Texts/SriLanka011.htm.
Karam, Azza. "Women in War and Peace-Building." *International Feminist Journal of Politics* 3, no. 1 (April 2001): 2–25.
Kaufman, Joyce P., and Kristen P. Williams. *Women and War: Gender Identity and Activism in Times of Conflict*. Sterling, VA: Kumarian Press, 2010.
———. *Women, the State, and War: A Comparative Perspective on Citizenship and Nationalism*. Lanham, MD: Lexington Books, 2007.
Kilmurray, Avila, and Monica McWilliams. "Struggling for Peace: How Women in Northern Ireland Challenged the Status Quo." *Solutions* 2, no. 2 (February 28, 2011). http://www.thesolutionsjournal.com/print/893.

Knight, Marc, and Aplasian Ozerdem. "Guns, Camps and Cash: Disarmament, Demobilization and Reinsertion of Former Combatants in Transitions from War to Peace." *Journal of Peace Research* 41, no. 4 (July 2004): 499–516.

Koenig, Rhoda. "Loyal Women, Royal Court Theater, London." *Independent*. November 13, 2003. http://independent.co.uk/arts-entertainment/theater-dance/reviews/loyal-women-royal-.

Kumar, Krishna. "Introduction." In *Women & Civil War: Impact, Organizations, and Action*, edited by Krishna Kumar, 1–3 (Boulder: Lynne Rienner, 2001).

———. "Civil Wars, Women, and Gender Relations: An Overview." In *Women & Civil War: Impact, Organizations, and Action*, edited by Krishna Kumar, 5–26. Boulder: Lynne Rienner, 2001.

Kumudini, Samuel. "Sri Lanka: The Link between Women's Political Representation and the Peace Process." Center for Humanitarian Dialogue. February 8, 2011. http://www.hdcentre.org/files/Sri%20Lank-%20a%20the%20link%20between%20women%E2%80%99s%20political%20representation%20and%20the%20peace%20process%20-%208%20February%202011.pdf.

Lawrence, Patricia. "The Watch of Tamil Women: Women's Acts in a Transitional Warscape." In *Women and the Contested State: Religion, Violence, and Agency in South and Southeast Asia*, edited by Monique Skidmore and Patricia Lawrence, 89–116. Notre Dame, IN: University of Notre Dame Press, 2007.

Levy, Clifford J. "Second Bomber in Moscow Attacks Is Identified." *New York Times*, April 6, 2010, A1.

Levy, Clifford, and Ellen Barry. "Russia Says Suicide Bomber Was Militant's Widow." *New York Times*, April 2, 2010, A1.

"Life as a Female Tamil Tiger Guerilla Relived by One of First Female Soldiers." *Telegraph*. May 8, 2009. http://www.telegraph.co.uk/news/worldnews/asia/srilanka/5283438/Life-as-a-female-Tamil-Tiger-guerilla-relived-by-one-of-first-female-soldiers.html.

Lilly, Carole S., and Jill A. Irvine. "Negotiating Interests: Women and Nationalism in Serbia and Croatia, 1990–1997." *East European Politics and Societies* 16, no. 1 (2002): 109–44.

Lobasz, Jennifer K., and Laura Sjoberg. "Introduction." *Politics & Gender* 7, no. 4 (2011): 573–76.

Lunn, Jon, Claire Taylor, and Ian Townsend. "War and Peace in Sri Lanka." Research paper 09/51. June 5, 2009. http://www.parliament.uk/briefing-papers/RP09-51.pdf.

MacKenzie, Megan. "Empowerment Boom or Bust? Assessing Women's Post-Conflict Empowerment Initiatives." *Cambridge Review of International Affairs* 22, no. 2 (June 2009): 199–215.

"Marion Price: Voice of Extremism." *Telegraph*. December 12, 2000. http://www.telegraph.co.uk/news/uknews/1378002/Marion-Price-voice-of-extremism.html.

Maunaguru, Sitralega. "Gendering Tamil Nationalism: The Construction of 'Woman' in Projects of Protest and Control." In *Unmaking the Nation: The Politics of Identity & History in Modern Sri Lanka*, edited by Pradeep Jeganathan and Qadri Ismail, 157–72. New York: South Focus Press, 1995.

McCall, Leslie. "The Complexity of Intersectionality." *Signs* 30, no. 3 (Spring 2005): 1771–1800.

McEvoy, Sandra. "Loyalist Women Paramilitaries in Northern Ireland: Beginning a Feminist Conversation about Conflict Resolution." *Security Studies* 18, no. 2 (April 2009): 262–86.

———. "Women Loyalist Paramilitaries in Northern Ireland: Duty, Agency and Empowerment. A Report from the Field." Paper presented at the Annual Meeting of the International Studies Association, February 2007, Chicago.

McGirk, Tim. "Palestinian Moms Becoming Martyrs." *Time*. May 3, 2007. http://www.time.com/time/magazine/article/0,9171,1617542,00.html.

McKay, Susan. "Reconstructing Fragile Lives: Girls' Social Reintegration in Northern Uganda and Sierra Leone." *Gender and Development* 12, no. 3 (November 2004): 19–30.

McKeown, Laurence, and Simona Sharoni. "Formations and Transformations of Masculinity in the North of Ireland and in Israel-Palestine." Unpublished paper, 2002. http://www.simonasharoni.com/Docs/MasculinityUnpublished.pdf.

McWilliams, Monica. "Struggling for Peace and Justice: Reflections on Women's Activism in Northern Ireland." *Journal of Women's History* 6–7, no. 4–1 (Winter–Spring 1995): 13–39.

MIFTAH. *Ninth Annual Activities Report (2009)*. Miftah, Jerusalem, 2010, http://www.miftah.org/Mact/MiftahActivityReport2009.pdf18.

Morgan, Valerie. *Peacemaker? Peacekeepers? Women in Northern Ireland 1969–1995*. Londonderry, UK: INCORE, 1996. http://cain.ulst.ac.uk/issues/women/paper3.htm.

Moser, Caroline O. N., and Fiona C. Clark, eds. *Victims, Perpetrators or Actors: Gender, Armed Conflict and Political Violence*. London: Zed Books, 2001.

Naaman, Dorit. "Brides of Palestine/Angels of Death: Media, Gender, and Performance in the Case of the Palestinian Female Suicide Bombers." *Signs* 32, no. 4 (Summer 2007): 933–55.

Nagel, Joanne. "Masculinity and Nationalism: Gender and Sexuality in the Making of Nations." *Ethnic and Racial Studies* 21, no. 2 (March 1998): 242–69.

Narozhna, Tanya. "Power and Gendered Rationality in Western Epistemic Constructions of Female Suicide Bombings." In *Gender, Agency and Political Violence*, edited by Linda Ahall and Laura J. Shepherd, 79–95. Basingstoke, UK: Palgrave Macmillan, 2012.

"Negotiating For Peace in Sri Lanka: A Behind-the-Scenes Perspective on Mediating Conflict Resolution." Wilson Center. April 20, 2006. http://www.wilsoncenter.org/event/negotiating-for-peace-sri-lanka-behind-the-scenes-perspective-mediating-conflict-resolution.

Ness, Cindy D. "In the Name of the Cause: Women's Work in Secular and Religious Terrorism." In *Female Terrorism and Militancy: Agency, Utility and Organization*, edited by Cindy D. Ness, 11–36. New York: Routledge, 2008.

———. "The Rise in Female Violence." *Daedalus* 136, no. 1 (Winter 2007): 84–93.

Ní Aoláin, Fionnuala, Dina Francesca Haynes, and Naomi Cahn. *On the Frontlines: Gender, War, and the Post-Conflict Process*. New York: Oxford University Press, 2011.

Northern Ireland Women's Coalition. Accessed June 13, 2007. http://www.niwc.org (site discontinued).

Norville, Valerie. "The Role of Women in Global Security." United States Institute of Peace Special Report 264. January 2011. http://www.usip.org.

O'Ballance, Edgar. *Terror in Ireland: The Heritage of Hate*. Novato, CA: Presidio Press, 1981.

Oliver, Kelly. *Women As Weapons of War: Iraq, Sex and the Media*. New York: Columbia University Press, 2007.

Pankhurst, Donna. "Introduction: Gendered War and Peace." In *Gendered Peace: Women's Struggles for Post-War Justice and Reconciliation*, edited by Donna Pankhurst, 1–30. New York: Routledge, 2008.

———, ed. *Gendered Peace: Women's Struggles for Post-War Justice and Reconciliation*. New York: Routledge, 2008.

———. "Post-War Backlash Violence against Women: What Can 'Masculinity' Explain." In *Gendered Peace: Women's Struggles for Post-War Justice and Reconciliation*, edited by Donna Pankhurst, 293–315. New York: Routledge, 2008.

———. "The 'Sex War' and Other Wars: Towards a Feminist Approach to Peace Building." *Development in Practice* 12, no. 2–3 (May 2003): 154–77.

———. "Women, Gender and Peacebuilding." Working Paper 5, University of Bradford, UK, August 2000. http://www.brad.ac.uk/acad/confres/assets/CCR5.pdf.

Pape, Robert A. *Dying to Win: The Strategic Logic of Suicide Terrorism*. New York: Random House, 2005.

Peterson, V. Spike. "Sexing Political Identities/Nationalism as Heterosexism." *International Feminist Journal of Politics* 1, no. 1 (1999): 34–65.

———. "Gendered Nationalism: Reproducing 'Us' versus 'Them.'" *The Women and War Reader*, edited by Lois Ann Lorentzen and Jennifer Turpin, 41–49. New York: New York University Press, 1998.

Peterson, V. Spike, and Anne Sisson Runyan. *Global Gender Issues in the New Millennium*. 3rd ed. Boulder, CO: Westview Press, 2010.

———. *Global Gender Issues in the New Millennium*. 2nd ed. Boulder, CO: Westview Press, 1999.

———. *Global Gender Issues in the New Millennium*. Boulder, CO: Westview Press, 1993.

Pickering, Sharon. *Women, Policing and Resistance in Northern Ireland*. Belfast: BTP Publications, 2002.

Planta, Katrin. "The 'X' Factor." International Relations and Security Network. October 12, 2010. http://www.isn.ethz.ch/isn/Security-Watch/Articles/Detail/?id=122420.

Porter, Elisabeth. "Women, Political Decision-Making, and Peace-Building." *Global Change, Peace & Security* 15, no. 3 (October 2003): 245–62.

———. "Participatory Democracy and the Challenge of Dialogue Across Difference." In *Gender, Democracy and Inclusion in Northern Ireland*, edited by Carmel Roulston and Celia Davies, 141–62. New York: Palgrave, 2000.

———. "Identity, Location, Plurality: Women, Nationalism, and Northern Ireland." In *Women, Ethnicity, and Nationalism: The Politics of Transition*, edited by Rick Wilford and Robert L. Miller, 36–61. New York: Routledge, 1998.

Price, Dolores, and Marion Price. "Death of a Soldier." In *Venceremos Sisters: Prison Writings of the Price Sisters*. Belfast: Cathal Brugha Cumann, 1974.

Proops, Marjorie. "Women Deadlier than the Male—Sometimes." *Sunday Mirror*, November 9, 1975.

"Resisting Terror: Women, Agency, and the Micropolitics of Sri Lankan Life." In *Women and the Contested State: Religion, Violence and Agency in South and Southeast Asia*, edited by Monique Skidmore and Patricia Lawrence, 83–87. Notre Dame, IN: University of Notre Dame Press, 2007.

Richter-Devroe, Sophie. "Defending Their Land, Protecting Their Men: Palestinian Women's Popular Resistance after the Second Intifada." *International Feminist Journal of Politics* 14, no. 2 (June 2012): 181–201.

———. "Gender, Culture, and Conflict Resolution in Palestine." *Journal of Middle East Women's Studies* 4, no. 2 (Spring 2008): 30–59.

Ross, Dennis. *The Missing Peace: The Inside Story of the Fight for Middle East Peace*. New York: Farrar, Straus & Giroux, 2004.

Roulston, Carmel. "Democracy and the Challenge of Gender: New Visions, New Processes." In *Gender, Democracy and Inclusion in Northern Ireland*, edited by Carmel Roulston and Celia Davies, 24–46. New York: Palgrave, 2001.

Rubin, Alissa J. "Despair Drives Suicide Attacks by Iraqi Women." *New York Times*, July 5, 2008, A1.

Ruddick, Sara. "Feminist Questions on Peace and War: An Agenda for Research, Discussion, Analysis, Action." *Women's Studies Quarterly* 12, no. 2 (Summer 1984): 8–11.

———. "Thinking about Mothering—and Putting Maternal Thinking to Use." *Women's Studies Quarterly* 11, no. 4 (Winter 1983): 4–7.

———. "Maternal Thinking." *Feminist Studies* 6, no. 2 (Summer 1980): 342–67.

Sa'ar, Amalia, Dalia Sachs, and Sarai Aharoni. "Between a Gender and a Feminist Analysis: The Case of Security Studies in Israel." *International Sociology* 26, no. 1 (January 2011): 50–73.

Sachs, Dalia, Amalia Sa'ar, and Sarai Aharoni. "'How Can I Feel for Others When I Myself Am Beaten?' The Impact of Armed Conflict on Women in Israel." *Sex Roles* 57 (2007): 593–606.
Sales, Rosemary. *Women Divided: Gender, Religion and Politics in Northern Ireland.* New York: Routledge, 1997.
Samath, Feizal. "Rights—Sri Lanka: How the War Gave Tamil Women More Space." Inter Press Service News Agency. April 20, 2010. http://www.ipsnews .net/2010/04/rights-sri-lanka-how-the-war-gave-tamil-women-more-space/.
Sarwar, Beena. "Some Mother's Son." *Countercurrents.* June 21, 2004. http://www. countercurrents.org/hr-sarwar210604.htm.
Schweitzer, Yoram. "Introduction." In *Female Suicide Bombers: Dying for Equality?* edited by Yoram Schweitzer, 7–12. Tel Aviv: Jaffee Center for Strategic Studies, 2006. http://www.e-prism.org/images/memo84_Female_suicide_ bombers_-_Jaffee_Center_-_Aug06.pdf.
Seva Vanitha Movement of Sri Lanka (Incorporation) Act (No. 10 of 1987), March 10, 1987. National Center for Biotechnology Information. http://www .ncbi.nlm.nih.gov/pubmed/12346608.
Sharoni, Simona. *Gender and the Israel-Palestinian Conflict.* Syracuse, NY: Syracuse University Press, 1995.
Shikaki, Khalil. "The Views of Palestinian Society on Suicide Terrorism." *Countering Suicide Terrorism.* Herzliya, Israel: Institute for Counter-Terrorism). http://www.ict.org.il/Portals/0/51563-Countering%20suicide%20 Terrorism.pdf.
Simpson, Mark. "Photographer Shot in Second Night of Belfast Rioting: Analysis." BBC News Northern Ireland. June 22, 2011. http://www.bbc.co.uk/ news/uk-northern-ireland-13869210.
———. "Real IRA Admits NI MI5 Base Bomb." BBC News Northern Ireland, April 12, 2010. http://news.bbc.co.uk/2/hi/8614723.stm.
Sjoberg, Laura. "Seeing Gender in International Security." June 5, 2012. http://www.e-ir .info/2012/06/05/seeing-gender-in-international-security/.
———. "Conclusion: The Study of Women, Gender, and Terrorism." In *Women, Gender and Terrorism,* edited by Laura Sjoberg and Caron E. Gentry, 227–39. Athens: University of Georgia Press, 2011.
———. "Looking Forward, Conceptualizing Feminist Security Studies." *Politics & Gender* 7, no. 4 (2011): 600–604.
———. "Women Fighters and the 'Beautiful Soul' Narrative." *International Review of the Red Cross* 92, no. 877 (March 2010): 53–68. http://www.icrc.org/ eng/assets/files/other/irrc-877-sjoberg.pdf.
Sjoberg, Laura, and Caron E. Gentry. "The Gendering of Women's Terrorism." In *Women, Gender and Terrorism,* edited by Laura Sjoberg and Caron E. Gentry, 57–80. Athens: University of Georgia Press, 2011.
———. *Mothers, Monsters, and Whores: Women's Violence in Global Politics.* London: Zed Books, 2007.

———, eds. *Women, Gender and Terrorism*. Athens: University of Georgia Press, 2011.
Sjoberg, Laura, and Jessica Peet. "A(nother) Dark Side of the Protection Racket." *International Feminist Journal of Politics* 13, no. 2 (June 2011): 163–82.
Skaine, Rosemarie. *Female Suicide Bombers*. Jefferson, NC: MacFarland, 2006.
Skidmore, Monique, and Patricia Lawrence. "Resisting Terror: Women, Agency, and the Micropolitics of Sri Lankan Life." In *Women and the Contested State: Religion, Violence, and Agency in South and Southeast Asia*, edited by Monique Skidmore and Patricia Lawrence, 83–87. Notre Dame, IN: University of Notre Dame Press, 2007.
Spackman, Conor. "East Belfast Interface: A Familiar Pattern Continues." BBC News Northern Ireland. June 21, 2011. http://www.bbc.co.uk/news/uk-northern-ireland-13860978.
Speckhard, Anne, and Khapta Akmedova. "Black Widows and Beyond: Understanding the Motivations and Life Trajectories of Chechen Female Terrorists." In *Female Terrorism and Militancy: Agency, Utility, and Organization*, edited by Cindy D. Ness, 100–121. New York: Routledge, 2008.
"Sri Lanka: UNIFEM Report: Gender Profile of the Conflict in Sri Lanka." Women Living under Muslim Laws. August 23, 2009. http://www.wluml.org/node/5489.
"State of Feminist Security Studies: A Conversation." Special issue, *Politics & Gender* 7, no. 4 (2011).
Steinberg, Donald. "Women and War: An Agenda for Action." In *Women and War: Power and Protection in the 21st Century*, edited by Kathleen Kuehnast, Chantal de Jonge Oudraat, and Helga Hernes, 115–30. Washington, DC: U.S. Institute of Peace Press, 2011.
Stephan, Maria. J., and Erica Chenoweth. "Why Civil Resistance Works: The Strategic Logic of Nonviolent Conflict." *International Security* 33, no. 1 (Summer 2008): 7–44.
Stern, Jessica. *Terror in the Name of God: Why Religious Militants Kill*. New York: HarperCollins, 2003.
Stern, Maria, and Malin Nystrand. *Gender and Armed Conflict*. Stockholm: Swedish International Development Cooperation Agency, April 2006.
Swamy, M. R. Narayan. *The Tiger Vanquished: LTTE's Story*. New Delhi, India: Sage, 2010.
"Swoop Thought to Have Sent IRA Girls on the Run." *Belfast Telegraph*. January 2, 1973.
Sylvester, Christine. "Tensions in Feminist Security Studies." *Security Dialogue* 41, no. 6 (2010): 607–14.
———. *Feminist Theory and International Relations in a Postmodern Era*. Cambridge: Cambridge University Press, 1994.

Telegraph. "Marion Price: Voice of Extremism." December 12, 2000. http://www.telegraph.co.uk/news/uknews/1378002/Marion-Price-voice-of-extremism.html.

Tickner, J. Ann. "Feminist Security Studies: Celebrating an Emerging Field." *Politics & Gender* 7, no. 4 (2011): 576–81.

———. *Gendering World Politics: Issues and Approaches in the Post–Cold War Era.* New York: Columbia University Press, 2001.

———. "You Just Don't Understand: Troubled Engagements between Feminists and IR Theorists." *International Studies Quarterly* 41 (1997): 611–32.

———. *Gender in International Relations.* New York: Columbia University Press, 1993.

———. *Gender in International Relations: Feminist Perspectives on Achieving Global Security.* New York: Columbia University Press, 1992.

Tickner, J. Ann, and Laura Sjoberg. "Feminism." In *Theories of International Relations: Discipline and Diversity*, edited by Tim Dunner, Milya Kurki, and Steve Smith, 185–202. Oxford: Oxford University Press, 2006.

Tilly, Charles. *Coercion, Capital and European States.* Cambridge, MA: Blackwell, 1992.

Ulster Home Cooking. Londonderry: DUP Center, n.d.

United Nations. "Women, Peace and Security." 2002. http://www.un.org/womenwatch/daw/public/eWPS.pdf.

United Nations Office for the Coordination of Humanitarian Affairs. "Human Security for All." Accessed December 23, 2012. http://www.unocha.org/humansecurity/about-human-security/human-security-all.

"United Nations Peacekeeping: Disarmament, Demobilization and Reintegration." Accessed March 7, 2011. http://www.un.org/en/peacekeeping/issues/ddr.shtml.

United Nations Security Council Resolution 1325. October 31, 2000. http://www.un.org/events/res_1325e.pdf.

UN Women. "Women Share a Vision for Israeli-Palestinian Peace." News release. June 3, 2010. http://unifem.org/news_events/story_detail.php?StoryID=1095.

Victor, Barbara. *Army of Roses: Inside the World of Palestinian Suicide Bombers.* New York: Rodale Press, 2003.

Van de Voorde, Cecile. "Sri Lankan Terrorism: Assessing and Responding to the Threat of the LTTE." *Policy Practice and Research* 6, no. 2 (May 2005): 181–99.

Waltz, Kenneth N. *Theory of International Politics.* New York: Random House, 1979.

Ward, Margaret. "Gender, Citizenship and the Future of the Northern Ireland Peace Process." *Irish Feminist Studies* 41, no. 1–2 (Spring/Summer 2006): 262–83.

Ward, Rachel. *Women, Unionism and Loyalism in Northern Ireland: From "Tea-Makers" to Political Actors.* Dublin: Irish Academic Press, 2006.

Ware, John. "IRA Girl Bombers Go to War." *Sun*. September 2, 1976.
Weldon, S. Laurel. *When Protest Makes Policy: How Social Movements Represent Disadvantaged Groups*. Ann Arbor: University of Michigan Press, 2011.
"What Is DDR?" United Nations Disarmament, Demobilization and Reintegration Resource Centre. http://www.unddr.org/whatisddr.php.
Wibben, Annick T. R. "Feminist Politics in Feminist Security Studies." *Politics & Gender* 7, no. 4 (2011): 590–95.
Wilcox, Lauren. "Beyond Sex/Gender: The Feminist Body of Security." *Politics & Gender* 7, no. 4 (2011): 595–600.
"Women Apart." *Newsletter*. March 29, 1973.
"Women's History: Sri Lankan Army Women's Corps." October 1988. http://womenshistory.about.com/library/ency/blwh_sri_lanka_women_military.htm.
Woodbury, Laura. "Reconstructing Gender Identity for Child Combatants in Post-Conflict African Societies." *Journal of International Service* 20, no. 1 (Spring 2011): 19–33.
"World Bank Civil Society Fund 2011: Theme: Gender and Demographic Transition in Sri Lanka." http://siteresources.worldbank.org/SRILANKAEXTN/Resources/233046-1298393467535/FINAL04042011Theme.pdf.
Yuval-Davis, Nira. *Gender and Nation*. London: Sage, 1997.
Zuckerman, Elaine, and Marcia Greenberg. "The Gender Dimensions of Post-Conflict Reconstruction: An Analytical Framework for Policymakers." *Gender and Development* 12, no. 3 (November 2004): 70–82.

About the Authors

Joyce P. Kaufman is Professor of Political Science and Director of the Center for Engagement with Communities at Whittier College. She is the author of *Introduction to International Relations: Theory and Practice* (Rowman & Littlefield Publishers, Inc. 2013), *A Concise History of U.S. Foreign Policy*, 2nd ed. (Rowman & Littlefield Publishers, Inc., 2010) and *NATO and the Former Yugoslavia: Crisis, Conflict and the Atlantic Alliance* (Rowman & Littlefield Publishers, Inc., 2002), and co-editor of *The Future of Transatlantic Relations: Perceptions, Policy and Practice* (with Andrew M. Dorman) (Stanford Security Studies, 2011). She is also the author of numerous articles and papers on U.S. foreign and security policy. With Kristen Williams, she is coauthor of *Women and War: Gender Identity and Activism in Times of Conflict* (Kumarian Press, 2010) and *Women, the State, and War: A Comparative Perspective on Citizenship and Nationalism* (Lexington Books, 2007).

Kristen P. Williams is Professor of Political Science at Clark University. She is the author of *Despite Nationalist Conflicts: Theory and Practice of Maintaining World Peace* (Praeger, 2001), *Identity and Institutions: Conflict Reduction in Divided Societies* (with Neal G. Jesse) (SUNY, 2005), *Ethnic Conflict: A Systematic Approach to Cases of Conflict* (with Neal G. Jesse) (CQ Press, 2011), as well as journal articles on nationalism and ethnic conflict, and gender and war. She is coeditor of *Beyond Great Powers and Hegemons* (with Neal G. Jesse and Steven Lobell) (Stanford University Press, 2012), and coauthor of *World Politics in a New Era* (Oxford University Press, 2012), with Steven Spiegel, Elizabeth Matthews and Jennifer Taw. With Joyce Kaufman, she is coauthor of *Women and War: Gender Identity and Activism in Times of Conflict* (Kumarian Press, 2010) and *Women, the State, and War: A Comparative Perspective on Citizenship and Nationalism* (Lexington Books, 2007).

Index

agency
    constraints on, 14–15
    definition of, 13
    feminist, 14
    intersectionality and, 13–15
    Palestinian women suicide bombers/martyrs and, 101–2, 107
    patriarchy related to, 13
    from Sri Lanka women's political violence, 131
    as women's political activism motivation, 146
Aharoni, Sarai, 7, 15, 109n45
Akhmedova, Khapta, 46, 49
Alexander, Jacqui, 13
Alison, Miranda, 4, 12, 14, 37, 113, 135
    on motherhood, 125
    on motivation, 39, 129–30
    on rape, 41
    on recruitment, 128
    on roles, 40
Alwis, Malathi de, 120–21
American Political Science Association, x
Anderlini, Sanam, 126
Arafat, Yasser, 86, 104
Ashrawi, Hanan, 85, 91
Association of Servicemen Missing in Action, 125–27

Balasingham, Adele, 122–24, 130–31, 136
Bandarage, Asoka, 123
Bandranaike, Siramavo, 120–23
Bandranaike, Solomon Wes Ridgeway Dias, 116
Bannon, Ian, 35, 44, 130, 154

Barghouti, Amal Kreishe, 95
Bat Shalom, 108n32
Beckwith, Karen, 32
Berko, Anat, 99–101
Beyler, Clara, 55n99
Bhutto, Benazir, 154–55
Blanchard, Eric, 8
Bloom, Mia, 4, 45–47, 101, 134
Bose, Sumatra, 96, 114, 118, 129, 140n45
Bosnia-Croat War, 25
Bouta, Tsjeard, 35, 44, 130, 154
Brunner, Claudia, 101

Cahn, Naomi, 158
case studies, 16–17
Center for Humanitarian Dialogue, 135–36
Chechnya
    suicide bombers in, 46
    women suicide bombers in, 49
civil rights movements, 35
Clinton, Bill, 86
Coalition of Women for Peace (CWP), 33–34
Cockburn, Cynthia, 10, 15, 62
    on Israeli-Palestinian dialogue, 95–96, 106–7
    on patriarchy, 65–66
combatants, 160. *See also* women combatants
community
    funding for, 164
    for LTTE women suicide bombers'/martyrs' defense, 132
    for LTTE women suicide bombers'/martyrs' support, 133

Northern Ireland peace activists for, 61–63, 77, 163
patriarchy related to, 150
Sri Lanka women's peace activism across, 125–26
in women's political activism, 35–36, 149–50, 163–64
for women suicide bombers' support, 49–50, 133
conflicts. *See also specific conflicts*
choices about, 2, 4, 13
domestic violence related to, 9, 11, 158, 164
escalation of, 122, 154–55
transformation from, 158
Confortini, Catia, 8, 10–12
Contested Lands (Bose), 96, 140n45
continuum of women's political activism, ix–x, 16, 146, 157
description of, 2, 28, 36
forms on, 3
range of, 17, 36
Corrigan, Mairead, 78n3
Cunningham, Karla J., 99, 103, 105
Cuomo, Chris J., 11
CWP. *See* Coalition of Women for Peace

DDR. *See* disarmament, demobilization, and reintegration
demobilization, 159. *See also* disarmament, demobilization, and reintegration
democracy, 32
MIFTAH for, 91–92, 109n35
SDLP and, 64, 80n23
in Sri Lanka conflict, 116, 118
Democratic Front for the Liberation of Palestine (DFLP), 96–97, 110n66
Denov, Myriam, 43–44
DFLP. *See* Democratic Front for the Liberation of Palestine
Dhanu, 46–47, 134
Dharmadasa, Visaka, 125–27
disarmament, 159. *See also* peace
disarmament, demobilization, and reintegration (DDR), 152, 154
UN on, 159–62
Disney, Jennifer Leigh, 13–14
domestic violence, 9, 11, 158, 164
Drumm, Máire, 70

Dudouet, Veronique, 3
Dzeko, Edin, 25

Eager, Paige Whaley, 4, 42, 128, 131
ecofeminists, 12
economics, 9–10, 17
Edwards, Maud, 13
Eerez, Edna, 99–101
Emmett, Ayala, 90
Enloe, Cynthia, 7

Farr, Vanessa, 14–15, 95
Fearon, Kate, 63
feminine traits, 12
feminism
ecofeminists, 12
goals of, 3
of LTTE, 14, 114–15, 130–31, 152
Palestinian women suicide bombers/ martyrs as, 100–101
tradition compared to, 31–32
women's movements as, 32
for women's political activism recruitment, 157
feminist agency, 14
feminist security theory (FST), 15–16
gender in, 8–9
insecurity in, 9
realism and, 6–7
social construction in, 7–8
theories in, 8–9
Fernea, Elizabeth, 89
FP. *See* Tamil Federal Party
Frerks, Georg, 35, 44, 130, 154
FST. *See* feminist security theory

Galtung, Johann, 9–10, 151
Gandhi, Indira, 154–55
Gandhi, Rajiv, 46–47, 132, 134
gangs, 163, 168n49
Gaza, 86–87
gender, 6, 71
as analytical category, 7
in FST, 8–9
intersectionality and, 15–16, 24n88
as power relation, 8
protection related to, 7–8
violent political conflict and, 145
gender discrimination, 161–62
gender identity, x
national identity related to, 32–33, 37

gender norms
    in intrastate wars, 29
    Palestinian women's peace activism
        as, 88–89
    Palestinian women's political activism
        and, 97–98
    Palestinian women suicide bombers/
        martyrs and, 104–5
    political violence and, 26–27, 36–37,
        50–51
    postconflict, 10, 22n50, 162, 168n48
    public sphere and, 26
    Sri Lanka women's political activism
        and, 123–24, 136–37
    women's peace activism related to, 1,
        10, 26, 148
    women's political activism related to,
        147–49
    women suicide bombers related to, 45
gender roles. *See also* traditional gender
        roles
    in Northern Ireland, 40–41
    Northern Ireland political violence
        and, 68–69, 78
    of Northern Ireland Protestant
        women, 73–74
    Palestinian women militants and,
        98–99
    Palestinian women's political violence
        and, 98–99, 105–6
    Palestinian women suicide bombers/
        martyrs and, 100–101
    political violence and, 43–44
Gentry, Caron, 4, 6, 14, 26–27, 36, 47,
    98
Goldstein, Joshua S., 39, 41–42
Good Friday Peace Agreement, 75
    NIWC for, 58–59, 63, 151–52
    violence after, 76–77
    women compared to men in, 151–52
Gunaratna, Rohan, 45
Gunawardena, Arjuna, 133

Hamas, 86–87
    for Islam, 105
    Riyashi and, 99–100
    women's elections in, 84, 150–51
    women suicide bombers and, 105
Handovic, Rasema, 25
Hasso, Frances, 88, 96–98, 102, 110n66
Haynes, Dina Francesca, 158

Helms, Elissa, 34–35
Human Development Index, 113, 138n2
Hunt, Swanee, 34, 63

identity
    gender, x, 32–33, 37
    maternal, 34
    national, 28–29, 32–33, 37
Idris, Wafa, 104
India, 115
international relations (IR)
    mainstream theories of, 6, 20n19
    mainstream theory of, 6
    realism and, 6–7
International Studies Association, x
International Women's Commission for
        a Just and Sustainable Israeli-
        Palestinian Peace (IWC)
    formation of, 92
    unified voice of, 94
    vision of, 93
    women's exclusion from, 163
intersectionality
    agency and, 13–15
    gender and, 15–16, 24n88
    in power, 15
interstate wars, 29
intifada (uprising)
    of 1987, 1, 86, 88, 90–91, 97, 99,
        110n66
    of 2000, 99, 103–4
intrastate wars
    gender norms in, 29
    interstate wars compared to, 29
IR. *See* international relations
IRA, 66
    Real, 76–77
    women in, 42
Ireland. *See* Northern Ireland
Irvine, Jill, 42
Islam
    Hamas for, 105
    language and, 119
    Palestinian women's political violence
        and, 103–6
    Palestinian women suicide bombers/
        martyrs and, 102
    in Sri Lanka conflict, 119–20
Israel
    map of, 87
    1967 Six Days' War in, 86

state-sanctioned violence from, 94–95, 110n50
Israeli-Palestinian conflict, 16–17. *See also* Palestinian women
    Gaza in, 86–87
    information on, x, 19n14
    IWC in, 92–94
    origins of, 85–86
    Oslo Peace Accords in, 86, 90, 109n45
    partition plan in, 86
IWC. *See* International Women's Commission for a Just and Sustainable Israeli-Palestinian Peace

Jacobson, Ruth, 65
Jacoby, Tami, 11
Jarman, Neil, 76
Jayewardene, Junius Richard, 116
Jerusalem Center for Women (JCW), 89, 108n32
Jerusalem Link, 108n32
Jones, Ann, 158
Jordan, Kim, 43–44

Khaled, Leila, 44, 47, 88, 98, 108n18
Kumar, Krishna, 29
Kumaratunga, Chandrika Bandaranaike, 121–23
Kurdistan Workers Party (PKK), 46, 48–49
Kuttab, 14–15

Lawrence, Patricia, 113, 118–19, 123, 129, 131
Lawsley, Patricia, 64
leadership
    of Dharmadasa, 125–27
    IWC for, 92–94
    MIFTAH for, 91–92
    Northern Ireland peace activists and, 65
    in Sri Lanka, 120–23, 136–37, 152–53
    of women combatants, 44
Liberation Tigers of Tamil Eelam (LTTE), 137. *See also* LTTE women suicide bombers/martyrs
    emergence of, 118
    feminism of, 14, 114–15, 130–31, 152

missing persons related to, 125–26
motivations in, 129–30
noncombat work in, 128
peace preparations and, 134–35
rape related to, 41
recruitment in, 128–29
suicide for, 113
virtues in, 129
women combatants in, 17–18, 43–44, 128–31
Lilly, Carole, 42
Lobasz, Jennifer K., 8–9
LTTE. *See* Liberation Tigers of Tamil Eelam
LTTE women suicide bombers/martyrs, 48
    community defense by, 132
    community support for, 133
    motherhood of, 133–34
    motivations of, 132
    opportunities for, 134
    status of, 132–33

MacKenzie, Megan, 22n50
marriage
    mixed, 52n17
    women suicide bombers and, 48–49, 52n17
masculinity. *See also* patriarchy
    concepts of, 10–11, 22n51
    male traits, 12
    postconflict, 162, 168n48
Maunaguru, Sitralega, 125, 127
McDonough, Martin, 75
McEvoy, Sandra, 4, 41, 74–75, 79n10
McKay, Susan, 162
McWilliams, Monica, 35, 63
Meier, Golda, 154–55
MIFTAH. *See* Promotion of Global Dialogue and Democracy
militarism, 11
Mitchell, Gary, 75
Mohanty, Chandra, 13
Morgan, Valerie, 27, 59, 78
Morrice, Jane, 64, 150
Moscow subway attacks, 2
motherhood, 65
    of LTTE women suicide bombers/martyrs, 133–34
    of Northern Ireland Protestant women, 75

in Palestinian women's political
   activism, 97
in Sandinista National Liberation
   Front, 39
in Sri Lanka women's peace activism,
   125–27
women suicide bombers and, 48–49
Mothers of the Plaza de Mayo, 34
motivations, 26–27. *See also* women's
      political activism motivations
   in LTTE, 129–30
   of LTTE women suicide bombers/
      martyrs, 132
   of Palestinian women suicide
      bombers/martyrs, 99–100,
      103–6
   for political violence, 38–39, 40–41,
      50–51
   for women's peace activism, 149–52
   of women suicide bombers, 45–48,
      99–100, 103–6, 132, 153–54
Muslims. *See* Islam
Muslim Women's Research and Action
   Forum, 120

Naaman, Dorit, 44
Nagel, Joanne, 72–73
Narozhna, Tanya, 47–48, 102
national identity
   gender identity related to, 32–33, 37
   public-private spheres and, 28–29
nationalism
   for Palestinian women's political
      activism, 88, 95–96
   of Palestinian women suicide
      bombers/martyrs, 102
   in Sri Lanka conflict, 114
   in violent political conflict, 147–48,
      152
Ness, Cindy, 37, 43, 45, 49, 104, 130
   on LTTE women suicide bombers/
      martyrs, 132–33
   on tradition, 40
   on violence context, 27
NGO. *See* nongovernmental organization
Ní Aoláin, Fionnuala, 158
NIWC. *See* Northern Ireland Women's
   Coalition
nongovernmental organization (NGO),
   121, 123. *See also specific
   NGOs*

nonviolent resistance (NVR), 3
Northern Ireland, x, 17
   civil rights movements related to, 35
   commonalities in, 62
   gender roles in, 40–41
   history in, 59–60
   involvement range in, 27, 57–58, 61
   involvement stages in, 35
   IRA, 42, 66, 76–77
   political violence outside, 70–71
   politics in, 60–61
   tradition in, 59–60, 73
Northern Ireland Catholic women
   age of, 68–69, 71–72
   bombs for, 66–68
   demonization of, 68–69
   gender equality and, 71
   men's imprisonment and, 67–70
   protection by, 67, 147
   recruitment of, 68
Northern Ireland peace activists, 57–58,
   78
   for community, 61–63, 77, 163
   against gangs, 163, 168n49
   leadership of, 65
   marching season related to, 63, 79n16
   from Northern Ireland political
      violence, 61, 79n10
   in political system, 63–65
   women's movement and, 62
Northern Ireland political violence, 81n73
   gender roles and, 68–69, 78
   Northern Ireland peace activists from,
      61, 79n10
   provocation of, 65
   religion and, 65–66
Northern Ireland Protestant women, 76
   constraints of, 72–74
   gender roles of, 73–74
   invisibility of, 74–75
   motherhood of, 75
   protection by, 74, 147
   tradition of, 73
Northern Ireland Women's Coalition
   (NIWC)
   focus of, 3, 151–52
   for Good Friday Peace Agreement,
      58–59, 63, 151–52
   men compared with, 151–52
   women's political activism of, 17,
      63–64, 77

NVR. *See* nonviolent resistance

O'Ballance, Edgar, 67
Ogilby, Anne, 81n73
Oliver, Kelly, 105–6
Oslo Peace Accords, 86, 90, 109n45

PA. *See* Palestinian Authority
Palestine Liberation Organization (PLO), 84
    Ashrawi for, 85
    goal of, 86
Palestinian Authority (PA), 86–87
Palestinian Federation of Women's Action Committees (PFWAC), 96–97
Palestinian women
    constrained agency of, 14–15
    underrepresentation of, 84–85
    women's political activism continuum of, 17
Palestinian women's activism
    context of, 83
    history of, 83–87
    relationship to men in, 84–85
    religion related to, 85
Palestinian women's peace activism
    citizenship and, 90–91
    definitions in, 90
    as gender norm, 88–89
    Israeli women's perspective in, 94–96, 106
    IWC for, 92–94
    JCW for, 89
    mediation for, 93
    MIFTAH for, 91–92
    summary about, 93
    WATC for, 89–90
    in West Bank, 91–92
    Women in Black for, 1, 3, 33, 90–91
Palestinian women's political activism, 17
    disloyalty and, 95
    gender norms and, 97–98
    motherhood in, 97
    nationalism for, 88, 95–96
    oppression related to, 88
    organizations for, 96–97
    restrictions on, 97
Palestinian women's political violence, 111n106
    choices of, 98–99
    gender roles and, 98–99, 105–6
    Islam and, 103–6
    in second intifada, 103–4
Palestinian women suicide bombers/ martyrs, 47
    agency and, 101–2, 107
    Arafat for, 104
    as feminism, 100–101
    gender norms and, 104–5
    gender roles and, 100–101
    Islam and, 102
    motivations of, 99–100, 103–6
    nationalism of, 102
Pankhurst, Donna, 10, 13, 22n51
Pape, Robert, 46, 48, 133
Parpart, Jane, 145–46
Pateman, Carole, 52n36
patriarchy. *See also specific cases*
    agency related to, 13
    Cockburn on, 65–66
    community related to, 150
    postconflict, 30
    traditional gender roles and, 34–35
peace
    definitions of, 10–11, 22n47, 90, 151
    militarism related to, 11
    women compared to men on, 149–52
    women's association with, 28–29, 33–34, 36
Peet, Jessica, 7–8
Peterson, V. Spike, 10, 30
PFLP. *See* Popular Front for the Liberation of Palestine
PFWAC. *See* Palestinian Federation of Women's Action Committees
Pickering, Sharon, 67–68, 73
PKK. *See* Kurdistan Workers Party
PLO. *See* Palestine Liberation Organization
politics
    in Northern Ireland, 60–61
    women's political activism as, 39–40, 160–61
political violence, 4, 54n57. *See also specific cases*
    economics and, 10
    examples of, 36, 57
    gender norms and, 26–27, 36–37, 50–51
    gender roles and, 43–44
    motivations for, 38–39, 40–41, 50–51
    outside Northern Ireland, 70–71

Popular Front for the Liberation of
    Palestine (PFLP), 44, 88, 96,
    108n18
Porter, Elisabeth, 31, 35, 160, 162
Posa, Cristina, 34, 63
postconflict. *See also* women combatants
    postconflict
    gender norms, 10, 22n50, 162,
        168n48
    masculinity, 162, 168n48
    patriarchy, 30
    Sri Lanka women, 135–38
power, 8
    intersectionality in, 15
Prabhakaran, Velupillai, 48, 114, 128–29,
    133–34
Premadasa, Hema, 121–23
Premadasa, Ranasinghe, 121
Price, Dolores, 57, 68
Price, Marion, 57, 68
Promotion of Global Dialogue and
    Democracy (MIFTAH), 91–92,
    109n35
Proops, Marje, 71–72
public-private spheres, 26, 37
    artificiality of, 149
    national identity and, 28–29
    status and, 53n36
    violence and, 9, 11–13
    women's peace activism related to,
        34
    women's political activism in, 148–49

Al Qaeda, 43

Rabin, Yitzhak, 86
rape, 9
    LTTE related to, 41
    women suicide bombers and, 46–47
realism, 6–7
recruitment. *See also* women's political
        activism recruitment
    in LTTE, 128–29
    of Northern Ireland Catholic women,
        68
    in Sandinista National Liberation
        Front, 41
reinsertion, 159
reintegration, 159–60. *See also*
        disarmament, demobilization,
        and reintegration

religion. *See also* Islam
    Northern Ireland political violence
        and, 65–66
    Palestinian women's activism related
        to, 85
    reinterpretation of, 105, 152–53
research
    limitations in, 5
    questions for, 4–5, 15, 18
revenge, 38, 129–30
    of men suicide bombers, 153–54
    of women suicide bombers, 1–2,
        46–47
Richter-Devroe, Sophie, 14, 95, 97–98
Riyashi, Reem, 99–100, 102
Roulston, Carmel, 61, 68
Ruddick, Sara, 34
Runyan, Anne Sisson, 10, 30
Rwanda, 115

Sa'ar, Amalia, 7, 9, 15
Sachs, Dalia, 7, 15, 24n88
Sales, Rosemary, 40–41
Sandinista National Liberation Front,
        55n79
    motherhood in, 39
    recruitment in, 41
Schweitzer, Yoram, 101, 132
SDLP. *See* Social Democratic and Labor
        Party
Seva Vanitha Movement (SVM)
    objectives of, 139n41
    Premadasa, H., with, 121
Sharoni, Shimona, 83, 88
Shikaki, Khalil, 49
Sierra Leone, 161–62
Simpson, Mark, 77
Sinn Féin, 70, 79n10, 81n50
Sjoberg, Laura, 4, 6–9, 36, 47, 54n57
    on agency, 14
    on motivations, 26–27
    on public-private spheres, 12–13
Skaine, Rosemarie, 4, 132
Skidmore, Monique, 113
Social Democratic and Labor Party
        (SDLP), 64, 80n23
Speckhard, Anne, 46, 49
Sri Lanka, 16. *See also* Liberation Tigers of
        Tamil Eelam
    leadership in, 120–23, 136–37,
        152–53

Sri Lanka conflict
  Britain in, 113–14, 127
  constitution in, 118
  democracy in, 116, 118
  independence related to, 116
  Islam in, 119–20
  language in, 116
  nationalism in, 114
  origins of, 113–18
  peace preparations in, 134–36
  precolonial Ceylon and, 116
Sri Lankan Women's Army Corps, 128, 141n79
Sri Lanka women
  as Muslims, 119–20
  political leadership of, 120–23, 136–37
  postconflict, 135–38
Sri Lanka women's peace activism
  across communities, 125–26
  motherhood in, 125–27
  UN on, 127
Sri Lanka women's political activism
  gender norms and, 123–24, 136–37
  goddess worship in, 123
  networking for, 123–24
  into violent activism, 124
Sri Lanka women's political violence
  agency from, 131
  notoriety of, 127
Steinberg, Donald, 159
Stern, Jessica, 154
structural violence, 9–10
suicide bombers, 44–45. *See also* women suicide bombers; *specific cases*
  profile of, 154
SVM. *See* Seva Vanitha Movement
Swamy, M. R. Narayan, 131
Syrian Socialist National Party, 45, 55n99

Tamil Eelam war. *See* Sri Lanka conflict
Tamil Federal Party (FP), 116–17
terrorist groups, 40. *See also specific cases*
  Moscow subway attacks by, 2
Thatcher, Margaret, 154–55
Tickner, J. Ann, 6–7, 9, 53n36
Tilly, Charles, 7
tradition, 40
  feminism compared to, 31–32
  in Northern Ireland, 59–60, 73
  of Northern Ireland Protestant women, 73
traditional gender roles
  maternal identity of, 34
  patriarchy and, 34–35
  in women's peace activism, 31–32, 34, 162
the Troubles. *See* Northern Ireland

Ulster Defense Association (UDA), 74, 81n73
United Nations (UN), 127
  on DDR, 159–62
  Security Council Resolution 1325, 146, 160–61
USAID, x, 159

Victor, Barbara, 4, 47, 102, 104
violence
  context of, 27
  cycle of, 11, 151
  domestic, 9, 11, 158, 164
  freedom related to, 26–27
  public-private spheres and, 9, 11–13
  structural, 9–10
violent political conflict
  gender and, 145
  imagination about, 145–46
  nationalism in, 147–48, 152
  trade-offs from, 147
  women's vulnerability in, 147

Ward, Margaret, 64, 150, 160
Ward, Rachel, 40–41, 57, 65–66, 73–74
wars. *See also specific conflicts*
  civil, 29
  interstate, 29
  intrastate, 29
  women compared to men on, 152–55
WATC. *See* Women's Affairs Technical Committee
Weldon, S. Laurel, 5
West Bank, 86–87
  Palestinian women's peace activism in, 91–92
Williams, Betty, 78n3
Williams, Kristen P., 110n50
Woman and War: Gender Identity and Activism in Times of Conflict, x
women
  movements of, 32, 62

problematic term use of, 15
representation of, 5, 157
Women and the Contested State, 127
women combatants, 154. *See also specific cases*
   acceptance of, 44
   in Bosnia-Croat War, 25
   leadership of, 44
   in LTTE, 17–18, 43–44, 128–31
   multiple roles of, 42–43
   rationalization about, 42
   women suicide bombers as, 1–2
women combatants postconflict, 159
   financial assistance for, 162
   gender discrimination of, 161–62
   resettlement of, 161–62, 164
   UN Security Council Resolution 1325 for, 146, 160–61
   weapons collections by, 161
women compared to men, 58
   assumptions on, 36
   in Good Friday Peace Agreement, 151–52
   on peace, 149–52
   perspectives of, 30, 33
   on war, 152–55
Women in Black, 90–91
   focus of, 3, 33
   mission of, 1
Women's Affairs Technical Committee (WATC), 89–90
women's peace activism, 165–66. *See also specific cases*
   choice of, 31
   dialogue across difference in, 31
   examples of, 1
   gender norms related to, 1, 10, 26, 148
   grassroots level of, 3, 30–31
   motivations for, 149–52
   politicization in, 29–30
   public-private spheres related to, 34
   roles in, 30, 146
   traditional gender roles in, 31–32, 34, 162
   tradition compared to feminism, 31–32
   as women's political activism, 3
women's political activism. *See also specific cases*
   assumptions about, 26
   community in, 35–36, 149–50, 163–64
   continuum of, ix–x, 2–3, 16–17, 28, 36, 146, 157
   definition of, ix
   gender discourses on, 6
   gender norms related to, 147–49
   importance of, 5, 157, 165
   of NIWC, 17, 63–64, 77
   as politics, 39–40, 160–61
   in public-private spheres, 148–49
   women's peace activism as, 3
women's political activism motivations, 5–6, 14, 26–28, 165
   agency as, 146
   of women and men in peace, 149–52
   of women and men in war, 152–55
women's political activism recruitment, 165
   family ties in, 155–56
   feminism for, 157
   from men's group auxiliaries, 157
   militancy from, 156
   special issue groups for, 156
women suicide bombers, 55n99
   acceptance of, 44
   characteristics of, 48–49, 153
   in Chechnya, 49
   choices of, 2
   community support for, 49–50, 133
   gender norms related to, 45
   Hamas and, 105
   in LTTE, 48, 132–34
   marriage and, 48–49, 52n17
   men suicide bombers related to, 1–2
   in Moscow subway attacks, 2
   motherhood and, 48–49
   motivations of, 45–48, 99–100, 103–6, 132, 153–54
   in PKK, 46, 48–49
   prevalence of, 45
   profiles of, 46
   rape and, 46–47
   revenge of, 1–2, 46–47
   from Syrian Socialist National Party, 45, 55n99
   as women combatants, 1–2
Woodbury, Laura, 168n48
Woodward, Shaun, 76
World Bank, 137

Xavier, Shereen, 135

7946/01